A TEARDROP ON A ROSE

The True Love Story Behind the Founding of Playgirl Magazine and Its Impact on Women's Sexual Liberation

Douglas Lambert
&
Jenny Lambert

Copyright © 2022 by DL & JL Holding Inc.

First Edition: February 2022

All rights reserved. Printed in the United States of America. No part of this book may be used or reproduced in any manner whatsoever without written permission from the publisher or author, except as permitted by U.S. copyright law.

This work may not reproduced, transmitted, or used in any form by any means electronic, mechanical, photocopying, recording, or otherwise, except for the use of brief quotations in a book review or analysis.

ISBN: 978-1-7352231-3-1

Pine & Palm Publishing

www.pineandpalmpublishing.com

Contents

Foreword	1
Introduction	5
1. "It Wasn't God Who Made Honky Tonk Angels"	11
2. "Shake, Rattle and Roll"	35
3. "Whole Lotta Shakin' Going on"	49
4. "Mystery Train"	69
5. "Mountain of Love"	102
6. "Wipeout"	116
7. "Misirlou"	139
8. "Blue Hawaii"	150
9. "Money"	163
10. "Superfly"	177
11. "I Heard it Through the Grapevine"	200
12. "Also sprach Zarathustra"	219
13. "She's a Lady"	231
14. "The Hustle"	241
15. "Fight the Power"	254
16. "A Teardrop on a Rose"	267
In Memoriam	281
Your Voice Matters	283

In Loving Memory of Jenny Margaretha Lambert

1942-2020

To my beautiful, passionate, and courageous wife who so delighted in being a liberated and sensuous woman and took such joy in championing gender equality and empowerment for all women. It is not possible, my precious Jenny, that any heart could love more than mine loves you. Thank you for returning that love in such full measure. We walked together as one soul in two bodies. Without you, there would be no story to tell, no life to rejoice.

Foreword

Looking back at the "first wave" of feminism beginning in the mid-1800s, the movement eventually won white women their right to vote in 1920. It happened with the passing of the 19th Amendment, an unbelievable 144 years after the ratification of the Declaration of Independence. It would not be until The Voting Rights Act passed in 1965 that all black women could vote too.

The 19th Amendment was a momentous but limited victory. In 1920, women asking for control over their own bodies, or to expect fair and equal treatment in education and the workplace, was still a bridge too far.

Fast-forward to the 1960s and 1970s, when the U.S. was a society caught up in rapid change and growing rebellion against all that was considered inequitable. Women were rejecting what they saw as the passive, one-dimensional role of their mothers. With this revolt came the "second wave" of feminism.

As with the demand for civil rights, the demand for women's rights was a pent-up explosion of indignation and frustration over the fact that equality and justice for all were being denied to large segments of American society, including women. A level playing field was something women hungrily craved from deep within their minds, hearts, and this time around, their wombs and vaginas.

A problem with both waves of the movement was the inaccurate image projected of angry women rejecting their femininity and demanding to be treated like men; or at least this is how those who disapproved of feminism sought to portray it. Jenny fervently believed this portrayal to be unfair and that it prevented widespread support of women's struggle for sexual freedom and universal equal rights.

In response, she quickly and accurately sized up the unpredictable times and understood the powerful role women would play in the coming cultural changes. From this thinking, her lightbulb idea was that there could be a huge niche for a vehicle that would convey the message that women *could* have both equality and sensuality.

Jenny envisioned this vehicle to be a women's magazine containing both sexually provocative material, such as male nudity, and applicable commentary on women's issues. The mission was to give voice to women's growing impatience with being treated as second-class citizens, as well as to their desire for freedom of sexual expression.

But the important practical question was: Would women want to look at pictures of naked men, and would they pay money to do so?

Jenny fervently said yes, and her husband Doug, wading through his struggle with male chauvinism learned from infancy in the mountains of Appalachia, put all his faith in the woman he so passionately loved. So they moved as quickly as possible to put all their business acumen and experience together to act upon this concept. Though they came from two very different worlds, Jenny and Doug had similar backgrounds of significantly poor beginnings with courageous, loving, but oppressed mothers beaten down by the denial of equal and just treatment. They were highly motivated both to make money and to help women get a better deal in life.

Hence, *Playgirl Magazine* was born. But not without complications. Among the pitfalls awaiting them was the necessity of prevailing in multiple court cases over Playboy magnate Hugh Hefner to gain undisputed ownership of the Playgirl name. Another was having to make the heart wrenching decision to step away from the Playgirl Club they had so passionately built together in the 60s. That nightclub had already become a venue for more liberated sexual expression, but now the 1970s were ripe for *Playgirl Magazine* to provide women with an even newer identity. Jenny and Doug strongly believed the magazine as conceptualized could become an incredible force in the modern women's movement.

One of the risks inherent in women achieving sexual freedom was that men would be the "primary beneficiaries," since unbridled sex with no commitment would play into their deepest fantasies. To offset this, Doug, Jenny, and their editor-in-chief knew it would be essential to connect sexual freedom with women's overall empowerment. Therefore, it became a top priority that the magazine contain a well-balanced diet of purposeful and instructive women-oriented journalism along with its sexually provocative imagery. The message they wanted to send was one of celebrating the very essence of the whole woman and all she was and had the potential to be in all arenas: personal, economic, cultural, political, and sexual.

As a result of this combined messaging, the Playgirl Identity created by the magazine made it as acceptable for women to take an active role in all aspects of life, including seeking out and being aroused by sexual stimuli, as it was for men. And importantly, the magazine offered a serious venue for meaningful conversation about women's growing sense of empowerment and their newfound sexual freedom.

There are those like Ruth Rosen, a top feminist historian, who say the 1970s era was "the most intellectually vital and exciting one in the history of women." Others assert that much of America as we know it today actually emerged from the 1970s, when women began to take charge of their own sexual decisions and experiences—to become their own "sexual agents." As a result, a woman's role in the whole of society went through a radical change.

That change, though occurring in spurts and stops, is still evolving today as women not only take control over their own sexuality, but also rightfully grow in political power, business success, and social influence. As they exert more clout in all areas of society, women are no longer asking but are demanding that they be heard, respected, and treated with equality and fairness.

In looking back at those critical transformational years of the 1970s, some go so far as to say that *Playgirl Magazine* laid the groundwork for offering a more realistic, whole, humanistic image of the complex nature of women; one which opposed the hypocrisy of the double standard of expectation for women's and men's sexual expression and behavior. Jenny and Doug believed that *Playgirl Magazine's* popularity helps to put into perspective women's battle with the conventional sexual culture up to that time. And although the magazine lost its focus, clarity of message, voice, and influence in the modern women's movement after being sold, its pioneer effort on behalf of women during those first five years of publication continues to exert an influence on the topic of women's liberation and sexual freedom even today.

Having to sell the magazine was one of the more painful experiences in Jenny and Doug's lives—their own version of "a teardrop on a rose," and why this book has earned such a title. The magazine was their baby, and like all proud parents, they had such high hopes and dreams for it.

Through it all, they remained proud of the role *Playgirl Magazine* played in helping women pursue and fight for their true worth and place on the world stage. They believed that if the succeeding owners had stayed true to its original vision and mission, the magazine would still be a strong voice and leader in the ongoing phases of the women's movement. And that movement has never been stronger or more important than it is today.

The original *Playgirl Magazine* celebrated all that makes a woman a woman, including her sexuality, intelligence, sensitivity, perception, expressiveness, capacity for love, and her infinite potential to exert power and influence around the world. Has all of this ever been done in one place before or since? It seems there is most definitely a place and, in fact, a need for such a forum today.

Introduction

"I Am Woman"

Jenny, 1972

I stared at the glistening fountain outside our Las Vegas hotel, unable to tear myself away from the thoughts suddenly bouncing back and forth inside my head.

Publishing a magazine was certainly an interesting idea. People loved reading them and bought them like crazy—including me. Nearly every person I knew kept up with at least one publication every week or month.

But publishing a magazine about lavishly spending money, like Douglas' friend back at the bar? That just didn't feel right. Not for Doug. Not for us. At least, not right now. Although we played the role well when we needed to, it was like Doug had said: "I know a lot more about entertainment, music, and sex than I do about jet setting."

No, if we were going to shift from the world of nightclubs to the world of publishing, it had to be for something we could really sink our teeth into. Something we enjoyed. Something meaningful to both of us. And yet...something enticing enough to keep us and our readers excited.

I continued gazing at our reflections in the water below, thinking. My husband wore that telltale smirk signaling the mulling over of his ever-present passion for growth, while my lips were pursed under heavy thoughts of willful innovation. There we stood, Douglas and Jenny—two minds that had already come together in the most extraordinary of ways when it came to building a successful business. And there we were, both still wanting even more.

That's when it finally dawned on me: We were already sitting on the idea for exactly the type of magazine the world needed.

Douglas pulled himself away from his thoughts as he moved to put his arms around me, but I ducked them and whirled to look him dead in the eyes instead. "I've been thinking. You said you would only publish a magazine if you knew the topic well, right?" He nodded slowly. "Well, judging by the success of the club, you clearly know a lot about making bodies look beautiful. You do it every day with our dancers." I paused to give him a moment to catch my drift, but he wasn't quite there. "Okay, yes, I help them with their dance routines, but you're the genius behind the music choices, the lighting, even their placement in the club. You truly know how to make women look and feel their most beautiful."

"So, a magazine filled with beautiful women?" he quickly argued. "Jenny, those already exist. You haven't forgotten about *Playboy*, have you? I'm telling you, there are no new ideas when it comes to magazines."

I couldn't help smiling now. "Yes there are. Because no one's doing a magazine filled with beautiful *men*."

I paused, watching as the initial idea plunged beneath the surface of his thinking. But, just like all the coins sitting at the bottom of the fountain bubbling behind us, the idea floated for a brief moment before sinking down onto hard stone. So I nudged it along. "Why don't we create a magazine that features a different nude male centerfold every month? Just like *Playboy* does with women?" He narrowed his eyes, signaling it was time to go in for the kill. "We already own the title: Playgirl."

As his jaw dropped ever so slightly, I could see his fountain of realization finally shoot up into the stratosphere, carrying all those sunken coins into the air with it.

And just like that, I had set off the whirlwind of events that would change our lives forever.

But I'd be lying if I said that idea burst forth like a flash of brilliance within just that single, solitary moment. Because the reality was, *Playgirl Magazine* had been a long time coming. I may not have recognized that fact until that moment, but it was always there. Its necessity was in the struggle of my mother's life, and all the mothers' lives around and before hers. It was in the struggle of my own grievances, and those of the other women I shared this world with. It was even in Doug's determination to make sure every single woman who walked in and out of our club felt coveted, sexy, and always safe.

Our subconscious desire to raise women up to the level of prestige and equality they so richly deserved had existed in both of us for a long time. Okay, maybe in me a little longer than in Doug. But neither of us had yet discovered an outlet through which to act upon this desire. No, not this desire—this need.

It would take an exceptional team of extraordinary people to pull off something like this the right way. And it would take even more incredible leadership to make that team function. But I knew without a doubt that Doug and I were the pair for the job. Because I knew us—our history, who we were, what made us tick, and how we made our decisions.

And only when you know us the same way can you truly understand why *Playgirl Magazine* was such a spectacular endeavor—not just for us, but for all women of the world.

Doug's family. Back row (left to right): Nell, Kenneth, Della (mother), Lee (father), Harold, Joe. Front row (left to right): June, Doug.

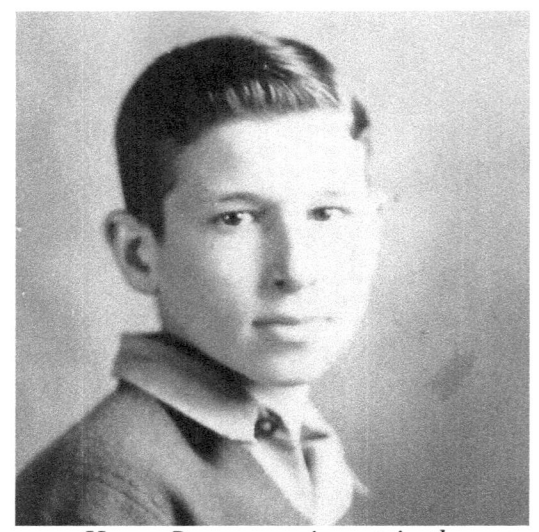

Young Doug growing up in the Appalachians

Doug in his army uniform

Chapter 1

"It Wasn't God Who Made Honky Tonk Angels"

Douglas, 1942

"Mama, Doug is in the kettle!" screamed my brother Joe.

My mother, hanging clothes a few feet away with her back to us, swung around. "God almighty, get him out!"

To this day I can recall little to nothing before the trauma of that warm summer afternoon of my eighth year. Mama was doing what she did every Monday the weather allowed: the backbreaking work of washing clothes in the front yard. She would boil water in a large, black iron kettle and then transfer it to wooden wash and rinse tubs. We kids would help by throwing kindling on the fire to keep the water boiling hot. When the water in the kettle got low, we would carry more from the nearby creek.

By this time, my older sister Nell and two of my older brothers had already moved away from home, leaving only my older brother Joe, younger sister June, and me. Fortunately, Nell was visiting that day. She and Joe later said I had stepped up on the bricks surrounding the kettle to throw my kindling in the fire underneath, then lost my balance and fell backward into the boiling water.

Joe and Nell each grabbed an arm and pulled me out as Mama ran to us. Having only overalls and undershorts on, my bare back was instantly scalded. "Wet one of the quilts in the creek and bring it fast!" Mama hollered to the others as she pulled off my pants.

I was crying from fright and going into shock. At that time, we lived about fifteen miles outside of a small coal mining town in southwest Virginia, deep within the Appalachian Mountains. My father was away with the only motor vehicle we had, but a main road was nearby. Mama sent Nell down to the road to flag the first vehicle that came along. Miraculously, within a short time a car did come, and the driver helped my mother get in, with me wrapped in a soaked quilt in her arms. Many times throughout her life, my mother said that fifteen-mile trip was the longest she ever took.

But the small town was not equipped for emergencies such as this. After several days, the doctor simply shook his head. "Mrs. Lambert, you best get him to the hospital in Charlottesville as soon as you can. There's nothing more I can do."

In those days, there were no ambulances in our neck of the woods and certainly no medical helicopters. Charlottesville, Virginia was about 275 miles away over some rugged mountain roads. Daddy was still away, and even if he had been home, it wasn't likely our old truck or I would have survived the hard trip. Charlottesville might as well have been across the globe.

"Then I'll be taking him home, doctor," my mother quietly asserted. The doctor shook his head again. "Without proper medical help, it's not likely he'll live through this at home."

Regardless, Mama did take me home. But not to die. That wasn't her way, and having had one son killed when run over by a wagon, she wasn't about to lose another.

Old Aunt Hannah, as we folks in the community called her, prepared a soothing salve which Mama gently applied to my back several times a day. Aunt Han also made pots of soup with every known healing herb the mountain could provide, and it was spoon-fed to me when I felt strong enough to eat. The routine became long and arduous for everyone involved.

Please Have Mercy

Rocking me for hours at a time with my stomach against her body and my head on her shoulder, Mama prayed. Nobody prayed as earnestly, tirelessly, or with more faith than my mother. "Lord, please have mercy.

Please don't take Douglas away. I couldn't bear it. He's so young and I love him so. Let him live, Lord." Her prayers weren't fancy, just simple pleas. But to my ears, this was music—the first music I remember. It was a soothing, humming sound, so comforting it reassured me that with God *and* Mama looking out for me, I was sure to get better.

It took more than a year to fully recover, but recover I did. The physical scars are still there today, and the traumatic experience sharpened my survival instincts. After that, I never felt there was any challenge I couldn't meet and overcome. Even the ever-changing mood and temper of my father no longer cowed me as before...except for the night Mama, June, and I hid in the attic during one of his particularly violent rages.

Having had too much to drink and angry about a "horse trading" deal gone wrong, Daddy was ranting and raving as he approached the house. Knowing from experience big trouble was ahead, Mama sprang out of her chair. "Go to the attic, quick!" she frantically urged while grabbing June and me each by the arm. Huddled together in the dark, quiet as mice, we waited while Daddy continued his rampage downstairs. Finally, all was quiet. "He's passed out," Mama whispered. "We'll be fine now." We crept back downstairs and sure enough, Daddy had fallen half on and half off the bed in a stupor.

Still frightened, June begged Mama to sleep with her, but Mama tucked us both in and reluctantly got into bed with Daddy. She knew if he awoke in the night and didn't find her there, she'd have even more hell to pay.

And so as with all people, there were some challenging times during those formative years. However, for every bad experience, there were offsetting good ones that gratefully seemed to linger longer in my mind. And what good thing didn't happen in real life happened in my always-racing brain, so full of happy fantasies that usually took me far into the future.

Sometime later, on one especially fine spring day, I decided to reward myself with a day out of school and away from chores. Nothing in particular came to mind that I'd done to be rewarded for, but as I said, it was an especially fine day and I figured I must have done something good in recent times. So I detoured to my favorite spot in the entire world: the grassy edges of an ambling riverbank.

There, the pointed ears of a pair of cottontails appeared. At eleven years old and full of youthful energy, it was difficult to keep my lanky body still so as not to scare the skittish rabbits. Gazing at the pair as they kept close together while searching for food, grooming each other, and staying ever alert to danger, my fascination with these alluring bunnies was a foretelling of my relationship with one captivating, life-changing woman. Of course, I could have no way of knowing that then.

As I watched, the rabbits suddenly scurried away as the blast of the whistle from an oncoming train unsettled the serenity of this peaceful green valley nestled in the Appalachian Mountains. This too was a foretelling of my future.

Motion of the Train

The train's determined forward movement as it roared over the mountains and through the valley seemed to be a daily reminder to us all that change was coming. And although young and still timid from lack of experience beyond my home and family, I felt the powerful presence of the train pull at me even then. It created a yearning in my belly for something more than life had offered so far.

As the train rumbled away, I had sharp visions in my mind of one day boarding one of those mighty Norfolk and Western machines and riding it to wherever my dreams would take me, quenching my burning thirst for direction, purpose, and adventure. Such was the main theme of so many of my adolescent daydreams.

Looking back, I know now that my parents and teachers viewed me as different and perplexing. School was boring, my mind continuously wandered, reading and writing held no interest, I couldn't sit still, and daydreaming kept me in constant trouble. So I finagled my way out of going as much as possible. But then, home didn't offer much relief because that meant doing chores, which were just as boring and frustrating as schoolwork.

During these years, there was a steady drumbeat in my head that came from a place far from the classroom, far from chopping wood, feeding livestock, pulling garden weeds, and, in fact, far from the mountains and hollers of Appalachia. I just didn't know where that place was. But I was on fire to find out.

It seemed everyone was frustrated with me, and I was frustrated right back. Although Mama remained patient and encouraging, my dad, in his stern and unforgiving manner, made clear that he considered me lazy and a ne'er-do-well. So, a big dilemma for my parents and teachers was: What to do with Doug?

"Doug, from now on you're workin' at the store every day after school and on Saturdays," Dad declared one day, as though he had come up with an antidote to snakebite. At that time, my father owned the only dry goods store in our little country community. Quickly taken with the business aspect of its operation, I was fascinated by the talk of merchandise displays, customer satisfaction, markups, markdowns, and profits. It all rang a bell with me that nothing else had before.

It was there in that little store I began to understand the vital importance of making money and how to do it. My dad was a born salesman and a shrewd businessman. He knew how to put the "glad talk" on customers and vendors alike, and how to quickly move merchandise in and out.

Under his sharp eye and sharper tongue, I learned invaluable lessons. I began a lifetime of developing and honing an ability to see and take advantage of moneymaking opportunities, and to come up with imaginative ways to get around obstacles that stood between me and success.

To me, *this* was real life—not plowing the cornfield or waiting my turn in the classroom. So I worked hard…although to my frustration, I only received a pittance allowance by my dad in return.

"Say Dad, what about me gettin' more pay for all the work I do 'round here?" I mustered the courage to ask one day.

"What about you payin' more for your board and keep?" was his sharp retort.

I frowned. "I don't pay nothin' for board and keep."

"Exactly," he grunted. No more was ever said about pay.

Born In 1934 during the Great Depression and growing up under the restrictions placed on all families by the rationing during World War II, I knew what poverty tasted like. Most all the people around us did. My father never held a job that produced a paycheck. Sometimes he was a storeowner, and at *all* times he was a "horse trader" or a "wheeler-dealer." Therefore, our family existed in a world of either feast or famine. But thanks to the "sometimes" store and my mother's hard work and resourcefulness with growing and preserving all manner of food, we never went hungry. And both my father and mother were very generous in sharing what they had—whether it was in abundance or short supply—with those less fortunate.

One of my first memorable experiences regarding wheeling and dealing was on one of our annual visits to the summer carnival, an event that got my adrenalin rushing and my curiosity about the outside world roused. On this particular day, my excitement could hardly be contained on the drive to the carnival grounds. With us all packed in, Dad wound the Packard station wagon (it was a time of feast) around the country dirt roads, banked on each side by tall, wet blades of bluegrass. Energized, my mind raced through the possibilities the day ahead held. As we approached the carnival, I caught wind of an idea through the open car window.

"I wanna open a hot dog stand and make lotsa money, Dad."

Dad shot me a curious sideways glance. "What'cha gonna call it?" his voice resonated in his gruff mountain drawl.

The response proudly shot from my mouth like a bullet from a carnival cannon. "Doug's!"

"Doug's!?" my dad mocked. "Are you crazy? If you wanna sell hot dogs, you'd better call it Hot Dogs. No one hungry is looking for a sign that says 'Doug's.'"

Business Lesson 101 was burned into my brain.

Over the years, I had watched my family and friends howl with delight as they took their turn on the Ferris wheel and merry-go-round. However, I always liked to browse the grounds and take in as much of the inner workings as I could while biting into a bright red candy apple. I particularly studied the boss men who barked out orders that kept the energy alive. Although I couldn't connect with reading and writing, the business dance that was necessary to make a carnival a successful moneymaker was clear to me, just as the running of the dry goods store was.

I sensed that the placement of the rides, the food stands, and the game concessions were carefully staged so that customers always had just a short walk to drop another nickel. The carnival planners had mapped out a path of thrills, wins, and enticements for spending hard-earned money. The carnival bait—exotic lighting, loud music, and suggestive females in skimpy costumes—called to me like cold creek water to a man dying of thirst.

By this time, I wanted a job outside my family's world of dry goods. I wanted to be paid cash rather than get an allowance reluctantly paid out by my father. And I wanted a job that offered excitement and adventure. In our small town, the options were few: stores like my father's, churches, a small hospital, and field chores. I wasn't interested in retail, medical work, raising money from the pulpit, and most certainly not farming.

But there was one other establishment in every town I'd seen: a honky tonk bar with a jukebox. Next to the blasts from the train whistle, the music from those nickelodeons spoke to my soul more than anything else.

MOONSHINE AND HONKY TONKS

At age twelve, I announced one morning to my parents at our kitchen table that I was going to work at the local honky tonk. My father's taunting laughter revealed his disbelief.

"Honky tonkin' at your age? What'll they have you do? Drag drunks out the door? Where do you come up with these crazy ideas, boy? You just forget that notion." He looked at Mama and shook his head. "Della, did you hear that?!"

Mama simply filled Dad's plate with a king-size helping of fried eggs, gravy, and hot biscuits, one of the many tools in her stockpile known to be a distraction when Dad was working himself up to a verbal blitz. Neither said any more about the subject for several days, and I decided to take that for acquiescence.

It's doubtful anyone would have called me courageous in my young days. I knew how to protect my hide. I hadn't saved a dog from a fire, or a friend from drowning, or confronted a school bully, but I walked into that dimly lit honky tonk unafraid and excited. My senses came to life. The music and laughter were ear-bursting loud, overwhelming cigarette smoke hung on every inch of the walls and furniture, bodies wreaked of hard work, locally brewed liquor lingered in the air and on glasses even after they were washed, and the cheap perfume nearly gagged me. It all blended together to make my ears ring, my eyes water, and my throat threaten to close up. I loved it!

The old wood floorboards creaked, but no one heard me. They were in a world of their own, pulled into the pulse of the tunes and the lyrics of all those great songs of postwar America. The shining jukebox served up songs that were the infancy of country and western music and the seeds of rockabilly. I instantly felt right at home.

The barkeep, a bald, bearded, barrel-shaped man with a once white apron around his considerable middle grunted to a patron three sheets to the wind. "Looks like a tadpole wants a mountain dew and a dance." This was when "mountain dew" was shop talk for mountain-brewed moonshine.

Young but tall for my age, I tried to appear mature and confident, which might have fooled a crocked mind, but not the barkeep. He jerked his head in my direction and had the attention of his other gritty, laid-back customers nursing their drinks.

I got right to it. "Sir, I need a job. One that pays real money." I was suddenly as interesting as the music and cheap liquor. The rumble of laughter seemed deafening, and I gulped in a breath and hoped my prominent ears weren't turning red.

"That so? Well, what can you do, son?"

"I can drive a truck. Been drivin' my daddy's for near a year now."

"And who's your daddy?"

Lee Lambert was fairly well known around the countryside, so I figured his name would be familiar to most of these people. Which is why I avoided it. "Leonard. We just moved here."

"Does he know you're here asking for a job?"

"Sure. We need the money," I lied. Why is it young people think they can get by with big, fat lies like that, especially in such a small community? But I wasn't thinking about what would happen tomorrow. I was fully focused on the moment.

"Send him down to Jakey's!" one of the customers bellowed. The guffawing began again, but after a pause, a set of keys came flying at me. Snatching them out of the air, I looked quizzically at the barkeep.

"You know where the train tracks split over in Jacob's Holler?" he asked.

"Yessir," I replied with conviction I didn't feel.

"Go on down there and find the barn just west of the bend. Then go about half a mile into the woods behind the barn and tell the man there, Jakey, that I sent ya'. Give him this envelope, and he'll give you something to bring back." He handed me a large, worn envelope from beneath the bar. "And you come straight back with it, you hear?" he commanded.

"Better call ahead so Jakey don't shoot him," shouted a man from across the room." Laughter again. But I stood solid.

"By the way, what's your name?" the barkeep asked.

"Doug, sir. Uh...Doug Hawkins." I wasn't quick enough to make up a first name for myself but figured my best friend wouldn't mind me using his last name.

"Well okay, Doug. Let's see how you fare at your first job."

This was too good to be true. I wanted with all my heart to become part of the Appalachian honky tonk social club, to be accepted into their circle of camaraderie, where storytelling, back-slapping humor, friendship, and the magical music from the jukebox constantly streamed through the room.

"What's *your* name?" I asked, trying to sound like one of them. But my ever-changing adolescent voice didn't support that effort.

"Name's Ezekiah. I own this joint." Mr. Ezzy, as I came to call him, and I were to become good friends.

By the time I headed out for the barn and the woods it was pitch dark, the only light coming from the headlights of Mr. Ezzy's truck. Straining to see and keep out of the ditches on either side of the road, I finally made it to the holler, to the barn, and beyond. The place was filthy, even by my young standards, and the four straggly men standing with lanterns in front of an old shed were daunting. But I got out of the truck.

They sized me up with suspicious stares. Although a hot night, a chill ran over my body. My legs threatened to not move. I wondered if I'd ever leave this place alive. No one would ever know what happened to me. Mama would grieve her heart out. My mind visited all these thoughts in just a few seconds. One thing I knew for sure, if I did make it out, was that the menacing appearance and manner of these men made me know I'd never, ever share anything I saw or heard here.

A man standing in the muck near the shed shouted, "Whatcha doin' here, boy?"

"Ezekiah sent me with this envelope to give to Jakey."

"Ezekiah wouldn't send a fuckin' kid."

"Well, he fuckin' did," I casually came back. I couldn't believe I'd said that. My mother was an uncommonly tolerant woman, but cussing and blasphemy were *never* allowed from us kids

"This is Ezekiah's truck and here's the envelope." With a trembling hand, I shoved the envelope at him.

Jakey opened it, took a look, and put it in his back pocket. Then he spit a splat of tobacco at my feet. "Okay, load 'em up," he said nodding toward a stack of heavy-looking boxes.

The four men stood with arms crossed or hands in pockets, watching as I walked to the boxes. "Sure," I said cheerfully, trying to sound like I did this every day. As I lifted and placed each box in the truck, my muscles were screaming for help. But I kept flashing a big smile, knowing I couldn't show weakness.

I snuck a peek at the jugs in the boxes to discover that I was now officially running moonshine. That is, if I got out of there all in one piece.

"Yo daddy know you're here?" one of the men asked.

"Don't got no daddy," I fibbed as I kept loading. "My family needs some money real bad, so I'm here." Lying, which was another one of Mama's deep lines in the sand, was becoming easier.

One of the men finally picked up a box and walked it to the truck, and the others followed suit.

"You got balls, kid," grunted Jakey as he spit again, off to the side this time.

"That's what the ladies tell me." I smiled back, wishing mightily that I felt as macho as I was trying to sound. One of the men let out a big "heehaw" in response.

As I got back in the truck, still not sure they'd let me drive away, Jakey said, "Tell Ezekiah he'd better find a man to do his dirty work."

"Why send a man to do a boy's job?" I shouted out the window.

Jakey laughed. "See ya next time then, kid."

My heart soared. Hot damn! I had just been accepted into the roughest, toughest fraternity in the mountains. For a brief moment, I thought this job was so great I'd do it for nothing—a consideration that quickly passed. Making money was already in my blood.

Back at the honky tonk, I put the small wad of dollar bills from Mr. Ezzy in the deep pocket of my overalls. Without counting, I knew it was more money than I'd ever had that was all mine. I swaggered up to the bar, accepted my free soda pop, and listened to the hum of conversation and the soft music coming from the jukebox as I gulped down my first swallow.

"So, how's it feel to have a job makin' real money?" teased a big-bellied guy at the bar.

"It feels fine," I allowed. "Mighty fine."

I noticed no one was laughing.

Nell and Wells

With all my older brothers and sister gone from home, I felt protective of my mother and younger sister June, but could do little to stop my father's assaults on our senses. Kenneth and Harold had gone off to fight in the war, and even though he was very young, Joe had moved over the mountain to find work in Pocahontas, Virginia. Nell, eager to be away from home and the tyranny of our father, moved to Bristol, Virginia and had started her family by this time.

Although there were frequent visits back and forth, I still missed her. Nell was the most outspoken person in our family. None of us ever had to wonder what she was thinking and feeling. Music seemed to be the driving force in her life, and was definitely the connection with her that had the greatest influence on me.

She was particularly drawn to the songs that told of hard times suffered by women. These stories were often of relationships gone wrong, soured marriages, painful divorces, drowning one's sorrow with drink, and masking the pain with good times in the local honky tonks. And of course, the songs broke both ways— men, through their own doing or circumstances beyond their control, had as many rough times as women.

"Doug," Nell would say with a sorrowful voice, "women have it hard. Look at Mama's life. Look at all the women who live in these mountains. Just think what they could be if they were given half a chance. It's not right." And as always after such serious observations, she added, "Now don't you ever forget the hardship your mama and all the women around here have suffered, Doug."

As much to herself as to me, Nell would often insist, "I'm not gonna live my life that way. No damn man is gonna keep me down. I swear it." I listened and heard the words she spoke, but still didn't understand what she really meant.

Kitty Wells, one of the earliest female country musicians, sat on the country music throne in Nell's eyes. "Nobody tells it true like sweet Kitty," she would declare. Nell was positive Miss Wells had experienced everything she sung about.

Kitty Wells secured her place in the hearts of millions of women when she bravely rebelled against Hank Thompson's hit song "The Wild Side of Life." It's a sad and sordid story of a good man whose beloved wife gave him up to return to her "honky tonkin', drinkin', and carousing days," with the husband's presumption that God had made such a cold-hearted woman as this.

Miss Wells' prompt reply to this was her release of the wildly popular "It Wasn't God Who Made Honky Tonk Angels." It stunned the male-dominated music industry. The song debunks the belief claimed in "The Wild Side of Life" that God makes such women, and puts the blame instead on the cheating husbands who forget they're married.

Radio stations were threatened if they played her song, and rumor had it that Kitty Wells' appearances were being cancelled because of the controversy. But the bell had been rung and there was no unringing it. Women wanted the song out there, telling their side of the story. The single sold one million copies and reached number one on the Billboard Country List. No other female country artist had achieved this status. And who do you suppose were buying these records? That's right—women.

I always imagined my sister was responsible for much of the radio playtime Kitty got. "Called up WOPI ten times this week and asked for 'Honky Tonk Angels.' So did my friends, and we're gonna keep calling," she proudly boasted. "Ol' Kitty'll make a fortune and show those sorry men what a free woman can do."

It's important to also note that although Kitty Wells' songs were now receiving consistent play time on radio stations, that wasn't the case with other female country artists. It would be another decade before their music would even begin to receive more fair treatment. And even today, the disparity between radio airtime for male and female country music singers remains gravely unacceptable. Regardless, Miss Wells was a pioneer and strong role model for women seeking equal rights and opportunities. No wonder women like my sister saw her as their spokesperson. I suspect even my aggrieved mother, who had suffered long and silently and would never speak of such troubles as told about in those songs, held her head a little higher when she heard "It Wasn't God Who Made Honky Tonk Angels."

Both the Wells and the Thompson songs conveyed the most popular theme of country music: Somebody done somebody wrong. And the ball of blame for the "wrongs" tossed back and forth between men and women excited and aroused the emotions of both. Needless to say, it was great for country music. There had never been such interest in or attention paid to it.

The honky tonk where I worked, Two Tone's Bar, reflected much of the life sung about in the songs on the jukebox. I witnessed firsthand these stories being played out in real life. I observed the intricate relationships between men and women in which they loved and hurt each other with equal passion. Some weekends I'd sweep floors, and if we were real busy, wash glasses and ashtrays. With hands in the dishpan behind the bar, I watched with wide eyes as women shook their boobies and butts in a sexual jitterbug; and I was acutely aware of not only my own excitement, but the effect of these provocative moves on men of all ages. Then, after several drinks and smokes together and a seductive slow dance or two, couples would leave the bar with their hands all over each other to do what my inexperienced mind could only imagine was something awfully good, like sampling all the candies from my daddy's store. This arousing experience left a lasting impression on my developing brain and rising hormones that came back to serve me profitably later on.

Whatever I couldn't figure out about life myself, Mr. Ezzy filled in with his graphic explanations and colorful language. "You wanna know sumpin', you just come to ol' Ezekiah. I've seen it all, heard it all, and done a fair 'mount of it myself," he'd say with a wink.

Although I didn't know it at the time, by my second day of work, Mr. Ezzy knew who my father really was. And Mr. Ezzy, being the better "horse trader" for that moment, persuaded Daddy to let me continue working under his watchful eye.

Yes indeed, the earthy, often bawdy goings on inside that first honky tonk added immeasurably to my education in the ways of the world and fed my budding mind and body. However, my happiest times there were when the crowds thinned and I'd splurge a whole quarter (extravagant in those times) on playing five of the numerous songs Nell loved and related to.

In fact, Nell was the first person to bring my focus fully on the fascinating connection between music and people's real lives. She demonstrated to me through her own life the incredible healing benefits of music (its rhythm, melody, and lyrics) as it triggers a safe and satisfying release of those pent-up emotions frequently on the verge of overwhelming us—those both hovering in the depths of our despair and those ascending to the heights of our bliss.

"Music is God's hand touching places in our hearts and minds that nothing else can touch," she would declare. "Ain't nothing else but music helps us get all that pain out of our soul and puts all that joy in it. Don't you forget that, Doug. Always listen to the music."

The honky tonk taught me how much truth there was to that. I took note of the songs people chose on the jukebox and watched their emotions rise and fall while their moods turned happy or sad as the music played. Thereafter, music became inextricably tied with the ups and downs and ins and outs of my own life. And all these many experiences were being stored and would serve me well in the future.

Even though I was witness to much of my father's offensive behavior, I was too young and into my own world through most of my childhood to fully understand the extent of the damage caused by the emotional and sometimes physical abuse my mother and the rest of us endured. I knew Mama's life was unbelievably hard and largely unhappy, and I knew that the source of most of her unhappiness was my father. But that was just our way of life: Avoid my dad's wrath when possible, look to Mama for what protection she could provide, enjoy the good times, and endure the rest.

Not having a consistent standard by which to judge our home life, it seemed normal to me at the time, for I don't recall feeling our lives were any different than those of our friends. But part of that *que será, será* feeling was likely because my mother and older siblings took the brunt of my dad's ill temper and domineering behavior.

While Mama suffered silently, my sister Nell did not—not with our father (the battles there were often fearsome to behold), and not with her husbands. As a result, it was Nell's plight of pain and unhappiness and, importantly, her expression of it through the music she loved, that caused me to first realize women simply did not play on an even field with men. At the time, however, that realization did little to alter my own behavior. Hell, I was a man—or soon to be one—so I didn't waste a lot of time dwelling on what was fair or not fair for women. I was growing up in a world dominated by chauvinistic men who were my models and often my heroes. Could I turn out any differently? No, I couldn't and didn't. But the impression of that inequality made an imprint on my being that surfaced and dramatically influenced my life much later.

Nell's story is actually not wholly unlike that of many women of that era who were saying "enough is enough" and striking out on their own. After divorcing an alcoholic first husband and then discovering that her second husband was cheating with one of her good friends, Nell felt it was time to take control of her own destiny. She tossed all of her husband's personal belongings on the front yard in the pouring rain, gave (as only Nell could) both the friend and the husband a fiery, no-holds-barred piece of her mind, and said goodbye to Bristol. With two kids and herself to support, she headed for Baltimore, where there were hopefully better job opportunities for women, and where she could mercifully put the past behind her.

Working and going to school, my sister, a single mom raising her children in the inner city, eventually became a psychiatric nurse at Spring Grove State Hospital. Going through this period of her life, Nell related all too well to the song "Heartaches by the Number," written by Harlan Howard and made a hit by Guy Mitchell. She identified with the repeated troubles voiced in this song and others like it, and there was comfort in the knowledge of shared suffering. However, as the Bible says to do, my sister girded her loins, confronted the hardships, and continued to move forward and find relief where she could. "That's what you have to do. It's all you can do. 'Cause time comes when we're all down there," she would instruct. "And don't you ever forget that, Doug." She never wanted me to forget anything she told me. And I never did.

Nell's healing salve was the music that spoke her language, confirmed the legitimacy of her plight, and let her know she wasn't alone in that struggle. She dreamed someday of being among those making this music that brought such solace to her and so many others. Nell wanted to sing of that seemingly futile search, in an often tragic world, for happiness that always appeared to be just out of reach. And high spirited by nature with a zest for life that couldn't be squashed, Nell also wanted to sing of the good times that gladdened her heart and flooded her soul with joy, temporary though it may be. Through her music, as she had through nursing, she wanted to make the hurt better for others as well as herself—even if for just the few minutes the music was playing.

With her kids finally grown and out of the home, Nell did just that. She formed a band and for a number of years performed in the Baltimore honky tonks and other venues in and around the city. Eventually she moved back to Bristol to be with family. And, in her 80s, Nell again formed a country music band, her goal being to perform on the stage of the historic Carter Family Fold in Hiltons, Virginia. Sadly, however, her heart that had broken, mended, and soared so many times before finally failed her.

Nell's memorial service, with the gracious permission of the Carter family, was held at the Carter Family Fold where, as part of the service, her band played with Nell's voice joining in on tape when they sang her favorite gospel "Wings of a Dove," written by Bob Ferguson and made hugely popular by Ferlin Husky in 1960. Some of her ashes were quietly spread around the stage, seeping down into the cracks between the old, worn boards. There on the stage in the home of the first family of country music, the music that sang her life, her soul was finally content.

Nell was one of the many women of that era who struggled against nearly insurmountable odds to be free and equal, to play a responsible role in life, and to have respect and dignity while unabashedly enjoying, on her own terms, good music, good lookin' men, and good times. Without even being aware that there was such a thing as the "women's movement," Nell defied the old rules and prejudices pertaining to women and was a forerunner for those women of the 1960s and 70s who battled for independence and equal footing with men. She was incredible, and I loved her so.

Musical Notes

The rambling Appalachian Mountain Range flows from Canada into Georgia. Like my grandparents, many of the people coming into the

Virginia and West Virginia part of Appalachia were Irish and Scottish immigrants, bringing with them their culture, stories and, importantly, their music. My grandparents always had at least a banjo and a fiddle among their valued possessions. Others had mandolins, mountain dulcimers, and autoharps. And it seemed nearly everyone in that generation and the ones to follow could play one or more instruments. Everyone except Doug.

Much to my deep regret and the disappointment of my family, the gene for musical talent skipped right over me. Thankfully though, I did inherit a deep love and appreciation for nearly all genres of music that has followed me my entire life.

Hard as mountain life was, our people were content with the basics, and they made their happy times by getting together, sharing stories, and playing music. No fuss was made; just gathering on a front porch, on church grounds, in living rooms, or by a stream where people picked, strummed, clogged, and sung to their heart's content. Through their music and dance they expressed joy, sadness, love, and bitterness at the sheer hardness of life, all while their fingers flew over strings, their voices joined together in perfect harmony, and their feet always moved to the music. That early style of Anglo-Celtic-influenced music became known as bluegrass, and as the guitar became more popular in the mountains, hillbilly country western music came into its own.

Over the years, some were lucky to add a radio or phonograph to their household. Access to these machines made all types of music available to us, if only on a limited scale. Our family was one of the first in the immediate area in which we lived to have a radio. This often made our house a gathering place on Saturday nights to listen to Grand Ole Opry from WSM Radio in Nashville.

I understood that music and the camaraderie that went with it affected people deep in their hearts. I felt an inner peace and even joy that stayed with me as I called a tune into my head. I was hooked, but I could not have known that music would largely define the rest of my life. As time went on, the jukebox and the honky tonk became the center of my world. They magically lifted me away from the here and now and provided glimpses into the future I was beginning to imagine for myself.

By the time I was in my mid-teens, my mother had secretly saved enough of her egg and butter money to do what she had dreamed and planned for many years: unshackle herself from an abusive husband

and an intolerable life. While my father was away for a few days, Mama packed what personal belongings she could, gathered up June and me, and with the help of family, made her getaway over the mountain to the bustling town of Bristol.

There, we lived a short time with Nell and her family while my resourceful mother negotiated a loan to buy a boarding house. Income from this venture served as my mother's nearly sole source of livelihood for the next twenty-five years, which enabled her to live a very modest but independent life free of abuse.

My dad came to Bristol several times and tried to get Mama to return through threats and harassment. When my brother Harold, now a tough ex-marine, found this out, he wasted no time getting to our dad. After coming back from WWII, Harold, like so many other men hardened from war, was more than ready for another fight, and considered butt--kicking a right he had earned. And there was no one's butt he was more eager to kick than Lee Lambert's.

Mama was never bothered again.

Throughout those years, although many other needs and wants were often done without, Mama never missed a payment on her mortgage. She built a reputation in the community as an honest, kind, independent, and hardworking woman of strong faith—a truly beautiful woman. And as such a woman, she certainly had suitors, but was very timid in that regard. She had vowed to never again be under the thumb of another man.

Mama was very open minded in her willingness to take in renters and boarders. However, in her soft-spoken, gracious way, she made it clear she would not tolerate inappropriate behavior made public. She may not have approved of what went on behind closed doors, but she didn't make it her business…unless someone was being treated poorly. As a respectable, clean, safe, and caring place to live, Mama's boarding house never lacked for residents, and stories of the colorful characters that came and went could fill volumes.

Bristol was also rich with musical history. In 1927, the first recordings of what came to be known as country music were made in an old warehouse in Bristol. These recordings forever more have been referred to as the Bristol Sessions—or to some, the "Big Bang" of country music. Included in these sessions were the original Carter Family and the Father of Country Music, Jimmie Rodgers. Johnny Cash called these recordings "the single most important event in the history of country music." Most people who know anything about music agree.

Today, Bristol is celebrated as the birthplace of country music. But to many, our mountain music was simply called "hillbilly music." The label seemed logical enough given that it originated in the rolling hills and backwoods of southern Appalachia. And the music certainly spoke to the lives lived by us all in that part of the country.

Although Bristol had much more to offer young folks like myself, I missed parts of my life in the mountains, especially the honky tonk. And I found school just as disagreeable in Bristol as it had been in all the other places we lived. Before the end of my eighth-grade year, I completely dropped out of school. I finally ended once and for all the years of misery sitting still all day in a classroom, trying in vain to concentrate, and suffering the agony and humiliation of not being able to learn to read and write as easily and readily as my classmates.

Today, I likely would be diagnosed with attention-deficit disorder and dyslexia and would receive lots of sympathy and extra help for them. And who knows what the outcome would have been? But a big part of what drove me was the need to prove myself *to* myself, as well as to the rest of the world. And a big part of any success I've enjoyed has been my ability to dream, imagine, think outside the box, and go places in my mind that many others do not, cannot, or will not. If that's part of having ADHD and dyslexia, then I consider any negatives those conditions may have caused me a fair trade-off for the positives.

That period of time did have its major successes too. Arriving in Bristol still shy about girls, a local young lady and her mother gave me my first sexual experience under the stars of the hilly countryside. To some that may indeed sound strange, and to them I say: Maybe it was, maybe it wasn't. But that's all the explanation you'll ever get.

Regardless of how it happened, it was an eye-opener. More than that, it opened every pore, raised every hair, and put aflame every fiber of my being. I never imagined such ecstasy was possible! Where had this rapture been all my fourteen years?! It certainly wasn't what I experienced alone under the covers when I thought everyone else was asleep.

However, already sworn to bachelorhood at that young age, I felt that even the promise of such bliss every night could not persuade me to consider marriage and a family. I had seen too much. And besides, it simply did not fit into my future plans.

Taking up Arms

While I was growing into manhood, our country was rebounding from World War II and finding itself in another war with North Korea. It was officially referred to as a "conflict," but both sides were shooting and bombing each other, and people were dying—that was war to me. And I wanted to play my part for my country.

In my eyes, becoming a member of the Screaming Eagles 101st Airborne Division was the most exciting way to do that. The Screaming Eagles were part of the U.S. Army, famous for their bravery in action, courage during the landings at Normandy, and the Battle of the Bulge. I had always eagerly consumed radio news about what was going on in the world, including with wars, and in my overactive imagination, I pictured myself a heroic warrior winning battles with sheer courage and brute strength under the flag of the Screaming Eagles.

On the day of departure for boot camp, all I could think about was earning my patch from the 101st Airborne Division. Dressed in their Sunday best, June and my mother waited with me for the Greyhound bus. Once boarded, I quickly got a window seat and began waving. My mother and sister ran to my window with tears rolling down their faces.

Up to that time, I'd never been away from my family, even for one night. I suddenly felt so completely alone and scared. I waved until June and Mama became the size of ants, then settled back to wonder what was ahead. For sure, it would be something different than I had ever experienced before.

After six weeks of boot camp, I was stationed in Aberdeen, Maryland, learning everything possible about weapons, ammunition, and combat vehicles. With growing confidence in my knowledge of ordinances and in myself, every step of training confirmed that I could tackle a task with a successful outcome. Weekends, when allowed off base, were spent with Nell in Baltimore, who had moved there with her two children. They lived in a one-room apartment in the inner city, and my bed was the floor. It didn't matter though—I was overjoyed to be able to spend time with family.

It was then I was also introduced to the world of nightlife, bars, music, and good times. With a bar on every corner and two in between, it was honky tonk heaven! So it wasn't like I was spending a lot of time at night on Nell's floor anyway.

At graduation, we were each given a hardbound book that chronicled our achievements through basic training. I looked at my picture among the other Screaming Eagles trainees and vowed to keep that book the rest of my life. And I have.

After graduating from their training program however, I was unable to make my way into the actual Screaming Eagles, because at that time they functioned only as a training unit. I was dismayed, but that perceived derailment at the time would prove to be one of the more fortunate changes of plan to occur in my life.

With that, it finally came time for my very first train ride. It was across the country to Tacoma, Washington, where the troop train was filled with soldiers being shipped out to the army embarkation center. Like all soldiers on their first assignment after boot camp, we were restless, hiding nervousness under the bravado of our uniforms and behind our boisterous clowning. I mostly watched. In many ways, I still felt like a boy pretending to be a man, and everyone else seemed the same.

Through the windows of the sleeper car, the landscape of America flickered by. I was at last on the "dream machine" of my youth. The familiar and always exciting sound of the train's whistle heralded the coming of my new life.

I had asked the conductor to wake me when we were crossing the northern Midwest. I didn't want to miss the aurora borealis, a wonderous natural light display in the sky. When you're not yet twenty and fresh out of the mountains, the world seems immense and everything in it fascinating.

Instead of the conductor's gentle shake, a rowdy pair of soldiers awakened me with their backslapping and roughhousing. Then I caught a couple of words being tossed back and forth between some fellows who obviously had been educated and groomed for an affluent life.

"You must be some kind of entrepreneur," I heard one say.

"My dad has several enterprises, and I'm going to work with him when I get back home," the other replied.

Entrepreneur, enterprise—the words landed on me like a prophecy. So important sounding. *Entrepreneur, enterprise*. Together, they were almost more than a mouth and a mind could get around; exotic and mysterious.

But first, that magnificent aurora sky!

The train gently rocked and rattled as it sped westward, where at some point I would board a troop ship that would take me from the embarkation center to South Korea—another leg on this great adventure I was on. Basic training had made my body and mind strong, and I felt mentally and physically armed and ready for any challenge.

Thoughts of where I had come from flooded my mind: my fight as a traumatized child to live, my mama's deep and abiding love, our small coal mining towns, the excitement of the annual carnival and the lessons learned there, my dad's tyranny, the good business training I got in the dry goods store, Nell's passion for music and practical advice, the excitement and hazards of running moonshine. And foremost burned into my brain and heart was the world of the honky tonks and jukeboxes.

We were packed into the ship and heading to Inchon Harbor in Korea. I was assigned to the U.S. Army's Ordinance Company, attached to the 24th Division at the demilitarized zone (DMZ). This strip of land served as a buffer between North and South Korea that was agreed upon during the standoff between the two. The DMZ was located about thirty miles north of Seoul, and, at that time, was the most heavily militarized border in the world.

A truck drove us through a never-ending monsoon and thirty miles of bumps and slush to our new home, about ten miles from the intensity of the DMZ. Hank, my buddy from Georgia who I'd befriended on the ship, shook his head. "Ain't seen so much goddamn rain and mud in all my life. How do they expect us to even piss in this stuff, let alone work and fight in it? This fuckin' shit makes Georgia's red clay look like the promised land." I grunted and nodded in agreement, wondering myself how I was going to survive this hellhole. But I knew I would. Because I had survived worse.

What I couldn't have known on that miserable day we arrived in Korea was how boring the routine of my army job would become, and how I would embrace that boredom to begin the design of my first "entrepreneurial enterprise." Yes, I finally did get my mind and mouth around those words.

Jenny, Mommi, and Trudy

Naldy and Ed

Jenny as a young woman living in Holland

Chapter 2

"Shake, Rattle and Roll"

Jenny, 1942

The Island of Java, the place of my birth and my first fourteen years, is one of 17,000 tropical islands, more or less, that today make up Indonesia. The days are hot and humid all year round, with a fairly long monsoon season. Entirely of volcanic origin, Java is a paradisiacal place with its lush green rain forests, jungles, colorful flora, and a great variety of exotic birds and wildlife. In fact, some of the most pristine beaches and marine parks in the world are there.

I was born as Jenny Sersansie in Jogjakarta in 1942. As many view it, Jogjakarta is the "soul" of Java, with its focus on fine arts and intellectual heritage. Although it is today a city of over three million with all the amenities and pitfalls of city life, it continues to passionately hold dear and protect its treasured customs.

Early in my life, our family moved to Jakarta, the capital city of Java. It has a very diverse population with its language, cuisine, architecture, religions, and art influenced by Javanese, Malay, Chinese, Arabic, Indian, and European cultures. Like our parents, my two brothers, my sister, and I spoke Indonesian, English, Dutch, and French.

I say all of this to draw the dramatic contrast between the life of my early years and that of Douglas' in the Appalachian Mountains of Virginia. We did, indeed, come from two entirely different worlds, though somehow, incredibly, we would eventually find each other, each the perfect soulmate for the other.

But I still had a lot of life to live before that fateful moment.

In the early 1940s, Java and most of the region was still under the colonial rule of the Netherlands, which it had been since 1800. My people suffered under this despotic control and deeply longed for freedom and self-rule. Therefore, early in the war when the Japanese conquered that part of the world, they were welcomed on Java as liberators. Our people figured nothing could be worse than the morale-defeating, and at times violent, suppression inflicted on them by the Dutch.

At first, the Japanese were quite lenient with the native people of the island and actually began a local political process that ultimately led to Indonesian nationalism. However, to the horror of many, those who were part of the Dutch hierarchy, especially the military, were rounded up and put in internment camps on and off the island. "Internment camp" was just a sanitized term for slave labor or concentration camp.

Poppi, my father, was a tall, slender, serious man from a large Indonesian family. He had made his career in the military and quickly advanced up the ranks to the level of sergeant major. Unfortunately, as such, he was one of the first to go to the camps. He spent two years of his life being starved, beaten, tortured, and made to work like an animal for the Japanese war cause. It's estimated that between four and ten million "Rōmusha," or what came to be known as forced laborers, in Java were taken to work in the camps. It has been reported that only approximately 52,000 were repatriated to Java. That my father survived is a testament to his incredible strength of mind and body and his unbreakable will to live.

In addition to the men who were "interned," thousands of women and children were also imprisoned in camps, and their treatment was often just as harsh. Starvation was a way of life, and general living and working conditions were inhumane. Women feared for their children, who were often taken away when they reached a certain age. People on Java, my mother included, knew that the women from the island of East Timor, only a few hundred miles from Java, were made to not only work like men during the day, but became sex slaves repeatedly raped by the Japanese soldiers at night. The Japanese referred to them as "comfort women," and a great many "comfort stations" were set up by the Japanese throughout Southeast Asia and the Dutch Indies Islands.

Women on Java, of course, lived in terror that this would happen to them. But it seemed in Java, only European, Australian, British, and especially Dutch women were sent to the labor camps, and not as readily to the comfort stations.

Bewildering to me, as I heard about this later in life, was that these atrocities against the women of Java as well as East Timor were not treated as war crimes or aggressively prosecuted. While much has been written and said—as it well should be—about the horrific plight of men during those tumultuous times, there seems to have been little public outcry against the treatment of women in the history of Indonesia; not only during the war, but again in the 1990s when Indonesian soldiers essentially treated the East Timorese women in the same inhumane way.

When the allies freed the islands and Poppi returned home, like most men of that era who had experienced the hell of war, he didn't talk about it. Nobody talked about it. In my life, I've learned there are some experiences too excruciatingly painful to put into words, and too horrifying for others to hear about. Maybe that's why people say some things are "unspeakable." And this seemed to be so with Poppi. Over time, though, he did share some details with Mommi, our mother, in very small measure. As we children grew up, she spoke of them to us on occasion.

When we were young, we had no understanding of it. But over the years of my adulthood, I've wondered what he felt and thought. Did he, as other men and women who have described being trapped in such barbarous situations, feel that awful shame, guilt, and powerlessness that goes with being unable to defend yourself and those around you against repeated and cruel aggression? As a dedicated military officer, Poppi must have felt some responsibility for others in the camps. And, undoubtedly, he must have felt so totally helpless to meet that responsibility. And did he have the tormenting nightmares and flashbacks, the depression and constant anxiety that have plagued others suffering from PTSD? As I said, some things are just too awful for words or even thought. How does one return home to family and a normal life and forget all that inhumanity? One doesn't. Not ever.

So, life with Poppi could be difficult, especially for our mother. However, she never complained, and as children our lives mostly went merrily on.

Mommi, like many mothers since the beginning of time, tried hard to protect us from most of the bad things inside and outside our home.

When things were becoming distressing inside, she would urgently say, "Children, go outside and play." We played barefoot outdoors and had great fun with our friends and each other, because we were not yet able to fully comprehend how dreadful those times could be for Mommi.

Our mother, from a well-to-do family of Dutch descent, was a fashion designer. She valued education and the arts and made every effort to expose us all to both as much as possible. That's when dancing came into my life. First was the beautiful Javanese court dancing with its traditional percussion, wind, and bowed instruments, colorful costumes, and disciplined hand movements. Those dances told heroic stories, or expressed the elaborate range of human desires and emotions. Then came classical ballet, with its beautifully complex music, elegant costumes, and precise full-body movements. I dearly loved every single thing about both forms of dancing! I delighted in the music and costumes of each, and felt especially proud when I had perfected ballet positions and movements like adagio, en pointe, plié, and of course, the pas de deux. I loved it all!

The other thing I realized early on was that I adored being in the limelight, though I was never particularly overzealous in seeking it. Instead, I humbly appreciated the attention when it came, and made the most of it while I had it. Naturally, I was thrilled when I was chosen as the soloist to dance to the beautiful "Blue Danube" waltz in our local theatrical program. "Mommi," I cried with joy after hearing the news, "they chose me to be the lead! I did it!"

"*Hebat!*" My mother exclaimed the Indonesian word for "fabulous." She pulled me into one of her big hugs. "My little starlet!"

Trudy, my older sister, also enjoyed dancing, and we had such fun practicing together, preparing for when we would be dancing with beaus. As my older sister, she would guide many of my movements, and neither of us ever directly spoke to the fact that the pupil was rapidly surpassing the teacher. I was proud of my progress, and Trudy was proud of me. That was enough for us both.

My older brother, Naldy, became an avid artist and played several musical instruments. Ed, the youngest of us, loved anything to do with music, especially rock and roll, and movies. It was this passion of Ed's that ignited and fed my own passion for all things entertainment.

Leaving Our Homeland

After the war, Jakarta was growing by leaps and bounds. It was fast becoming the great financial and industrial megacity of over ten million it is today. People from all over the world were pouring in.

However, immediately after the war, the Dutch tried to resume control of the East Indies. But this time, the people of the new Republic of Indonesia resisted, which resulted in a bloody armed conflict and a diplomatic battle with the Dutch Empire. In 1949, The Netherlands recognized the United States of Indonesia's Declaration of Independence, and a liberal democracy was established. There was great excitement and optimism for the future in the whole region!

Despite this incredible growth and positive prognosis for improved life, our family's destiny lay elsewhere. Plans were being made by my parents to immigrate to Holland, where it was believed life would be more peaceful and offer more opportunities for their children. To uproot with four children and leave one's homeland takes courage, as well as an overwhelming desire for something better. My parents had an abundance of both.

But it turned out Poppi was to remain behind in Jakarta. We children didn't understand why that was, and it was only much later in our lives that we would learn.

So, incredibly, my mother, who had never been off Java, was to take us to this new land by herself. The day in 1954 when we left behind our relatives, friends, and the only way of life we knew in order to emigrate from Indonesia, I was too young to be fully aware of just how brave of heart my mother was to undertake this pilgrimage alone. To us children it was an unbelievably exciting adventure that would lead us to fantastic happenings we couldn't even imagine.

As we arrived at the dock and rounded the boardwalk leading to the ship, I stopped in my tracks. There was the largest manmade thing I had ever seen: the enormous passenger vessel M.S. *Johan van Oldenbarnevelt*! I felt a sudden surge of terror and grabbed my mother's arm. "It's *so* big!" I managed to whisper.

Smiling, Mommi reassured me, "Not to worry, little one. In time, it will get smaller. You can be sure of that." One glance at my mother with her head and shoulders held high and a look of confidence on her face consoled me completely. With Mommi by my side, I was ready to embrace a future that I felt in my gut could only be wonderful.

The thirty-day voyage was tedious, and our mother proved right; the ship did seem much smaller with each day. But we found plenty of distractions. Mommi had her hands full keeping us all out of mischief, especially my brothers. Or at least that's how I like to remember it. They found everything about the ship interesting and set out to explore every inch of it. Mommi constantly kept an ear alerted for the call of, "Man overboard!" It's a wonder she ever managed to sleep during those thirty days.

Trudy and I were at the age where cute boys and men were a fascination. And there were plenty of them on the big ship. I'm sure that was no small concern to my mother either. "Don't talk to the boys. They will think you are *pelacur*," Mommi would warn us against being thought of as "loose women."

"Yes, Mommi," was our dutiful reply. "We won't talk to them." We tried out best not to, but she hadn't said we couldn't flash a smile at whoever looked our way—and plenty did!

Our mother also used this time and wonderful opportunity to educate us about what we were seeing and experiencing. And it was such a great gift we didn't even consider it education. We were simply in awe of all that was going on around us and the sensations we were experiencing.

As we sailed through the Indian Ocean and Arabian and Red Seas, Mommi enthusiastically pointed out, "The Red Sea is bordered by six countries, and the odd colored algae is what gives it its reddish-brown color." Sailing up the Suez Canal she shared the history of the Canal, dating back to the Pharaohs, and the persistent efforts through the years to connect the Mediterranean and Red Seas. At the Port of Aden in Yemen, she pulled guilders (Dutch money) out of her purse and told us, "Go ahead, buy something beautiful you will want to keep forever." Trudy and I bought exquisite scarves made of silken fabric our eyes had never beheld before.

As we sailed around the Strait of Gibraltar, the Bay of Biscay, and finally through the English Channel, we became progressively more excited as we anticipated our arrival in Holland, our new home. The Port of Rotterdam was becoming the largest port in Europe, and for many years it was considered the world's busiest port. The frenetic activity of ships moving in, around, and out of the port was at first dizzying and even intimidating. But we were together in this as a family and united in our determination to find our way in this new and unfamiliar land. We huddled together and remained undaunted by the unfamiliar and by the speed with which our lives were changing

Being multilingual, including Dutch, each of us had a huge advantage as we adapted to our new life in Holland. But there were, of course, other challenges. For me, initial painful concerns were in the personal differences. "I look and sound different from everyone else," I cried in my mother's arms as she attempted to comfort me, reassuring me of the beauty found in all people regardless of skin color, hair color, religion, or language. There had been plenty of Dutch and other Europeans in Jakarta, but Indonesians were far in the majority there. Previously, my mind simply did not register that the differences mattered. But now being in the minority, I feared they would.

As we adapted to our new way of life, Trudy and I discovered an outlet that brought fantastic joy and fun into our lives: the Dutch-Indonesian Social Club. Here, bands blared out popular music to which we could dance ourselves into a frenzy, and we did! The image of America as the Wild West was still a norm, and the locals called any music from the United States "cowboy music." This made it all the more alluring to my sister and me.

On one occasion during one of these frenzied dances, Trudy yelled over the music, "This is like having sex standing up!" Shocked, I almost fell over right there on the dance floor! I knew nothing more about sex than what we saw in the movies, and assumed the same was true for Trudy. Our parents drew a firm line in the sand about romance and boys. Dancing was the closest we were allowed to get to that line. Had Trudy, I wondered, gone over it? Not likely, since she would have been as afraid of Poppi's anger and Mommi's disappointment as I was.

The peak of our happiness was when the clubs hosted rock and roll dance competitions. Those events were the highlight of our lives! And one such event turned out to be providential. We met two brothers, Bram and Renee, who seemed hilariously funny to us—not the brothers themselves; they were ultra "cool," as we said back then. It was the fact that we liked two brothers and they liked us, two sisters, back. Over time, our friendship with these handsome fellows became a decidedly serious matter.

The only connection we had to our beloved rock and roll music while at home, however, was a tiny transistor radio. We turned it up as loud as it would go and blasted music from the United States and Europe. Poppi had finally and mysteriously joined us in Holland by then, and the music drove him mad, but his complaints were mostly good humored. On the other hand, Mommi, spurred on by our enthusiasm and the beat, beat, beat of the music, would often join in and dance with us around the house.

There were many fun times, but with Poppi's arrival to finally live with us in Holland, there was again a rising sense of stress at home. Unfortunately for Mommi, she would take the brunt of that stress as my siblings and I continued to enjoy exploring and growing in our new world.

A Surge of Independence

Our eight years in Holland passed quickly. During that time, partly to get away from home as we finally started to realize the stresses inside those four walls, Trudy and I moved together from Rotterdam to an apartment about forty miles away in Amsterdam. A relative guided me to a job at the Bank of Amsterdam, and, not yet out of my teen years, I experienced that first intoxicating surge of independence—although I was still secure in the knowledge of Trudy's continued presence.

Before long, we located an exciting choice of clubs where we could continue our love affair with dancing. We also continued our friendship with Bram and Renee, and I could tell that Trudy and Renee had drawn very close.

One night, Trudy burst through the door of our apartment, outwardly flushed and excited. "Jen! Renee just proposed! And I said yes, yes, yes!" she twirled around the room in a flurry of bliss.

This proposal wasn't a surprise, and, yet, I suddenly found the news hard to absorb. It left me with mixed emotions. Trudy was my best friend, my partner in fun and mischief, the sister I adored, depended on, and looked up to. We had always been inseparable. Thoughts of no longer being number one in her life left me with a sudden feeling of being alone. But I loved Trudy so very much, and seeing how she glowed made me truly thrilled for her. "That's...wonderful Trudy. Really, it is!" I tried my best to show my support and love.

But she caught on and frowned. "This is a good thing, Jen. A loving marriage can be wonderful. Don't you want the same? How about you and Bram?"

I remained silent, unsure of the answer she was looking for.

"I know he cares for you a lot," she continued. "Has he ever mentioned marriage?"

Trudy's question was a practical one, since Bram and I were seeing a good bit of each other. But at that point, I felt much too young, immature, and still caught up in having fun to understand or give much thought to serious love and what marriage was really all about.

"I know he cares, and I care about him," I told her slowly. "But we don't seem to feel what you and Renee do. We're just...good friends."

"I think he would like to be more than just good friends, Jen."

"Maybe, but I'm not ready for marriage. There's so much I want to experience before settling down." But even as I said these things, I felt the growing panic at the thought of being alone and without Trudy. Who could I share these feelings with if not Trudy herself, the person I had shared every important thought, deed, and feeling with all my life? These thoughts collided within me. "I'm scared, Trudy. I'm scared to lose you."

"Oh, Jen. You mustn't be. We'll still be close and see each other every day. I promise. So long as you want me, I will always love you and be here for you."

"But it won't be the same after you're married! How can it ever be the same?" I was now crying. The tears were both for Trudy's happiness, as she was so very happy, and also selfishly for what I was about to lose. What would I do without my Trudy?

Whether spurred on by Renee's marriage or true love, I'll never know, but Bram did eventually propose. And I accepted for all the wrong reasons. I wanted someone to laugh, dance, and have a good time with. Someone to live with and keep me company; someone who would provide the emotional support and sense of security I still needed. Marriage with Bram seemed to offer all of that; maybe not on the deep level I shared with Trudy, but I was willing to settle for even just a surface sense of those things. In retrospect, I was still immature and not ready for marriage. And yet, I was not strong or independent enough to turn away from it.

It was 1962 now, and our lives were once again changing. My family—all of us except for Naldy, who had made a complete life for himself in Holland—was immigrating to the United States! My parents consistently sought out better lives for themselves and their children, and the United States was the ultimate destination for those desires. Though both Trudy and I were hardly children by now; we were still young, but we both had husbands. Thankfully, Renee and Bram were plenty eager to explore life across the ocean, so it meant that, minus Naldy, we would all remain together as a family.

It had always been a far-out dream of mine to go to America, the land of infinite excitement and opportunities. Not only did I want to live there, but I also wanted to become a citizen, to be an American in every sense of the meaning of it!

The next several months were a flurry of activity as we prepared for our new adventure, once more taking comfort in the knowledge we would all be together. We again traveled by ship, but this trip was a short ten days—even though it seemed like a thousand. Mommi, Poppi, Ed, Trudy, Renee, Bram, and I were as happy and excited in our anticipation of living in America as children on Christmas morning. It was as though we each held our own secret reason in our hearts for wanting to reach the United States of America. For me, it was simply the ultimate destination of the world.

The S.S. *Groote Beer* finally arrived in New York Harbor, and when we got our first glimpse of the Statue of Liberty through the fog, every one of us had tears running down our cheeks—just as millions of immigrants before us had. She was such a beautiful, noble lady inviting us to come stay awhile, or maybe forever, and enjoy all the many glorious benefits offered by this great country, including realizing whatever dreams we may be coming with. How could anyone from another country seeking a better life not be indescribably uplifted and deeply touched to the core of their being by that experience?

We set foot on American soil for the first time at the Port of New Jersey and made our way to New York's Grand Central Station. I immediately loved everything about this new country: the hustle and bustle, the clatter and noise of busy traffic, the flashing neon lights, the smells, and the hurrying people too distracted to pay me much mind even when they bumped into me. All of it compounded in a way that made me feel more alive than I knew was possible.

At Grand Central, we boarded a train to meet our American sponsors in our new "hometown" of Toledo, Ohio, where we would begin our lives as Americans.

A New Life

Ohio was very much mainstream middle-America when we arrived in the 1960s. We were accustomed to the diversity of people, food, dress, and language found in Indonesia and Europe. Here, the primarily white population, with a much smaller black minority, along with the unfamiliar physical setting, food, dress, and language at first made it seem as though we were on another planet. While it was a little scary, those very differences made it exciting to my young mind. We were in America!

Toledo proved to be the ideal place for my family to become assimilated into American culture. We were immediately accepted and welcomed despite the differences in our physical appearance, language, and mannerisms. Our mistakes and missteps as foreigners in this new place were kindly indulged, and we quickly met people who seemed eager to include us in their family of friends and their activities. Although much seemed strange, we found comfort and reassurance in each other. And the eagerness of our friends and neighbors—these ordinary, wonderful Americans—to put us at ease and guide us around that necessarily huge learning curve made the experience a tremendously positive one. As a result, I often look back on that special time with gratitude and warm memories.

Being adept at learning languages and already able to speak English, from the get-go I picked up on the informalities of American speech and acquired the lingo of casual conversation. And my friends even said it was with only enough accent to make me sound "worldly" and "charming." This made it easier for me to become an insider. And, as a shy, self-conscious young woman so full of both fear of rejection and an overwhelming desire to be included, how I reveled in being on the inside with my new American friends!

Over time, there was a growing sense of personal freedom and confidence happening inside of me. And yet, that feeling of anticipation was marked by both excitement and a degree of vague anxiety. For what reason, I did not yet know.

Doug in the NCO office

Doug and his army buddies

Korean rockabilly band playing in the NCO Club

Korean girls dancing to rockabilly

Chapter 3

"Whole Lotta Shakin' Going On"

1956

Doug: Arriving in Korea during the dreaded monsoon season, our troop was immediately transported by trucks to our base just ten miles from the demilitarized zone. As we were hauled through the torrential rains and knee-high slush, the sense of danger we had been prepared for seemed so real we felt we could reach out and touch it. Our minds and bodies were on red alert. The penetrating dampness from the rain, humidity, drenched foliage, and our wet clothes not only soaked into our skin, but into our very souls.

Every aspect of this strange and foreign land seemed so completely different than that of the Appalachian Mountain region where I grew up. "Well," drawled Hank, "if we're dead, we sure know we ain't gone to heaven. No siree, we for sure ain't there."

"Did you expect to be?" I replied.

He shrugged. "Just thought I'd have more time to make it good with the Lord. Me and him ain't spoke for a while."

"Well, Hank ol' buddy, you'd better start talking." Remembering the close collaboration Mama and the Lord had when I fell into the scalding water, I wondered if maybe this would be a good time to do some talking myself. But not having visited with Him much when times were good, it didn't seem right to go knocking now.

To cope with my new reality, I spent a lot of time in my head, which wasn't anything new for me. This was going to be an adventure all right, and I resolved to turn it into one as positive as possible. But right off the bat, I wasn't at all sure how to do that.

Every new recruit was assigned a job. The process began with a mandatory meeting with the U.S. Army's 55th company commander. I arrived nervous but determined to not appear weak, reflecting on the days I had first faced the barkeep and the moonshiners—and even my own dad.

"What can you do, corporal?" the captain asked as he referred to his checklist of jobs to be filled.

"Sir," I didn't hesitate, "I do bookkeeping." A stretch, but I had learned to keep the numbers balanced while working between the bar and moonshine dealers. Granted, it was my own unique method of bookkeeping. "I also have experience working in bars, mainly managing and transporting inventory." He would never know that meant running moonshine. "As well as building maintenance and that sort of thing."

He explained the two jobs that were open. One was driving trucks back and forth to Seoul. I considered the coming monsoons and immediately asked about the other job.

I left the meeting as the newly appointed Labor Noncommissioned Officer in charge of 300 local civilians. Having been cleared and approved as "friendly," these village men were hired to support the dangerous mission of our American military by maintaining and hauling ammunition.

My new job was to supervise the payroll, perform general administration, and monitor clearance of these locals. Plus, based on my bar experience, the captain added the management of the Noncommissioned Officers (NCO) Club to my job description. Well, they called it a club. It was actually a nearly empty Quonset hut, a weird looking, half-barrel metal building that could be used for pretty much any purpose. But the "club" would have to wait.

My immediate job was to manage the 300 Korean civilians and make sure our military had ammunition to fight with if the North Koreans ever decided to come over the DMZ and take back South Korea. The captain also gave me an education about the circumstances on the base needing attention. We called this an "earful" back home. "Here are your problems, Lambert. Your civilian workers tend to wander off, meaning they aren't here on the job when they're supposed to be. The other problem is that when our soldiers are off duty, they visit the local villages, which puts us smack in the middle of a goddamn mess. They get drunk and chase women, the villagers get upset, fights break out, and our VD rate is probably the highest in the entire U.S. Military." He poked his finger at me. "So your job, corporal, is to be shit-sure we have 150 civilian workers here and working at any given time, and that the soldiers are armed and ready when needed."

Was he kidding?! I wanted to look around and see how many other Lamberts he was talking to in the room.

Thankfully, I was assigned two experienced assistants who I sent to round up the civilian workers. Approaching the group for the first time, my stomach curled when I got a big whiff of something foul, kind of sour and rotten smelling. "Good afternoon. I'm Corporal Lambert, and it looks like I'm in charge here. So, the first thing on the list is to get rid of that fucking dead rat!"

Those who understood English, including my assistants, burst into laughter. Once the interpreter made my remarks clear to the rest of the civilians, they also erupted into laughter. I froze and waited for an explanation.

"Um, sir," one of my assistants quietly informed me as he turned his back to the civilians. "What you smell is their lunch." He explained that kimchi is a traditional Korean dish, a spicy fermented mixture of cabbage, vegetables, garlic, radish, and green onion. "We call it...pungent," he noted, trying to keep a straight face. All the locals seemed to understand this word and agreeably nodded their heads. I took a breath, trying to ignore the odor.

"So. 'Pungent' is the first official Korean word I've learned," I joked. Everyone cracked up again, and if there was any ice between us, it had just melted.

After my tour of the labor camp, it was clear these people had been shortchanged. They needed more tents, bunks, food, and a separate mess hall. I didn't know what to expect from the supply sergeant, so I beefed up my numbers. What the sergeant approved was just about the exact amount needed to keep my workers off the ground, reasonably dry, well fed, and hopefully willing to stay on the base.

As far as the rest of the base, we got busy cleaning every corner, updating the food supplies, and ensuring every soldier had adequate munitions they kept above the standard of spit and polish. And, importantly, the area to cook kimchi was moved to a separate tent. The locals liked having their own private mess hall, and we all liked being a little further away from the...pungentness.

Word of the improvements was getting back to the brass, and I was enjoying being in their good favor. However, a well-run organization meant I had increasingly more free time on my hands, which ordinarily isn't a bad thing. But in this case, there weren't many options for how to use that free time, which resulted in a good bit of boredom.

I made the mistake of writing home about the doldrums this boredom had put me in and got a quick reply from Mama reminding me about "idle hands being the devil's workshop."

"I'm sure there's plenty of folks there needing help," her letter added. "And it wouldn't hurt for you boys to have a nice vegetable garden to eat from. So, Douglas Lambert, you find yourself something worthwhile to do and do it!"

As always, Mama was right. But gardening wasn't my thing, and although my mama would walk ten miles and back to give comfort to a neighbor, it was a blow to my character that I didn't inherit that degree of goodness. So, what was left? The so-called NCO Club. I had neglected this part of my duties because it was in such dismal condition that I hadn't let much of my mind go there.

"Be careful what you ask for, you just might get it," my father often reminded me. And so it was with the NCO Club. The Quonset hut had no bar, and it was dirty and empty except for several tables, chairs, and an old billiard table. But a few soldiers were so bored they would make the trek to the club through ankle deep muck for a flat, warm beer and maybe the extra thrill of a pool game with warped cues.

Here, finally, was my "thing to do." My challenge. It wasn't exactly what Mama had in mind, but maybe it would keep the devil at bay—and that would please her no end, since the devil seemed to particularly covet my soul.

TEX AND THE VILLAGE GIRLS

In the club, I tried to encourage conversation to get some feedback from the occasional customers we served. However, they seemed resigned to the way things were and passed off the lame NCO Club with a running dialogue of, "What do you expect? It's the army."

One night, a fellow I hadn't seen before came in and was doing some high powered "good ol' boy" talking with the few guys. His stories and jokes were dominating the attention and getting plenty of laughs. Myself a "good ol' boy," we made a quick connection, and he talked freely.

His name was Thomas, and he was from Fort Worth, Texas. People called him Tex, and it would suit him fine for me to do the same. Tex had a girl who he planned to marry when he got back home, and he would follow in his father's career tracks as an oil rigger.

What Tex lacked in social graces and education (which I lacked), he more than made up for with his infectious enthusiasm, good humor, and down home practical common sense. When I asked why soldiers rarely came into the club, he rolled his eyes and glanced around the room. Then taking the last swig of his warm beer, Tex wiped his mouth on his shirtsleeve, burped, and said, "Come with us to the village this Friday night and you'll see. The drinks are a hell of a lot better, and you can dance with a real girl." He gave me a knowing look, a mock salute, and headed for the door.

That Friday night, I hit the local village bar with my new Texas friend and his buddies. The minute we stepped inside, my pulse increased a few notches. The local drinking hut was a large room with makeshift tables and chairs. The bar was unpainted, and the dance floor was pieced together with remnants from other building projects. It made my Appalachian honky tonk joint look like a luxury establishment, and it wasn't much of an improvement over the Quonset hut back at base. But the beer was cold, the liquor potent, and the place was packed with girls flashing smiles and dancing for drinks and tips.

It didn't take long for men who would sweat and pull together by day to turn into brawling rivals at night under the influence of alcohol and women. And the first to get into a fist swinging free-for-all was Tex. He was dancing with a girl whose boyfriend had taken offense and picked up a chair as a weapon. I liked a good brawl as well as the next guy, but having no dog in this hunt, I ducked into a safe corner and watched. And as fists were flying, a plan was coming together in my head.

Get Go-Go Going

The next day, I made my first munitions and labor checks, then met my battered pal at the NCO Club and took him into my confidence. "Tex, I've got a new plan to keep the soldiers on base *and* get them into our club." He gave me a look out of the one eye still open that let me know he absolutely did not believe me. His hangover was not helping him summon any of his famed enthusiasm for my idea either.

"I'm telling you, this so-called club is really a honky tonk waiting to happen! We've got the shell of a club, but there's no fun, no magic, no life. We've got a shitty record player with scratchy, out-of-date records, warm beer, no liquor...and where are the girls? We need girls!" Tex glanced around silently, sadly confirming there were definitely no girls in the place. "I'm going to fix all that," I said. "Watch. This'll be the most popular hangout in South Korea."

"Corporal, you are one crazy dude," Tex responded slowly, shaking his head.

Confidently looking him in his good eye, I said, "You just confirmed my plan is a winner!" A big knowing grin was all over my face. It was hard to contain my excitement, and Tex was getting caught up in it.

"So then what's next, hot shot?" he asked.

"What's next is to liven this place up. And I know just the person who can help."

The carefully packed box of 45s from my sweet sister Nell arrived in about three weeks' time; just enough to scratch out my plan on more than a few mess hall napkins.

Launching a search for a jukebox, my team thankfully found a cheap one in Seoul that was trucked up to our base. Tex viewed the jukebox with curiosity and admiration. "Man, you damn sure know how to get an ol' mule movin'!" With mounting excitement, he asked, "You got any Bob Wills and his Texas Playboys to play on that thing?" Right then and there I knew my beautiful beat-up jukebox was going to be a hit.

The construction unit was happy to build us a somewhat respectable bar. We found a decent cooler to keep the beer cold and ordered some brand name liquor. It didn't take long for the workers to spread word that we were spiffing up the NCO Club. There I was, halfway around the world, a few miles from the most dangerous militarized border in existence, creating the next step up from an all-American honky tonk.

Little did I know it was soon to be one of the world's first go-go clubs.

Keeping up with the latest hit singles and bands from back home was a big part of the job. Pressing new arrivals to get the buzz on any up-and-coming hit tunes wasn't difficult; most of the guys were happy to ask their mothers, wives, and girlfriends to send them some 45 records. Music around the world was changing and the U.S. was the hub for this riveting revolution. The hillbilly music from my childhood had evolved into rockabilly, a sound having the soul of country and bluegrass with a hard driving beat. Between 1955 and 1957, rockabilly went national thanks to three huge hits: Carl Perkins with the first recording of "Blue Suede Shoes," Elvis Presley's sultry "Heartbreak Hotel," and my personal favorite, recorded by Jerry Lee Lewis, "Whole Lotta Shakin' Goin' On." And shakin' was just what I had in mind for my new club.

Although thousands of miles from the United States and having little means of communication except mail, I tried to stay as current as possible with what was going on in the music and entertainment industries so as to keep the NCO Club relevant and popular. By now, this business was not just in my blood, but rushing through my veins like the rapids of the Chattanooga River after a spring flood.

A great assortment of records was regularly arriving from home, always immediately slipped into slots on my beloved jukebox. It stayed busy playing three songs for a quarter, and the extra money went back into club improvements.

Tex, always making sure country western music was well represented, waved several more records sent by his girl: "Dear John" by Jean Shepard, "Your Cheatin' Heart" and "I'll Never Get Out of This World Alive" by Hank Williams. However, he continued to grouse. "Dougie, you've done a heap of good for us boys, but we still ain't got any girls!"

"Sad ain't it?" I replied. "Want to hear the really bad news? Apparently there's a regulation that civilian entertainers aren't allowed on a military base this close to the DMZ." Tex hung his head, but I wasn't done. "Don't fold your cards just yet. I think it's time I have a talk with the captain." I made for the door. "And by the way, Tex," I added over my shoulder, "don't you think maybe that girl of yours is trying to tell you something with those records she's sending?" An empty beer bottle whizzed past my head and shattered against the wall.

A few minutes later, I saluted the captain and he saluted back. "Okay, corporal, what is it now? You only show your sad face when you want something." *Damn right*, I thought. Why else would I want to come to the attention of high command?

He gestured for me to sit in a chair and rubbed his brow, looking as though he was unsure about sharing his next words. "You've done a hell of a job with the locals and with that piece of crap we called a club." Not one to throw around compliments, I knew the captain was sincere.

"Thank you, sir," I replied. "But there's still work to be done." In front of him was the paperwork I'd submitted covering every detail of my request. "Sir, I have the solution to your main problem here on base." I quickly went on before he could ask me to define the problem. "I believe we have a safety-first issue at hand, and the NCO is prepared to do the groundwork to put a correction plan into action. If I could just speak to the general about this, I believe we could get his approval to implement this plan right away."

The captain's face reflected his disbelief over me suggesting going over his head to the general, and I knew I was risking whatever goodwill I might have with him by even hinting at such a thing. But I also gambled this was the best way to get the captain's full attention and his most immediate response.

"What's the problem that's so urgent to solve? Did I miss that part?" he asked. Without waiting for a reply, his face grew redder and his voice grew louder. He jabbed his infamous finger at the clause in my paperwork and punctuated every word as he bellowed, "On...base...live...entertainment? What kind of solution is this to any problem we might have?! No way in hell will there ever be live entertainment on this base! You know as well as I do there's a regulation against it. And be fucking sure of this: We are *not* going to the general or anyone else with this fucking twaddle. We're in at *war*, soldier! Are you crazy!?"

Twaddle? What the shit was twaddle? I had no idea, but crazy I knew! I sat up straight. The worst was over, and now was the time to get him to approve my plan.

"Sir, you're absolutely correct. We are in a war. So, let's go back to the original problem you told me I had to solve when you first made my assignment. Our men are leaving the base for entertainment, which creates safety and readiness issues, as well as problems with the local communities. So, what happens if we offer entertainment appealing enough that the men choose to stay right here on base? Problem solved."

I plastered a look of relief on my face intended to increase his confidence. "Yeah, I'll grant you it's a little off the wall. But we know if we can keep the men on base, not only will they be safer and happier, but the base will also be more secure in the event of an attack. Isn't that the desired outcome?"

He stayed silent, rubbing his stubby chin as he pondered the appeal of my solution.

"There's even little to no extra overhead involved because the club's income will pay for the extra costs of providing the entertainment." The captain looked back at my paperwork. But I wanted to get ahead of what he was going to say next. "And you are one hundred percent correct, captain. Asking for live bands is asking for a lot, considering the regulation forbidding it. We've already got a great jukebox stocked with 45s. So let's scrap the band. Instead, let's just start with," I cleared my throat, "girls."

The captain was silent. I was experiencing a miracle. "And they'll wear costumes which will make it very...legitimate. I'm thinking a special swimsuit costume. More like a dress, and we'll cover it in fringe to make it look like they're showing more skin." The captain was still breathing normally, and his red face was now a healthier shade of pink. So I began closing the deal. "Sir, when the men are off roaming the villages looking for a little fun and entertainment, it puts our base in a highly vulnerable position. If there ever was a DMZ breach and North Koreans came over the border, we'd have to go to a dozen or more villages to find our men and drag them back. A livened-up NCO Club is the perfect solution. The men would never want to leave the base."

The captain went back to reading my request, and I managed, with some effort, to keep my mouth shut now. Suddenly taking a piece of paper from his desk drawer, he began to write. "Corporal, I hate to admit it, but what you say makes sense." Handing me the paper, he said, "You'll get my support for the girls, but we still need to jump a few hurdles set by some higher-ups in Seoul."

The next few weeks were a blur of paperwork, all forms in triplicate that covered every detail of operating an NCO Club in the U.S. Military.

I dreaded the thought of being called in front of some sort of committee (I did my best work one-on-one) to defend what those higher-ups may see as outright insurrection, but I had a speech written down and rehearsed in my mind just in case. The appeal would basically be the same as presented to the captain, with the current success of the club as supporting evidence. The fact that I was having a hell of a good time and taking advantage of an opportunity to teach myself the nightclub business while gaining invaluable experience was my own private agenda. It was a win-win for all sides.

The day for my speech in front of the committee did eventually come. My recollection of that meeting in Seoul is vague, probably clouded by my first ever anxiety attack. Guided into an enormous room, I found myself standing in front of a table of seated men, some in uniform, some not. We all properly saluted, and I sat. A uniform with the most decoration indicated I should speak my case, and I summoned up all the confidence and conviction I could muster. My intent was to make it short and to the point.

But as it happened, I didn't need to worry. I gave my speech, and no questions were asked. The paperwork was signed and stamped and included both girls and...*bands*! I actually had approval for bands, which was key to my plan. The men at the table gave me big smiles and wished me luck.

I set up an office to run the base's newest attack-ready plan: my version of a honky tonk smack at the DMZ border.

Life in Korea was now getting interesting. Each day, I insured the stability of my munitions unit, then scheduled meetings with various Koreans who were sourcing talent.

"You're in our budget," I told the region's "entertainment agent." He was more than pleased to provide me with girls who auditioned for coveted dancing positions, and local bands who wanted performing opportunities on the American military base. The pay would be solid and steady. I promised absolutely no hanky-panky with the girls unless they wanted to participate, and also requested the inclusion of safe transportation for the women to and from the base. My wheeler-dealer friend eagerly shook my hand and offered me a shot of America's finest whiskey.

I reflected on my plan: Girls in fringe dresses dancing on a bar. Live bands shaking the room. Jukebox music between acts. A built-in customer base of soldiers looking for a little piece of American heaven. What I didn't know then was that I had just founded one of the first go-go dance clubs five years before the trend exploded in America.

About a week later, Tex, with a drink in hand and an adoring girl on his arm, slapped me on the back. He was yelling over the pulsating music, and over his shoulder I kept one eye on the gyrating girls working up a frenzy among the guys who were hollering for more. On its very first weekend, the NCO Club was packed to a sold-out crowd of soldiers. Before long, the troubles in the villages were becoming virtually nonexistent as the men spent more and more time on base. My plan worked both to the benefit of the army and to my personal learning curve.

Excitement was growing about performers who were building names in the U.S., so we booked an act calling themselves The Kim Sisters, and they proved to be one of the most popular acts we had. I wasn't positive they were The Kim Sisters of Las Vegas fame, but they were close enough. No one trapped at the ends of the Earth, as those servicemen felt they were, cared about the Sisters' bonafides. The only credentials that mattered to those love-starved men were that the girls were ultra sexy, talented sirens who sang their hearts out.

Life in the army was going remarkably well. The boring days were long gone, and I had earned the respect of those below and above me. By this time, the club was such a big hit that I planned to approach our beleaguered captain with my next scheme...or rather, plan...for expansion. However, before I could convert it from mess hall napkins (my preferred blueprint material) to a typed report, my orders to return to the States came through.

Saying Goodbye

It was bittersweet, but the time had come to move on. Saying goodbye to friends like Tex, who had shared the good, bad, and ugly of this incredible experience, was hard.

"Come see me in Hollywood," said one of my buddies as we both packed for our return. "It's a ball, you'll love it there." He wrote his contact information on a piece of paper and added, "Thanks for making it a good ride, Mr. Go-Go Man."

He was just one of many soldiers passing contact information to me. While some were from various parts of the country, the guys from California were the most insistent that I make a move to the entertainment capital of the world. The message given to me by many of these men was that the NCO Club had made their lives in an often demoralizing place so far away from home more bearable, leaving a memorable impression on them. As a man not given to sentimentality, I was more than a little surprised at how very touching and meaningful this was to me. And it was no small factor in stoking the fire in my belly that kept alive the dream of an ever bigger and better "Quonset hut" back in the United States.

Early one night before shipping out, the captain and I enjoyed a drink together at the NCO Club. Having been through some good times and bad together, we shared a certain kinship, although neither of us spoke much on a personal level. But I felt comfortable sharing what I was feeling at that moment. "Captain, I know I've been a big pain in the ass at times, but I'm mighty grateful to you for your support. I put my heart into the club, and I sure hate to leave it. Besides, who back in the States is gonna hire a munitions man?"

"Yep, you're a *royal* pain in the ass!" he agreed. "But you more than made up for that. You provided an oasis for these homesick boys, and that enabled them to be better soldiers. As far as your future, I think our country is about ready for you and your go-go club," he laughed. "I say take your honorable discharge and what you've learned here and aim for the stars." My captain's encouraging words were more prophetic than either of us could have imagined.

Over my last few months serving, I watched as the live bands became polished performers. With my guidance, their performances were paced for maximum mood and energy, the lighting focused for the most dramatic effect, and the alcohol provided a reasonable choice of quality. My jukebox more than did its job of bringing a great variety of popular music to this rather isolated spot in the world: hillbilly, rock and roll, rockabilly, country power ballads, and some of the great pop classics—music that linked us all to home, family, friends, loved ones, and normality. I was proud of what had been accomplished, of course, with a great deal of help and support from those around me.

And in no small feat, some of the soldiers had found romance, even deep and abiding love, in that club. It made me wonder if my own soulmate was out there somewhere. I sure hoped so. Going it alone was...well, pretty lonely.

THE JOY OF MY LIFE

JENNY: The most important event in a woman's life was about to take place in mine.

Out of my marriage with Bram came the most magnificent gift imaginable: my son Michael! Giving birth to this perfect little being was a truly wondrous and sacred experience to me. In life, there are usually just a few critical happenings that significantly change us from deep within. Giving birth, especially for the first time, is most definitely one of those times.

Not only was I in awe of this beautiful baby boy and amazed that my body could have produced something so wonderful, I was also instantly aware of the huge and daunting responsibility I had for this baby's life, now and into the future. If that doesn't take some of the frivolous immaturity and self-absorption out of you, nothing will. And it did for me—not all I would have liked, but some.

However, despite the love Bram and I shared for Michael, it was becoming clear to me that my marriage would not bring the fulfillment both my husband and I wanted and needed, and this cast a shadow over all things good at that time.

When I finally shared my feelings with Mommi, she of course expressed deep concern. "But Jenny, Bram is a good man and a good provider. He loves you and Michael. Marriage is not something you just cast aside because you have an unhappy day. You must give this serious thought."

"But I *have* given it a lot of thought. For a long time. Yes, Bram is good to Michael and me, and yes, he does give us the basic necessities we need. But I just don't love him as a wife should love her husband, and I don't think he loves me that way either. How can that be a good thing—to stay together without the happiness that only two people deeply committed to each other can know?"

"There's more to marriage than love, Jen," Mommi said as she sighed. It was a dejected response, a side of her I hadn't seen much before. But I shouldn't have been surprised—she had stayed in a less-than-happy marriage, even an abusive one at times, in great part because in her mind it was best for us children, and in part because that's what women of her generation and cultural background did. This conversation was hard for her to fully wrap her mind and heart around.

But it was vitally important to me that she understand, and that I have her support. "Mommi, Bram is a valued friend, but we don't share a common dream we can be excited about and work toward together. And we don't have the deep love, passion, and intimacy between us that would get us through whatever bad times may be ahead. And you know there will be those times. No matter how compatible two people are, there are always rough patches to work through."

Still looking at me as though I was speaking a language foreign to her ears, Mommi shook her head. But I pressed on. "I'm still young, and I need those things in my life, just as Bram needs them in his. But we can't give them to each other."

Although I had an inkling at the time of how critical those ingredients in a marriage were, I really didn't understand and appreciate the full extent of their importance in keeping a relationship vibrant and strong enough to sustain it through the hardships, pitfalls, and landmines that lie in the path of all marriages. "I want to be more than just a wife or a woman whose main concern is that she belongs to a man. I want to be my own person, to become all that I can be, free to explore all the possibilities life has to offer. I can't do that married to Bram, Mommi." I shook my head angrily. "Sometimes I feel this raging fire burning inside me, but I have to smother it and the passion that fuels it, because it's my place to do so. And when I have to do that, I feel like I have nothing. I can't stand the nothing. This vacuum of emotion makes me feel completely empty, sapping the drive that makes me feel alive and makes life worth living."

I was desperate for understanding and support, because my growing dread was that if I remained in this marriage, a vital part of me would die. However, I also knew that a divorce would bring hurt to others I deeply cared about, including my husband and, down the road, possibly our son. Even though this is a conflict experienced each day by thousands of women and men, at the time, I felt so alone in facing such a lifechanging decision.

"Jen, you have to consider more than just yourself. What about Michael? He needs his father. Please, please think hard about this," Mommi said, echoing my internal concerns.

"I have, Mommi. And just think: What would Michael's life be like if I stayed married to Bram and continued to be miserable? Would I not only resent Bram but Michael too? Could he grow up happy with me being so unhappy?"

At some point in our ongoing conversations, there were fewer protests, and I could tell Mommi was listening with her heart more than with her mind. Finally, one day as I was once again pouring my heart out, she took my hands in hers, looked me in the eye, and with seldom-seen tears, she shared a part of herself that now seemed eager to escape after being pushed far down and locked away for a long time.

"I too wanted those things, Jenny. I had dreams and desires. I had talent and ambition. I wanted to be loved and to love back with passion. I know about the burning inside, and I know about the emptiness. But I lived in a world where women with ambition and who sought independence were not smiled upon. A world where a woman's uniqueness was squashed under a man's ego, where we could only shine as bright as our men allowed us to shine. A world where women had to turn their heads away from the wrongs and injustices, the pain and the suffering, as though they didn't exist. A world where a woman with children could not raise them alone. There were no good choices but to submit and bear it. My comfort was in God and in my children. There was no use in wanting more."

"Oh, Mommi." I wrapped my arms around her. "I know your life has been hard and often unhappy. But you've never complained." And then I thought, *who was there to complain to?* And my mother would have thought such complaining would not have made a difference and would have only been an undue worry to others. No, Mommi would not have done that. So, she took her burdens to only her lifelong source of strength: her God.

"But today, in this world, I see it can be different," Mommi continued as we hugged. "And I do want it to be different for you. We must make it different. Jenny, you have a right to be the person you want to be, and although I may not always agree with your decisions, I'll always love you and do my best to help you."

My heart was swelling with my mother's incredible compassion and understanding.

"You know, maybe when I was young, there *were* better choices for me and other women, but we simply didn't have a big enough appetite for a different life, a different way of doing. Or maybe most of us didn't have the strength and courage to fight for that life. But, *putriku*," she called me her princess, "you *do* have the hunger for more out of life and for a better way. And you do have the strength to go after it. I don't know where that will lead you. Maybe a good place, maybe not such a good place. Either way, my heart and my love will be with you."

The tears running down both our faces were not only for the hope we shared for my life at that moment, but for the loss of hope she had once experienced in hers. I only hoped that striking out on my own could replenish a little bit of that hope for my mother now.

Thus, divorce from Bram became inevitable. And the pain, feelings of self-doubt, and guilt I experienced were just as inevitable. It was an agonizing, soul-searching time for me. Since there had been no significant conflict between us and he had done nothing wrong, Bram couldn't understand my need to be out of the marriage. Even though I knew he felt the same way I did about our emotional relationship, he was a man of logic, and on paper, we worked. I don't blame him for being upset about my seemingly sudden need to flee. What I was surprised about, however, was that in his anger, he decided he wanted full custody of Michael. That resulted in an even longer and more hurtful battle between us.

How horrible I felt for causing such distress in one I loved so much. Of course, Mommi understood, but it was still a very sad and stressful time for her too. And Poppi...well, he had his own concerns about my situation.

"And how exactly do you expect to support yourself and Michael? Will Bram help?" he asked. I wondered if his main worry was the possibility of us becoming a burden to him.

"Of course Bram will take care of Michael, but since this is my decision, I can't ask Bram to take that responsibility. I'll take care of Michael and me." But Poppi seemed skeptical. This was a time full of angst and very low self-esteem on my part. I was so afraid of losing Michael and full of guilt because of the unhappiness I'd caused people

I loved. But despite all of this—or maybe because of it—my divorce ultimately resulted in some much needed personal growth.

Only in my early twenties at this time, I had never really known what it was like to feel entirely responsible for anyone, including myself. I'd always had my parents, then Trudy, then Bram. Now, the decisions I was making, including not accepting any help from Bram, would put me, for the first time in my life, in the position of having full and total responsibility over not only myself, but for a child. As I saw it, I had no choice but to do it...and no doubt that I could.

And so, I began life as a single, working mother. My heart was with Michael, and I loved him dearly. He seemed to be the only thing good and right about my life at that time.

As a result of my banking job in Amsterdam, where I had been noticed and praised by the people above me, a career in banking seemed to be the most practical plan for my future. But working in that world previously had not been satisfying. Not in the way I so desperately wanted it to be. And even though I had the love of my family and friends, I still felt lost and empty.

At this point, it seemed I could only feel happy and fulfilled on the dance floor—just as it had been since childhood when I was first fascinated by ballet and the thrill of the spotlight. It was on the dance floor where I felt most free and able to express myself as a complete person. And it was there I found the passion that was missing from my life. It was a drumbeat that got louder and faster with each day.

THE CALL OF THE WEST

It wasn't just my own drum pounding louder and faster; it was the world's drum! Change was in the air everywhere, especially in America.

Almost everything I knew of the United States as seen in movies, magazines, music, and fashion seemed to come from Hollywood. Once again, that seductive siren song turned my head and heart westward—to what, I wasn't sure. But I was certain I had to go. Toledo was a great starting place as we integrated into American life, but dreams came true in California—and that's where I wanted to start fresh and take control of making my dreams a reality, whatever they were. I wanted it for myself, and I wanted it for my son.

Not only was I ready to move on, but Ed, my younger brother, was too. His mind and heart were still filled with music and entertainment. The idea of being in Hollywood was indescribably exciting to him. While it was easy for Ed and me to embrace such a move at our young age, it took big-time spunk for my parents to make that decision.

"You want to go where!?" Mommi uttered in disbelief. To her, a place as far away and as different as California was the same as another country in some other part of the world. "But why?" she asked. "What's wrong with Toledo? It's a good place. The people are good. Trudy is here. Our lives are here."

"Yes, it is a good place. But there are more opportunities in California. Life is better there, more exciting, richer."

"You want to leave your home and family and make a million dollars in California? You think it will be that easy? What would a girl alone with a baby do in California?"

"Well…I wouldn't be alone if you and Poppi came with me," I offered guardedly.

"Poppi and me leave Toledo? What on earth would we do in California? We know nobody, we would not have jobs. Where would we live? And what about Michael? His father is here. Michael needs to grow up knowing his father."

My mother was a woman of great inner fortitude in so many ways! But over time she came to understand this move was vitally important to me. And she understood how much her help was needed. Eventually, she and Poppi were willing to uproot once again and move west. And once the decision was made, they did so with a wonderful spirit of expectation and adventure, which added to my own excitement even more.

As she always had been and always promised to be, my mother was totally supportive at an important time in my life. I depended on her strength and wisdom so very much. I loved my mother for many reasons, and this was just one more.

Though our hearts were saddened by the prospect of being separated from our beloved Trudy for the first time ever, we packed up, left Trudy behind to enjoy her life as a wife and mother, and headed for Los Angeles, California; modern day Canaan; land of milk, honey, and golden opportunities.

Front row (left to right): Jenny, Mommi, Trudy

Jenny and her family move to the United States

Doug returns home from the army

Chapter 4

"Mystery Train"

Doug: The army issued me a ticket to return home to my mother in Bristol. Like all young people coming back from military service who were not returning to an already established life, I struggled with getting my footing.

Exposure to a world and experiences that were 180 degrees different from all that I knew before had changed me. I wanted even more out of life now. But back home, the dreams and exciting ideas for my future held in Korea clashed with the reality of my situation. I was still a poor, uneducated country boy with few resources at my disposal that would help me get ahead.

So, restless and adrift, I stumbled around a good bit trying first one job then another, and doing my share of hell raising around town with some other high-spirited guys. One thing I found out for sure was that "working for the man" just didn't work for me. I guess that was one other trait I inherited from my father. As far as I knew, for better or worse, he was always his own boss.

"Douglas, they're hiring over at the pharmaceutical plant. It would be a steady job, and the pay is good," Mother eagerly informed me several days after I had walked out on a job where the boss didn't seem to understand I didn't take well to being "bossed." So, just like that, I applied for and got a job at S.E. Massengill Company, making my best effort to conform—not so much for my sake, but for my mother's.

As an office assistant position, it was actually an excellent job in most people's eyes. "You'll learn the pharmaceutical business from the ground up. There's plenty of room here for advancement for sharp, ambitious people," they assured me.

If you made it to one of the top positions at S.E. Massengill, you'd have it knocked in that town as far as money and prestige went. At that time, the plant was one of the largest employers in Bristol. But how many years would that level of success take? And what good would living in a big house atop Holston Hills be if I was a bloody insane idiot?

But there was nothing more promising in sight. And Mother, sure that Moses had been given an 11th commandment he carelessly left off the tablets which read "Thou shalt have and keep a steady job with a regular paycheck," was not to be ignored.

So, I reluctantly became a nine-to-five man.

Mother was bubbling over with happiness to be able to fix me her specialty gravy, biscuits, ham, and eggs each morning, send me on my way with a brownbag lunch, and have me back home in the evening for a hot supper. This was sheer joy to her, and I tried my best to keep that joy going for as long as I could.

Until I just couldn't.

During the three or so months at home, there was much time to reflect. Although still cocky and full of piss and vinegar, I had grown up enough while away to be more aware of the incredible strength and outstanding character of my mother (who, for some reason, I had begun calling Mother instead of Mama immediately upon returning home). I was better able to see the difficult life she had lived and was still living—albeit now without the added burden of a cruel and repressive husband and seven kids to worry about. I better understood that whatever grounding I possessed came from the unconditional love of my mother and the model of decency, goodness, and courage she was to me.

Impressed upon my mind still at that young age was the image of two prominent women in my life: my mother and my older sister, both who I loved and admired very much. The one endured untold hardship over many years, patiently biding her time before making her move to independence because there was little opportunity in her younger days to do differently. The other, in a newer age, took the bull by the horns and fought her way from the get-go to a better life.

However, I'm not proud to admit that even in the face of my awareness and appreciation of these women's lives, I continued to look at the world through male eyes and therefore did not make the connection that both their pain and hardship was the product of discriminatory, oppressive, unfair, and unequal treatment in a male-dominated world.

In fact, after my experience in Korea, I was feeling pretty much like the alpha male myself, ready to go out and conquer the world, including as many women as might come my way. Yes, I was still a male chauvinist—and you may justifiably add the word "pig" to that description.

Although I was happy to be reunited with my family, I couldn't get the thought of Hollywood out of my mind. It became crystal clear to me that I could not be satisfied living the slow-paced life with limited opportunities the Appalachian region offered. The club created in the Korean Quonset hut was still in my blood, and I was sure I could recreate it in the States. But it wasn't going to happen where I was.

The way I saw it, the army had given me an opportunity to prove I could make a business work. I got job training and loads of experience all paid for by the government. In my case, it was better than a college education or the job training others coming out of the service were getting at government expense. Besides, I wasn't any good in school and hated every day of it. I'd be miserable trying to make a go of it again. And I already knew the entertainment business was my calling, and had a pretty good idea of how to make good at it. I just needed the right opportunity. So I was itching to get out there and get started, and knew I could never be satisfied if I didn't try. I also knew I'd have to do it my way, however flawed that way may be. Because in my stubborn, youthful arrogance, there was no other way.

Life during this time in Bristol was not all work and no play though. Although state law prohibited the sale of hard liquor, roadhouses and bars served cold beer. There were also plenty of girls eager for a good time, and I had several buddies who, like me, were sowing their wild oats. Our main interest after a day's work, and especially on weekend nights, was to have a good time.

Although I tried to stay away from trouble, having partially learned that lesson in Korea, it still seemed to home in on me like sonar seeking its target. And, with the same accuracy, it always seemed to find me.

One particularly rowdy night after jumping into a brawl to help my friends (or maybe they jumped in to help me, who's to say?), a beer bottle was smashed over my nose. Blood spewed everywhere as I crashed to the floor, unconscious.

My friends piled me into their car and drove me the short distance home. I was still out cold when we got there, and Mother had them carry me into the house and put me on the bed. She called a doctor, and he advised staying in bed with ice on my nose through the night. Although there'd be swelling and some dizziness, he stated I'd be okay the next day. He was right except for the incredible headache and searing pain all over my face, especially my swollen, broken nose.

Mother, as she had done before, sat up with me through the night in a rocking chair by my bed to make sure I didn't bleed to death or go into shock. The next day when I came to my senses, she said in her somber I've-just-talked-with-God-and-here's-what-we've-decided voice, "Douglas, we need to talk."

But before she could go on, I had my own message I needed to admit. "Mother...I have to leave Bristol. As much as I love you, June, and the rest of the family, I can't make it here. I'm dying from the inside out."

Tears sprung from her eyes, "I know, son. I know." She was squeezing my hand with both of hers. "I prayed so hard for you to come home safely and that you would settle down and be happy here. But you're not happy and you're never going to be. Even though I cried that whole year you were in Korea, your time there was good for you. You grew up some. But you're not doing any growing here. So, though it'll break my heart again to see you leave, I know you have to go."

Hallelujah! Mother, God, and I agreed! My mother loved me more than life itself. I knew that because she told me so many times, and to give her blessing to me leaving was proof of it. It was time to get on that train again, and this time it would be a ride to a future full of the unknown.

My nose healed, my hopes for the future returned, and the day came to once again leave Bristol, my friends, and my family.

But I was more than ready and prepared. My sister June, now a beautiful young woman, and my mother saw me off with tears flowing, just as they had before. Boarding the train that would take me along the old Santa Fe Railroad route, I didn't look back. I was too busy looking forward. Mile by mile the past was replaced by dreams of what was to come. Mile by mile I disappeared into my future.

Traveling West

The train had a scheduled two-hour layover in Gallop, New Mexico. I walked a few blocks to the nearby cantina (just another word for honky tonk), where its mistress, the jukebox, was waiting. The magnificent machine served up a selection of music that appealed to the mixed audience, locals of both Mexican and American heritage. I dropped my coin into the slot and my first pick was "Mystery Train," recorded by Elvis Presley three years earlier. Junior Parker had written and recorded it originally, giving the song his distinctive soul sound. However, Elvis' later cover version was a big hit across cultures and had become a sort of anthem. And "Mystery Train" certainly felt appropriate for this point in my life.

A Hispanic couple next to me at the bar smiled. The man flashed a big grin and commented in a heavy but amiable Mexican accent, "Señor, it is hard to sit still when Elvis sings." I smiled and nodded in agreement. There we were, assembled in a cantina in the middle of nowhere, men and women from all walks of life, rich and poor, travelers, day workers, and white-collar office workers, all united by great music. The beat, the lyrics, the energy, and the message were threads that tied strangers together.

My thoughts were interrupted by the train's whistle blast, sending up her own sweet tune to alert us that the Santa Fe was ready for departure.

"Which side?" I asked the conductor as I boarded. He grinned and pointed me to the row of seats on the right. I had learned to ask which side of the train would reveal the best scenic views, and it had become a great way to get to know the conductors who performed their jobs with pride and shared their personal stories, often about the families they so proudly supported.

Hearing about their lives not only helped pass the time, but instilled in me a further desire to get out there and start making a life of my own.

Yes, the West Coast was calling. And I was on my way to answer the call.

Legendary Hollywood

In just a few days' time, there it was: The famous Hollywood sign. It stood like an enormous crown high above Hollywood and Sunset Boulevards. Those iconic white letters announced the city, calling out to the dreamers and schemers with a promise of power and fame. And I was now one of them.

Taking a short trolley ride from the train station to West Los Angeles on the outskirts of Beverly Hills, I found my way to a hotel called The Regina. It wasn't the fanciest place in town, but with its art deco design and classic Los Angeles look and feel, it met all my expectations. Plus, it had weekly rates and the location was central.

I settled into the hotel and within a few days realized the people milling around looked like characters in the old Damon Runyon movie *The Lemon Drop Kid*, which they showed at least two dozen times on base in Korea. My new neighbors were a collection of questionable yet likable people. I eventually learned they included con artists, mobsters, showgirls, strippers, prostitutes, and serious gamblers. My mother would have done some serious praying had she known I was hanging out with the likes of these people. Not that she wasn't anyway.

I spent my days exploring the area, amazed that things could cost so much just because they came from a place called Beverly Hills. And yet, somehow the fruit did seem plumper, the ladies thinner, and the men almost more groomed than the women. In the eyes of nearly everyone I met, excessive money seemed to make everything function a whole lot better. But I had already learned that.

Most evenings, a group of The Regina residents would gather just off the lobby area where a small but satisfying bar service was offered. Their stories were often obscene and provocative, and the laughs came easily. It didn't take long for me to be accepted. But I took a lot of ribbing about my hillbilly dialect from this cosmopolitan crowd.

Brian, a stout, loud Irishman who had a heavy brogue of his own, was one of the friendliest. He seemed perpetually unemployed. His lady friend, Tornado Tonya, was a dancer at the El Rancho and other popular clubs in the area. Brian called her Thelma.

Then there was fast talking Tony who offered up a new "can't lose" scheme to make a "quick grand" every day. I kept a firm grip on my wallet anytime Tony was around.

I never delved too deeply into anyone's "action," and avoided being pulled into any of it myself. The most notorious and menacing of the characters to grace The Regina was Mickey Cohen, a well-known mobster. Cohen, as I understood, lived on Moreno Avenue, a posh area of L.A., and he came around and slummed it at The Regina from time to time. Maybe it was because one of his lieutenants, Bill, was a regular there.

Cohen was an unimpressive short, balding man who appeared to be in his late forties or early fifties. Although I didn't know all the gory details at the time, I knew enough to tread lightly around him. I took heed to the fact that he had a long and violent criminal racketeering career around the country and particularly in the L.A. area. He was rumored to have been high up in the organized crime arena, having very close ties with such figures as Bugsy Siegel and Al Capone's younger brother, Mattie. Supposedly Cohen was involved in the whole spectrum of organized crime, including protection scams, drugs, prostitution, gambling, and murder. This was 1958, and he had spent several years in prison for tax evasion. I gathered he had not been out too long.

Bill, a smooth talking, darkly handsome guy who looked to be in his early forties, took a liking to me. On several occasions he offered me a job with his "organization" without going into detail as to exactly what that job would be. He would say, "You'll do well in my line of work, Doug, because you're not a wiseass, you're a go-getter, you're quick on the trigger, and can be trusted." Then he would laugh real big, slap me on the back and add, "But you're too goddamn innocent and green! I like that though. I like that about you."

The only thing remotely tempting about the offer was the money Bill assured me I'd be making. At that point, the funds I'd brought with me from Bristol were quickly evaporating, and I had no serious prospects ahead. But I had to tell him, "No, thanks," as graciously as possible. Bill clearly thought he was doing me a favor, and I was genuinely appreciative, but this was not a person whose wrong side—or right side—I wanted to be on. There are some decisions in life about the roads we take or don't take that prove particularly smart. This was definitely such a decision.

As with Bill, all the folks at The Regina seemed to want to take me under their wing. I gathered it was in large part the fact I gave off an aura of innocence and country boy "greenness," as Bill said. Though I have to say in this environment, I felt I was quickly becoming "citified." Not only were all these folks fun and entertaining, they offered the additional value of having their fingers on the pulse of the town.

Brian invited me to the El Rancho one evening, where we watched the burlesque dancers bump, grind, and tease to a provocatively slow, sexy beat. "The crowds seem to be getting smaller," Brian whimsically observed. I figured he was thinking about Thelma and her career interests.

I considered what I was about to tell him, taking a deep breath before speaking. "Burlesque has had its day, Brian. It's over. Doesn't mean anything to the new crowd coming in. Rock and roll is where it's at nowadays."

Brian thought for a moment and begrudgingly agreed. I didn't add that rock and roll, and what was becoming known as go-go dancing, were served up with a sexual energy and a lighter side that didn't necessarily speak to the older set. Likely, Brian was sadly thinking the same as me: that Thelma was already beyond the better side of forty and probably wouldn't have much appeal to the young rock and rollers.

But there was no question in my mind about the positivity of the coming change.

At the End of the Trail

I decided if I was ever going to have a club of my own, I'd better make some specific moves in that direction. I had seen enough of Hollywood and Beverly Hills to learn that prices were inflated, and it was probably the most expensive place I could be. Plus, I felt a need to break away from the people and temptations at The Regina. So I began exploring outlying towns where I could live and hopefully thrive on a smaller budget.

With a slogan of "Welcome to Friendly El Monte," this city about fifteen miles east of L.A. seemed as good as any to get away from the expense of the downtown area while still remaining in a thriving residential and commercial community. Not a bad place to consider starting a business.

During lunch at a local coffee shop, I struck up a conversation with a guy in no hurry to be on his way. "Have you lived here long?" he asked.

"No, but I'm thinking about making it home," I replied.

"You'd be thinking smart. It's a good and growing community, the last stop for settlers who came west. The end of the famous Santa Fe Trail."

"No kidding?" I stopped him. "The Santa Fe Trail, as in the route for the railway? I took that train to get here."

"Yeah. El Monte was the end of the road for the Santa Fe Railroad. In its early days it had a reputation as a rough town where men settled disputes with guns and knives. Now we tend to talk things over first before going for our weapons," he said with a belly laugh.

I soon moved into a low rent hotel in a predominantly Hispanic section of town that made The Regina look like the Taj Mahal. For a few bucks a night, I got a scantily furnished room with a community bath down the hall and a view overlooking the most run-down section of town there could possibly be. What time I wasn't sizing up the town on foot, I spent staring out my window and thinking.

After a few days of poking around and talking to anyone who would answer my questions, I determined that even here, some pretty good "bridge" money would be needed to open and operate the kind of club I had in mind. As eager as I was to get started, jumping into the nightclub business without sufficient startup and operating funds would likely end up in failure. I needed to make some big money fast.

Two of the attractions from my window were a bar directly across the street and a neglected garage with a "For Rent" sign several buildings down from the bar. The bar offered cheap beer and a jukebox that seemed to play the right songs without taking any money from me. And the garage offered a solution to my desperate situation.

Sitting on a stool at the far end of the bar over the course of several nights, I noticed one particular fellow who came in most evenings around six, had one beer, then left. He was quiet but friendly, and while he kept to himself, he didn't push away conversation either. He wore work clothes with grease smudges, and his rough hands, though clean, had evidence of oil and grit around the fingernails

I took my shot. "Hi, I'm Doug Lambert. Comfortable place for a beer." He reached out to shake my hand and introduced himself as Danny.

"Good to meet you, Danny. Something tells me you might have the same interest in cars as I do."

"Yeah. Worked on them all my life. I could take apart and put together a car or truck blindfolded," he shared without appearing to be bragging.

I prodded a bit further. "You work around here?"

"Nah, in a body repair shop across town. But I live nearby."

We moved on to easy conversation about our car preferences, sports, and the choices on the jukebox. Gradually over the next week or so, we developed a casual friendship. We didn't get much into our personal lives, but we enjoyed our talks.

One evening, Danny stated he was beat from a long week of work...a week that had only just started. But he added a chuckle to lighten his complaint.

"Business must be good then?" I asked.

"It's okay enough to get me a beer at the end of the day." I liked his matter-of-fact manner and tendency to not play himself up.

But my interest in Danny was more than just casual. As we had visited over these days on our barstools, I had sized him up very purposefully and decided he fit into my plans. So I finally asked, "Ever thought about having a business of your own?"

"Not really. Just like having a steady job and good paycheck each week."

I could see my mother's big smile of approval.

"Well, maybe there's more to life than that. How would you like to go into business with me in an auto repair shop?"

He just stared at me. "Doing what? I already have a job."

"There's a garage down the street with a rent sign. It has enough space for you and one other good body man, and I have the sales skills to bring home all the business the two of you could handle. But most importantly, you'll be your own boss."

He laughed. "I don't doubt you could talk the boxers right off a man's ass." Then he paused, thinking. "What would my steady cut look like?"

I took a swallow of my beer. "I guarantee it would look far better than it does at the job you have. People in California are crazy about their cars. Cars are a status symbol, and they want them to look great. I think you and I could give 'em what they want and more. But I don't know how long that garage is going to be available, so the time for both of us to jump in is right now."

Danny pushed back, explaining he only owned the tools to do simple repairs. "The expensive work needs special tools. Where would we get them? I don't have any extra cash to put into a deal like that."

"I'll take care of that part," I assured him without feeling any assurance myself.

"They're pretty pricey."

"How much?"

"Three hundred."

My first thought was they might as well be three thousand, but I made my face smile and stuck out my hand. "Deal."

He stalled again by dragging on his beer. Figuring I had said enough, I kept quiet and did the same, letting him do his decision-making. Finally, he looked me in the eye and returned the handshake. "Deal."

We ordered another round to cement our agreement and began discussing our first steps. Though I made sure to infuse everything I said with an air of confidence, I still suggested he hang onto his job until I nailed down the money for the tools. Just in case.

An Angel from Heaven

That night and all the next day, I did a lot of staring out my window. I was working my brain like I never had before. Success was so close I could smell it, and I knew in my gut this was the path to it. But there was one seemingly insurmountable obstacle in the way of that path: that first three hundred dollars.

Part of my rent included a basic ten-minute cleaning and bed-making service each day. A short, rather plump Hispanic lady in her fifties had been coming to my room over the weeks I'd been there to provide the service. Lena (short for Magdalena) spoke pretty good English, though with a heavy accent. But we had gotten on chatting terms, since I was often in my room when she came.

She shared that she had at least a couple of grown kids, a husband who had been killed, this job during the day, and a job she didn't go into detail about at night. She alternately called me "good boy" (probably because of the manners Mama taught and enforced) or "young boy" (I was twenty-two, but being very slender, looked younger).

On this particular day sitting at the window in the room's one chair, I didn't look around or speak beyond, "Hello," when Lena came in.

"What's the matter? You are sick?" she asked.

"No, ma'am."

"You are worried?"

"Yes, ma'am. Very worried." I had shared some of my life with Lena, particularly my dream of opening a nightclub. When I'd talk, her half closed, weary eyes would light up and stay completely focused on my face.

She also liked it when I talked about my mother; her kindness and gentleness, her faith, and her deep love for all her children. "Good mama, good son," Lena would say.

"Do you want to tell me about the worry?" she asked now. I felt as close to Lena as anyone in my immediate world right then, and while talking wasn't going to help, I decided it would feel good to give voice to all that had been spinning in my head. So I let loose on this tired little cleaning lady who seemed about as down on her luck as I was.

"So, three hundred dollars is all that is keeping you from your dream? No problem. I can loan it to you."

I stared at her in disbelief. "What did you say?"

"I have three hundred dollars for you."

"But where would you get money like that? And why would you loan it to me? You hardly know me."

"You are a good boy and you have a dream. I have the money but no dream. So what good is it to me? You will pay me back when you get your club."

"But Lena, I don't know when I can pay it back. You must need your money for yourself, or for your family."

"No, I don't need the money until you pay it back. Then you'll buy me a fancy drink at your club, no?"

I had no expectation that this improbable fairy godmother either had three hundred dollars or, if so, that she would actually hand it over to a near stranger. So after a skeptical, "Thank you," I went back to my thinking and worrying.

But true to her word, the next afternoon when Lena came to my room, she handed me a torn and dirty envelope containing three hundred dollars in small bills. My heart practically took wings and flew out of my body. I threw my arms around this angel from heaven, kissed her plump cheek, lifted her off the floor, and twirled her round and round.

Leaving the room, Lena turned and smiled, the only smile I had ever seen on her face, and said, "Now your dream is mine."

Although I had no way of knowing it at the time, that would be the last I would ever see or hear of this mystifying woman.

Over the next few days, I was as busy as a switch engine. Talking the garage owner into accepting thirty-five dollars as a down payment on the first month's rent of one hundred dollars, I then made a deal for the tools and arranged to have a big, bright sign painted on a piece of used lumber that couldn't be missed—not "Doug's" and not "Danny's"—but "AUTO BODY REPAIR." Daddy would be proud of that sign.

Danny quit his job and together we worked to get the garage ready for business while also interviewing for another mechanic. In between, I pounded the pavement meeting salesmen at the local new and used car lots. They all had a solid turnover of cars from sales or trade-ins, many needing body repairs and detailing. Finding cars to work on wouldn't be a problem.

Within weeks, we had a waiting list and were looking for a third mechanic. As I had guessed, Danny was a pro and ran the garage superbly, which left me free to build the business. Before long I had the three hundred dollars put aside to return to Lena, but she was no longer coming to the hotel. I asked the owner about her and was simply told she no longer worked there. I could find no one who knew anything about her. How could that be? Why wouldn't she stay in touch and let me pay her back? Did she not expect me to do so? Had she become ill, maybe even died?

More than once in my life I've wondered about this incredible experience and how completely gratifying it would have been to hand that money—plus generous interest—back to Lena, then treat her to the finest drink money could buy. Instead, I put three new hundred-dollar bills in an envelope and carried it in my pocket for as long as I lived in El Monte, hoping Lena would find me or I would find her. Without this remarkable woman and her miraculous gift, and without Danny sitting on that barstool and possessing the very skills I so desperately needed to make my plan work, I'd likely have gone back to The Regina and ended up in prison—or worse.

Doing some preliminary research and brainstorming, I sat the startup for my eventual nightclub at a minimum of $25,000. All the advice I'd heard and read about regarding a new business was to first and foremost be prepared to go for at least three years before expecting to start pulling a profit. That meant I still had lots of work ahead of me.

Pushing the club idea to the back of my mind and keeping my nose to the grind with the auto business was one of the hardest things I've ever done. However, the fear of jumping the gun and starting too soon with too little money and ending up losing everything kept me going. I was determined to never again be where I was that day looking out my seedy hotel window, quickly sliding into a state of total despair. But my dream of a nightclub was never far from my mind, and I saved every nickel and dime I could to that end.

Although our business was bringing in good income for Danny and me, I realized that to make the big bucks, we'd have to have more volume. The problem was our small building. So we agreed to open additional garages in nearby towns. This meant I needed outside funding.

I had struck up a kind of friendship with Johnny, a local businessman who owned several service stations and a car lot. In addition, he had what seemed like a lucrative "bookie" business on the side. He had heard from his sales team that our garage repairs were increasing the price they could charge for their used cars. This impressed Johnny, and he began looking at me with new respect.

Over coffee, I laid out my plan. An excellent listener and very business sharp, Johnny quickly grasped the strong potential for my proposal to expand. But I needed an investor. Luckily, Johnny liked to make money and wasn't afraid to take a risk when he figured the odds to be in his favor. It was a match made in heaven.

"Prove yourself to me, Lambert, and I'll be your silent partner on up the line." He gave me a knowing look. "I'm sure you have ambitions beyond auto repair shops."

"You bet I do. But first we're about to make the auto body repair business the sexiest in town."

"Sexy? Car painting? You're one crazy hillbilly." Johnny slapped the table with the flat of his hand and burst out laughing.

Crazy? I knew I was on the right track.

Candy Apples

My "crazy" scheme was to add a specialty service to our auto repair shops.

Joe Bailon, an artist who used cars as his canvas, had invented a spectacular new paint style. His first paint color was called candy apple red, and it would become the rage among car lovers. These were the first cars to have their exteriors transformed from ordinary and dull to brilliantly shining gems. The cars were painted a shade of red that reminded me of the sweet sugar coating on candy apples at the carnivals I loved as a kid.

Manufacturers weren't bringing vehicles off the assembly line with candy apple red paint. So, the business concept of candy apple painted cars seemed like a winner. Soon these gem-colored cars would become available in green, pink, and yellow, reflecting the mood of the millions of fans who idolized the surfer lifestyle, which was symbolized by bright neon-colored surf shorts and shirts, and blond-streaked hair. This new tendency represented youth, vitality, sexuality, and a more laid-back way of living. Our cars were going to fit into this trend just fine. I knew without a doubt we were on the brink of tapping into an exclusive group of consumers who were either very wealthy or very willing to spend their last dime on a sexy, rare, expensive candy apple paint job. This trend was my "shining" opportunity to make the money I needed to build my dream club.

Curious about our fast-growing new investment, Johnny made a rare appearance at our main shop. "How's it done?" he asked as he accepted a tour of the place.

"We start by adding a metallic base coat. It gives the car a rocket ship look." I slowed my pace to emphasize the process. "Then we add a translucent color coat, which gives a depth that completely alters the dynamic of the car. Finally, we apply a clear coat of gloss, giving the entire car a blinding shine." I looked directly at Johnny. "I told you it was sexy. But it's also seductive, exotic, and feeds the owner's ego, all while advertising his or her…availability."

Johnny let out a large puff of air and turned to me. "Nobody will care what the fuck it costs."

"Exactly," I agreed, smiling. "There's a whole spectrum of colors to come: green, blue, orange," I added. "And you'll see lots of press about Zsa Zsa Gábor's Rolls Royce, Danny Thomas' Lincoln Continental, Dean Martin's station wagon—I swear, a candy apple red station wagon! Oh, and Sammy Davis, Jr. is having his Vega wagon done, and Joe, the inventor, is building the Oldsmobile Toranado for the *Pink Panther* movie. We'll have plenty of free publicity."

Johnny was drooling right along with me. We were like two kids in a candy shop. A very lucrative candy shop.

"I think candy apple green will be my favorite color," laughed Johnny.

I smirked at him. "Because that's the color of the money that'll flow our way?"

"You got it," he said emphatically.

We had a solid team in Danny as the shop boss and the men who worked under him, consistently increasing efficiency and profits. We moved the specialty paint operation into a separate building and added an auto sales business so we could sell our dazzling cars to people who came from all over to claim a custom candy apple car.

I saw the specialty cars as part of other trends breaking out around us too. Beaches overflowed with bikini-clad temptresses who were willing to give their hearts (and more) to surfer boys. When Jan & Dean sang "Surf City" and The Beach Boys rocked out to "Surfin'," kids in Kansas and Oklahoma believed they could one day take part in the seductive beach scene; that they too could experience the California dream. And we would be happy to provide them all with cars to match those dreams.

It was now January 1964, and I received a call from Brian, of The Regina days. He and Tony wanted to take me to the newly opened Whisky a Go Go club on Sunset Boulevard in West Hollywood. All my talk back then about my go-go club in Korea and the new wave of rock and roll had piqued their curiosity, and they thought going to the club with me would make it all the more exciting. As with all great inventions and ideas, I wasn't the only guy with a vision of scantily dressed girls dancing on bar tops. Chicago already had a Whisky a Go Go and New York had another go-go version, the Peppermint Lounge.

Two whiskeys in, I shouted to Brian and Tony over the blasting beat of music. "I'm tellin' ya, the winds of rock and roll are blowing across this country, and they ain't ever gonna stop blowing." Music was impacting every aspect of our lives—how we dressed, styled our hair, danced, drank, and even how we felt about sex. "Hell," I yelled, "rock and roll makes everyone feel young and sexy."

The Whisky was officially a "disco" where recorded music drove the night, but the owners had added several unique touches. Johnny Rivers fronted a three-piece band, and their live performances let the crowds respond in a more energetic, interactive way. Customers didn't clap to recorded music, but the applause was wild after each of the group's rousing songs; an affirmation that people were happy to justify spending top dollar for a night out on the town with live entertainment.

The club's famous décor and setup actually arose from its lack of space. The Whisky's sexy dancers and female DJ were suspended over patrons' heads on an elevated platform, offering a great view of mini-skirts, skimpy tops, and gyrating bodies. While craning my neck to look at them, I reflected on the fact that my Korean go-go club had been in action a year or two before The Whisky first opened its doors in Chicago in 1958. I must have been smiling about it, because the bartender smiled back. "You doin' okay?" he asked, gesturing to my drink.

"Yes, but I'd be doin' great if you'd move out of the way so I can see the twins," I joked back.

He chuckled and moved aside to give me full view of what fantasies are made of. The club had employed a set of beautiful dancing twins who had worked out excellent choreography—a dynamic, double treat of wiggles and shakes to the pulsing beat. While I shared with Brian and Tony more details about my Korea experiences, we never took our eyes off them.

Neither Brian nor Tony had served in the military, so they were enthralled by stories of Korea: the threat from the North, the kimchi, the weather, and most of all, the Korean dancers and sexual scene I had created.

"So, you guys like our dancers?" the bartender came back and asked.

"Like 'em?" bellowed Brian, slapping me on the back. "Hell, man, this soldier invented go-go girls!"

"Then this round is on me!" replied the barkeep. Smart move. What's the price of three drinks when you can keep customers for another few hours buying plenty of their own?

It was good to see Brian and Tony and catch up on the gang at The Regina. But I'd be lying if I didn't say the most intriguing part about our outing together was everything I was learning about this incredible business—not to mention, all the things I already suspected about the business that were now being confirmed before my very eyes.

Mysterious Disappearance

Danny had become a trusted friend and partner, although I knew nothing about his background. He was a quiet man and didn't talk much about his life outside the shop. We actually shared an apartment, but were so rarely there at the same time that it was like living solo. We still made time to share a beer and discuss business once a week, and I left our relationship at that. I respected his need for privacy, whatever the reasons.

Our business was going great, and it had been a fun run. But I was just about at the financial point where I could start pulling away and turn my full attention to the enterprise that had taken top billing in my head and heart since coming back from Korea.

Danny and I had talked about it a number of times over the last few months, and he had indicated he was comfortable taking the reins as long as there was some initial oversight by me and, of course, business input from Johnny.

Then around three o'clock one morning, Danny pounded on my bedroom door, hollering my name. Thinking he was drunk (which was unusual for him), or maybe sick and needing help, I jumped up and opened the door. "Doug, I need some money. How much do you have in your wallet?" he practically panted at me. Groggy, I found my wallet and counted out less than two hundred dollars.

"Thanks." His voice was desperate and his breathing fast and shallow. Rabid fear was in his eyes. "You've been a good friend, Doug. But forget you ever knew me. You'll never see me again."

I was dumbfounded. "But...but why? You're a part owner in our business! Things are going great!" I stammered.

"I can't explain, but I'm out. The business is all yours. Here's my handshake on that, just like when we started. Good luck to you pal, and have a good life." With that, he picked up the small bag he had packed and was out the door. I stood in the dark silence in my shorts and undershirt, scratching my head and trying to grasp what the hell had just happened. It just didn't make any sense to walk out on the deal of a lifetime. Unless...

There were only two times up to that point when I had witnessed that kind of fear or had come close to it myself. My mind jumped back to that first day arriving in Korea and being transported to our base. We were consumed by a terrifying, pervasive sense of dread and anxiety, made worse by not even being sure where the danger would be coming from. I could see it in the eyes of the other men and knew they could see it in mine.

The other time was in more recent years when I was at The Regina. One of the men staying there was desperately trying to scrape up enough money to pay off a gambling debt. He was practically on his knees begging each of us for money. Was Danny in that kind of trouble? Why hadn't he confided in me? Maybe I could have helped. Or maybe he was beyond help. Or he didn't want to drag me into it. There were any number of possibilities that could lay claim to your life if it got off track, and standing there, half naked in the dark, my mind was latching onto anything and everything.

Seriously considering going to the police, asking around town, or quizzing the other men at our shops, I reminded myself of Danny's emphatic words: "Don't try to find me." Looking around corners and under rocks for him could end up putting him in greater danger. And me as well.

So, right or wrong, I decided against it. It was one of the strangest and scariest circumstances I'd yet faced, and one of the few times I felt helpless about taking charge of a situation. But Danny was gone, and I had to decide what to do next.

A chapter in my life was closing. Danny ran the auto repair and paint business with skill and care, and there was mutual trust and respect in our partnership. It was impossible to think about replacing him. Besides, my own fear was ever present, and more than once a day I looked over my shoulder. If Danny owed money and his debtors couldn't find him, what would keep them from knocking on my door to collect?

Much of the time during those days following, I was as nervous as a buck during hunting season. Those fears sometimes bordered on the irrational, including thoughts of a connection between Johnny and Danny. Johnny was a fairly big-time bookie. Would he have let Danny get himself into a bad situation? Surely not. Wouldn't Danny's absence put the business, of which Johnny had a piece, in jeopardy? As I said, all kinds of thoughts streamed through my head at different times of the day and night. Perfectly innocent strangers walking down the street became hit men. Car beams at night in my rearview mirror became stalkers. But even as alarming and eerie as Danny's disappearance was, I knew I had to move forward, and quickly.

The timing would at least work to my advantage, since I had nearly reached my financial goal. The first item of business was to settle with Johnny. I felt sure there'd be no problem on his end. While I had shared Danny's abrupt exit with Johnny, I didn't indicate that Danny would never come back or want his share of the business.

"When we sell, I'll take Danny's share and put it into a joint account with your name and mine on it. If he returns, it's his. If not, you and I split it. You can take your share and run with it, or consider investing in my club."

Looking at the books, Johnny seemed happy with the deal. My plan was to always have Danny's share ready for him in case he ever did show up. Which he didn't.

As dawn came up one morning, I drove twenty miles out to Surfside Beach to breathe in the cool ocean mist, comparing it to the valley breezes back home. The blurry reds and blues of sunrise on the California coast reminded me of the subtle jeweled tones of a jukebox. On this morning, my senses were calmed as my mind focused on moving ahead. Visions of my club began overriding every thought—and fear. The actual physical appearance of it was like a photograph captured by my mind, so clear, bright, and real.

With the foam of the spent waves gently reaching in to wash my feet, my mind floated back to boyhood and that day in the tall grass by the river, watching the pair of rabbits. I remembered the sudden trill of the train's insistent whistle, the rumbling of the engine, and the clacking of the wheels on the tracks, all announcing the coming of change.

As it was then, so it was that morning on the beach. As each wave broke, I could feel the coming change in every fiber of my being. And I was ready for it. I desperately wanted to be part of it. Thinking of the rabbits again, I found myself remembering how happy they seemed as they foraged together in the grass, and how glad I was that they had each other.

Jenny: My family settled into an affordable and safe Los Angeles suburb, close enough to enjoy the excitement of the city, but without out as much of the expense and congestion. At first, Michael and I lived with my parents in their small house, but I quickly found a banking job to bring in income and was able to get an apartment of my own. During the day, Michael continued staying with my parents, since he was still an infant, and putting him in daycare was not an option I would consider.

After a while, knowing Michael was being left in Mommi's eager and capable hands, I felt comfortable enough to go out with friends on the weekends for some fun and relaxation. Most of these girls were single and without children, but there were a couple, like me, who were single moms. Young and not yet settled, we all enjoyed the loud, energetic music, streaming lights, and happy chatter and laughter of the clubs. But by far, the best part was that I could dance, dance, dance to my heart's content.

Each of my girlfriends had hopes of meeting the love of their life at the clubs—someone who would passionately sweep them off their feet and whisk them away to live happily ever after. But that wasn't my objective. And what made being at the clubs even more fun and liberating for me was that romance was not at the forefront of my thoughts; finding the best dance partner was!

My friend Corrine was gushing about a guy I'd danced the last three sets with as we sipped drinks at our table. "Oh Jenny, he's an absolute dream! He *must* have asked you for a date by now, with the way you two were dancing."

"Yes he has, and I said no," I told her resolutely. She frowned. "Come on Corrine, you know I'm not interested in dating right now. I just want to have fun. Feel free. Besides, Michael's the only man in my life," I said matter-of-factly.

"But he's so cute!" she said, staring me down like that was all I needed to hear to change my mind. I frowned right back at her. "Well then can I have him?" she asked, laughing.

"He's all yours. I've got another partner lined up anyways," I told her as I nodded toward a tall, firmly built man in a purple striped shirt standing over by the bar. "He asked me for the next dance. I'll see what kind of moves he has on the floor."

Corrine rolled her eyes and smiled. "And off the floor, maybe?"

I laughed and smacked her arm playfully. "You go, girl. Get out of here and get your man before someone else grabs him."

Although I was always relatively shy and most definitely didn't think of myself as a "showoff," being on the dance floor transformed me. My shyness and the negative thoughts about myself ingrained from childhood fell away. Dancing had always come as naturally to me as breathing. But in this atmosphere and with this music, it seemed my mind went into a zone, and my body responded independently and spontaneously on its own.

Maybe my ballet training helped. Back in Jakarta, when I'd get too creative during a ballet lesson (which was often), my strict teacher would whack me on the bottom with a thin baton she carried. I wondered what my teacher would say if she saw me dancing this way now. Or worse, what my parents would say.

But to me, it didn't matter. Rock and roll was more electrifying and empowering than I had ever imagined anything could be, and I was having the time of my life. As I danced with "purple shirt," I saw Corrine rubbing up against my ex-partner as they kept rhythm with the music. *Guess I'll be driving home alone tonight*, I thought, smiling to myself.

At first, my fascination with the clubs and dancing did come from my love of the music, the fun of mixing it up with friends, and forgetting for a short while the worries of making my way as a single mother. But at some point, I realized there was so much more to what I felt on the dance floor. It wasn't about shaking my booty better than anyone else, or attracting the best dance partner, or even feeling flattered that others were copying my moves. Yes, all that was great for my ego, but it gradually dawned on me that what happened to me on the dance floor went deeper than those surface feelings. I tried to explain it to my mother, who was struggling with understanding my near obsession with dancing, while at the same time keeping her promise of always being supportive.

"It's this 'zone' I keep trying to explain to you, Mommi. It's a place in my mind where anything and everything seems possible for me to achieve. It's a place where I can be and have whatever I want. I feel free and in control. It's like I'm as good as anyone else on Earth! Nothing else makes me feel that way."

"But what about your job at the bank? You do well there. They like your work. You have a good income for a woman. Doesn't that bring you satisfaction, or make you feel successful?"

"Sometimes," I replied. "But it's not enough. I can't spend my life in the bank and be happy. I know that for a fact."

As the 1960s wore on, my life seemed to be a whirlwind of work, fun with Michael, and of course, dancing. Despite all this, it was a lonely time. I went on dates, but not with anyone serious. And I was reaching a point where I longed to experience that special passion people in love seemed to feel.

But there was plenty of other passion to feel too. The 60s were proving to be a pivotal time in history, and the air was full of energy and excitement. Our senses were bombarded with fast occurring changes taking place on every front: more casual dress, longer hair worn by males, and skimpier clothes worn by females. Even the scents people liked changed. Evening In Paris and Old Spice were out; more herbal and musky scents were in.

Fun, sporty cars were hitting the market big time: GTO, Stingray, Cobra, the wildly popular Ford Mustang, and what I personally dreamed of, a candy apple red Camaro.

And, to top everything off, more drugs and more sex were definitely in.

It seemed what reflected (or maybe led to) those changes most was the music. It was loud, uninhibited, and increasingly explicit in its pleasure-loving message. And yet, at times it was sober and poetic as it expressed a selfless message, bringing our attention to society's failures and to the human suffering all around us. When summed up, the music of the 60s expressed how we all (primarily of a certain age) were feeling inside at that time: restless, conflicted, needy, compassionate, full of both love and rage, and ready to rock the boat.

Sure, having a good time with fewer restraints was high on every young person's list, and we went after it with a passion that only comes from long pent-up feelings. But more and more, the young were also focusing on the wrongs in society and the suffering represented by our country's involvement in the Vietnam War and the denial of basic civil rights to minorities. Much to my satisfaction, included in those concerns was the long-neglected issue of women's rights.

Yes, civil rights and the war were getting the most attention. There were increasing demonstrations around the country that would start off peaceful and too often end up in violence as the demonstrators were scattered by police. But women were making noise too as they tried to bring attention to their cause. As it did with minority men, the Civil Rights Act of 1964 declared women could not be discriminated against in the workplace. But that was just a bunch of words on paper. All minorities and all women had to fight to try and make those words mean something. And they are still fighting today.

The Civil Rights Act was first proposed to protect people on the basis of race, color, national origin, and religion. I say people, but "people" did not include women in the Act's original design. That's an interesting sidenote every woman should know. They should also know that women ended up being included in that law by accident. Or at least unintentionally, when a Virginia congressman suggested including women in an effort to kill the bill entirely. He figured that although some men could see the justification in protecting the rights of other men, regardless of color, etc., few men at that time would ever agree that women should be treated as equal to men. Therefore, it was assumed they would vote against the bill. But thankfully, for other political reasons, the bill passed and was made into law.

Now came the even harder part: enforcing it. And as I said, that battle is still going on today.

Praise is Not Enough

An important fact that women of today should take away from those times is that as recently as fifty-five years ago, women were not legally (and not in the minds of most men) considered to be equal to white men, men of non-white races, men of any religion, or men originally from countries outside the U.S. As a result, women in this country were denied the respect, dignity, basic God given rights, equal freedoms, and privileges guaranteed to men by the Constitution of the United States.

Although slowly progressing in my bank position, I was very aware my advancement was not equal to that of my male coworkers, despite my often-praised job performance. It was frustrating to see men much less capable than me move ahead of me in both pay and position.

One day, fed up with it, I went into my immediate supervisor's office, shut the door hard, and sat down. Smiling, he said, "Hey, Jenny. What's up?"

Without smiling back, I laid out the specific example of my concerns (though there were many) I'd chosen for this conversation. "I've been here six months longer than Robert, and I've been given more responsibility and special assignments than he has during that time. Yet he now makes more money than me and has a higher position and title than me. Why is that?"

"Well," he said looking surprised but still managing to smile. "That's not hard to understand. You're given those responsibilities and assignments because we know you can handle them better than anyone else. There's no one better at their job than you, Jenny. And this bank appreciates you and all you do."

It was just a bunch of pure, baffling deflection of my real question. I'm sure my face reflected my effort to make sense of what he had just said. "Then why don't I get paid at least the same or more, and have the perks that come with a higher position? If I'm the best at my job, shouldn't I be paid the best of everyone here?"

"Not exactly."

My brow furrowed even harder. "Then what do I need to be doing differently to earn what I'm owed?" I'd learned long ago to try and provide a solution before placing blame. But I sensed that tactic wasn't going to work here.

He then, in all seriousness, looked me up and down, paused indiscreetly to focus on my breasts, and replied, "Honey, unless you can turn yourself into a man, which would be a crying shame for the male population of this world, there's nothing you can do differently. This is how things work, and this bank is no different than anyplace else."

I exploded. "I can't believe this! You mean just because I was born a woman instead of a man, I can't be paid fairly for my work or hold positions equal to my ability?"

He was no longer smiling. "I didn't say that. Men have families to support, and they get more respect from businesspeople involved with the bank. Customers like to deal with men. They take men more seriously. Thinking they have a man handling their banking gives them more confidence. So, the bank has policies and customs of doing things a certain way."

I was livid now. "You're saying even though I, a woman, am the one actually doing the work, a man should get all the credit and rewards from that work simply because he's a man?"

"Now, Jenny, simmer down. I don't make the policies. It's always been this way." Attempting another smile, he added, "You've heard the old saying 'behind every great man, there's a great woman,' right? Well, you're one of those great women." And he plastered that fake smile on his face again.

No, I hadn't heard that "old saying," and hearing it for the first time now just made me angrier. It was at that moment I was sure I would leave my job. And I vowed I would not take another job where I couldn't receive fair and equal treatment in exchange for my hard work.

But where would that be? From what my supervisor had said, there was no reason to believe it would be different anywhere else.

I was trembling from sheer anger and disgust. Every ounce of my being wanted to slap this man right across his smiling lips and storm out then and there. But I couldn't, because like those men who got credit and payment for *my* work, I too had a family to support.

I silently left his office, instead relishing in the fact that soon enough, those bastards were going to have to find another "great woman" to get behind them—and hopefully while back there, she'd give her "great men" a hard kick in their sorry asses.

I shared my work experience with friends outside the bank and wanted to hear their own stories of unfair treatment, both at work and at home. While everyone agreed women were not treated equally, not all had the same view of the inequity as I did. Some simply shrugged and said, "What's the big deal? This is just the way things are, have always been, and will always be. There's nothing we can do about it." And my least favorite reply was, "Men will be men. Can't live with them, can't live without them." What was that even supposed to mean? It was a non-answer, a non-stance one way or the other. I understood that some things were just easier to ignore, but I couldn't. Not this.

Thankfully, like me, most women were no longer willing to just lie down and take it. But knowing exactly what to do about the injustices was the big question.

My thoughts about the treatment of women weren't profound, and certainly weren't based on facts and statistics. They were just what I had observed throughout my life at home, at work, and seemingly just about every place else. The difference now was that those observations took on new meaning and legitimacy. The injustices were real, and I finally felt I had a right to say out loud that they were wrong, and to publicly challenge them.

As I talked with and listened to more women—married and unmarried, those who worked outside the home and those who didn't—it became clear that a lot more needed to be done to bring "women's rights" issues to the forefront of women's thinking. I wanted all women to believe, as I did, that we no longer had to be satisfied with or accept limitations, and could now fight the abuse inflicted on our mothers and grandmothers.

Just talking about it didn't feel like enough, but as a single working mother, I didn't feel called to join demonstrations around the country (though I admired those women who did). And, although my breasts were more than able to hold their own, I did still wear my bras on occasion and didn't have any extras to burn.

But with or without me, women of all ages were now breaking the chains of traditional roles: marriage, motherhood, matron of the home and, for some, long suffering domestic victims. The country was on fire with literal and figurative bra-burning and the demand from women for not only sexual freedom, but freedom and equality on all fronts. They were awakened to the desire for great sex, gratifying emotional attachments, and respect—rather than settling for wedding rings and promises unkept.

THE RESPONSIBILITY OF FREEDOM

With the arrival of the birth control pill in 1960 and the legalization of abortion, this sexual freedom was coming even faster to women. The availability of the birth control pill changed women's view of sex more than any other single happening. It was no longer just a problematic issue with an uncertain outcome. Now sex could be looked upon by women the same as men: as a fun experience to which they were entitled. This was largely in part because they no longer felt burdened by the fear of pregnancy if and when they decided to have sex—something men never even had to think about when they were having fun sleeping around.

But not all was necessarily right and good with uncontrolled sexual freedom—either for men or women. With freedom comes responsibility. I saw around me the disaster that can result, particularly for women, from exercising sexual freedom without considering the responsibility. And I saw the damage men could inflict by being tempted by the freedom and ignoring the responsibility.

It always seemed odd to me that my single friends tended to confide in me and ask for my advice, because I felt the least qualified to give out advice. But I tried my best.

One such friend was Janice, who I met at one of the clubs. She was a very pretty, bouncy, slender girl with her short blonde hair cut into a bob. She had come to California from the Midwest to get into modeling or acting. But like so many who had come with high ambitions, she ended up doing something else entirely: waitressing at one of the more exclusive restaurants in town. There, she had gotten involved with Ted, a wealthy, married customer who had no intention of changing his status for her.

Janice sat me down at a diner one afternoon, holding back tears. "Jenny, I need help. I'm pregnant…and Ted is the father."

"Oh, Janice…" was all I could think to say. I knew Ted had just recently told Janice he was ready to be rid of her. I had no doubt a baby would do anything but make his resolution to leave her even stronger. "I thought you were on the pill?" I asked.

She finally let the tears fall. "I am! But sometimes I forget to take it. Or I run out. I don't remember which one happened this time."

"And you're sure you're pregnant?" I tried to be the voice of reason, because it was all I could think to be on the spot.

"Yes," she sniffled. "I haven't gotten my period in three months. So I went to see my doctor."

I sat and waited for her to say what I thought might be coming. But she didn't. "So…what are you going to do?" I prodded gently.

She grabbed a napkin from the dispenser on the table and wiped her eyes. "I have to have an abortion. I can't support a baby! Not on my own."

I patted her arm, trying to be comforting but not at all sure it was doing any good. "Are you sure that's what you want? I hear some women regret it afterwards, when it's too late. Or some end up having reproductive issues and can't have children later when they *do* want them. I'd hate for that to happen to you, Janice."

"I'm not ready for a baby. I like my life the way it is. If I had a baby without a husband, I'd have to go home and get help from my parents. I don't want that. And besides, my parents may not even let me come back home if they find out why I'm coming." She was desperate, and her voice was pleading. I felt terrible.

"Well, what did your doctor say?" I tried to continue exploring all avenues.

"He doesn't do abortions. But there are doctors who do. I have a name. I just need to borrow some money and have someone go with me, to look out for me. I know I can trust you, Jenny."

There it was. The ask I had been expecting. And it was a dilemma I had no easy answer to. If I didn't help her get the abortion, she would find a way on her own and could end up like one of the awful horror stories I'd heard about. On the other hand, I had been brought up by parents who were very strict Catholics, and as such, were firmly opposed to abortion—among many other things. By this time in my life, I had rejected and even rebelled against much of their strict thinking, which had resulted in tremendous strain between us. But there was still enough influence from those teachings that made me feel queasy about the idea of abortion. Was it the same as "killing" the baby? I didn't know. Either way, would there ever be a good enough reason to do that? I was extremely torn, not at all sure helping Janice would be the right and responsible thing for her—or for me. I felt "damned if you do, damned if you don't."

Janice did get her abortion, even though I could never bring myself to go with her. After losing touch for a number of years, we met for lunch and caught each other up on our lives. Janice spoke poignantly of that day, and the child she had "not allowed to live" (her words). But I certainly wasn't judging her. Who's to say what's right or wrong for any other person? Right and wrong are never clear-cut poles of each other. Instead, the truth lies in that murky gray area between the two. Every situation is unique and should be treated as such. And at that time, much as it unfortunately does today, abortion resided in a very murky gray area.

Illegal drugs were another nightmare during this time. The most frequent problem I encountered was when people I knew got into legal problems from marijuana use or selling small amounts of it. At that time, pot was legally considered as bad as the harder drugs out there (and there were plenty of those as well). That meant a young person's career and maybe their whole life could easily be ruined by simply going to a friend's house for a get-together, being around small amounts of pot, and ending in a jail sentence.

But even more tragic was when someone became addicted to the hard stuff, and that addiction took over their life until they were a mere shell of the person they once were. And very often, even that shell would crack and underneath it would be nothing—a life lost to the tragedy of a rapidly growing epidemic. I was fortunate to never lose anyone close to me to drug use, but I had friends who weren't so lucky. Their stories kept me away from all drugs and frivolous alcohol consumption, and I grasped fiercely onto the natural "high" for life I'd been blessed with. That made it easier to follow my instincts away from it all.

But during those turbulent 60s, it was hard to escape the sorrow of the national tragedies that happened within five years of each other, when three figures who were trusted and looked to for leadership were shot down by assassins. John Kennedy, Martin Luther King, Jr., and Robert Kennedy may have had different motives for their beliefs and activism, but they all had the charisma of rock stars that wildly excited people, gave us hope for the future, and caused people (particularly those of us who were young) to jump on their bandwagon. After this loss, the country was stunned and largely left swaying in the wind as it waited for someone to step up and fill the void.

John F. Kennedy's beautiful wife Jacqueline had imprinted on our nation a new level of sophistication, grace, and dignity as she stayed above the fray while her Prince Charming often strayed from what she called "Camelot." And then, at one of the most destabilizing times in our country's history, Mrs. Kennedy, who had to do much of her grieving publicly, presented a calm, composed, and stately image to all Americans as they grappled with their own grief and anxiety. It can be said that at this perilous time for our country, a *woman* stepped up and modeled exactly what the nation needed: strength, confidence, and above all else, courage. It was marvelous to behold, especially for women like me at the time who so aspired to uphold everything Jackie O represented.

That a woman filled this role was a sign of the changing times, and I was changing right along with them. I became independent, self-supporting, and enjoyed fun times out on the town; either alone, with a date, or with my girlfriends. I was now an expert at using make-up to great advantage, and instead of a shorter schoolgirl cut, my hair hung loose below my shoulders or piled high on my head. My clothes were modern and revealing in all the right places, my scent was a natural musk, and my taste for music was wild and loud. As a result of this boosted confidence, I was becoming more assertive and willing to speak up and out, especially when it came to me or my family and friends being treated with fairness and respect.

There I was, Jenny Sersansie, a shy little girl from an ordinary family in Indonesia, living in the most exciting place to be at that time: Southern California. And I was caught up smack in the middle of one of the biggest upheavals the country had ever seen. I couldn't help but wonder what my role in all of it might be. Would I even have a role? Deep within me since childhood had been this sense that fate had something important and wonderful for me to do in life. But doesn't every young person feel that way?

Since my divorce, I had not found a man who set my soul on fire, and I was unwilling to settle for less. But by this time, I had reached a point in my life where I deeply longed to share that passion with someone. I was dissatisfied with my job, yet had no other career in mind or training and experience that would lead me to something better. I seemed about as unsettled and adrift on a personal level as the country was on a national level. But I did have two vitally important loves in my life.

The first was Michael, who was no longer the "babe in arms" I had carried from Ohio to California. He was growing into a sharp, handsome young man who continued to bring me and his Oma (grandmother) such joy.

The other was my dancing. On the dance floor was where I still felt the most alive, sure of myself, and optimistic about the future.

But would those loves be enough?

Don Taylor, Playgirl Club bouncer

Exterior of the Playgirl Club

Playgirl Club cocktail servers

Chapter 5

"Mountain of Love"

1964

Doug: After selling the auto repair and painting business, Johnny and I signed a new agreement that made him part of my next enterprise. Like a racehorse jumping out of the starting gate, I was raring to go.

Quickly up to my neck with all the startup requirements, I worked long hours through the day and into the night, which was a really good thing. It kept my mind from wandering too often to Danny's disappearance and would-be hooligans.

First thing was to make a deal on a great location I'd found: a pool hall on Valley Boulevard that was a bit of a dive and had an enormous neon-red sign that flashed "BEER." The legal paperwork to get a business open, especially like the one I had in mind, was a pain in the ass. But I persisted and eventually succeeded, considering it part of what I knew would be a steep learning curve ahead.

My experience in Korea proved a big advantage as I readied the inside physical setting: shopping for used, cheap furnishings, arranging the bar and tables around a central stage for the girls, providing some space for dancing (though that was more limited than I'd have liked), situating the lighting just right to create both a sense of coziness and excitement, and ordering a wide selection of beer and liquor.

And of tremendous importance was bringing in the right "talent." That meant girls. Again, my Korea experience was invaluable as I interviewed and auditioned girls, girls, and girls until I found the few that best fit the image of what I wanted for the club. Not a bad way for a single man to spend his time!

At night, I scouted the competition. Along Valley Boulevard was a short, straight run of buildings converted into spaces for food markets, beauty salons, eateries, and booze joints. El Monte was in dire need of some great entertainment, and I was just the person to bring it to the neighborhood.

As I "researched" the local bars and pool halls, I made some casual friends along the way, both men and women who would become my future customers. The ploy was to lure them away from their boring barstools and introduce them to a real night out.

A nearby supper club and lounge had a big draw: a 350-pound piano player with a warm smile and warmer personality, who wore an endearing maroon velvet vest and a bowler hat. With his size and his talent at the piano, Don Taylor was not only the entertainment, but he was also the keep-your-eyes-on-things guy. His large stature made his presence instantly known, while his gracious, cheerful, and well-mannered personality made him liked by all. At the start of each break at this club, Don would jolly the customers by exchanging friendly handshakes and comments.

But from my perspective, the most important thing was that no one intimidated him.

After a fair amount of watching, one evening I decided to finally approach Don while he was on break. "Sure do enjoy your music, Mr. Taylor. Can I buy you a drink?" I asked. The room was filled with people focused on their own drinks, and to them, Don's playing was probably just inconsequential background music. So he seemed to genuinely appreciate my comment and offer.

"Thanks pal, glad someone is getting some pleasure from it. A beer would be welcomed. I'm dry as a desert toad." While the drinks were coming, I dropped a few coins into the jukebox, slow tunes of course. "You're going to put us out of business with that slow music," Don said, grinning. Clearly, he was on to me.

So I jumped right in. "Then let me hire you for my new club, and I'll pay you better than what you make here." We both took a swig of our beers.

"You must like piano playing an awful lot," Don finally commented coyly. He knew I was serious, and he was pacing himself.

"Actually, there's no piano in my plan. Only a jukebox and some gorgeous girls dancing in tiny costumes."

He laughed. "Man, that sounds like the place to be. But I've already got a job I like. They treat me well, pay me good, and I don't wear this vest because I have to." Don was letting me know he was a person to be respected, and his attitude strengthened my confidence that he was the right man for the job at my club.

"Your vest would be welcomed as a bouncer's uniform. The girls are going to need someone to protect them, and who could do that better than you? I know you'd be a key to the success of my club. Think about it, and let's talk again soon." I threw down ample money to cover the check, shook his hand, and left him to consider my proposal.

Even though it was near torture to force myself to wait a few days and give Don time to consider dancing girls versus piano keys, I made myself do it. But the night finally came when I dropped by to see him again and ask what he thought.

"So you're really planning on opening your club, huh?" he cut straight to the chase.

"I'm hiring twin dancers next week, and I'd like you to meet them. Get a good feel for them, y'know? Since you'll be their protector and all."

With that one line, I could see the wheels in Don's head were finally turning my direction. Salary, schedule, and benefits were now just formalities.

Come to Play

The club came together more smoothly than I had believed possible. This concept had been bouncing around in my head for years, and each bounce helped complete the picture. Now within days of opening night, I applied the final touches.

Remembering my daddy's lesson, I replaced the "BEER" sign with a flashing neon job that read "GIRLS." I wasn't in love with the club's name though. It seemed crass, but I had a deadline to meet to get the sign ready for opening night. So "Girls" was it for now. In addition to nailing down Don Taylor as my bouncer and second set of eyes, I hired the Whisky a Go Go twins at more expense than I wanted to take on. But I figured it would pay off in the long run.

Finally, the big night came. I put on the new tan suit and striped tie I'd bought for the occasion, even though dress was generally becoming more casual. I wanted to make sure I presented a clean cut, high end, and successful image.

Standing at the front door ready to open for business, I took one last look around. It seemed surreal. A dream come true. My mind quickly flashed back to that old rough and hewn honky tonk in Appalachia where I learned so much about life. Then it flashed forward to the metal Quonset hut in Korea where I learned so much about this business. Without either one of those experiences, I doubted I'd be standing there watching this long-held vision come to life.

As I looked at the room, that breathless moment on the brink felt frozen in place. But in minutes, my club would be alive with energy and excitement.

And so it was.

Customers waiting outside rushed in. Bartenders mixed drinks served by hustling, smiling waitresses in miniskirts and low-cut tops. The jukebox pounded out loud, rousing music as beautiful girls kept time on the bar with their scantily covered bodies. Customers crowded the dance floor, everyone laughing and hollering to friends across the room. And the cash register sang its own lusty tune: *cha-ching, cha-ching, cha-ching.*

If life had ended for me right then and there, I'd have died an unbelievably happy man.

The dancers were a huge hit. They were also given plenty of protection and respect because on my property that was a priority. What they did off the clock and away from the club, however, was their own business and their own right. With plenty of input from me (being a man who knew what men liked), the twins developed a routine that made them the talk of the town. The classy, happy atmosphere of the club attracted a healthy mix of guys and girls, couples and singles. The lighting, seating, and décor created an upscale yet fun and laid-back ambiance. And just for added insurance, I kept the price of a drink competitive until we built some loyalty. Anything illegal, including drugs, was not tolerated under my roof.

There was no doubt in my mind that our establishment was superior to the other clubs in or around El Monte, and the customers reflected that opinion. They tended to be sharp dressers and acted as they were treated: first class all the way. More dancers were hired and in between entertainment sets, customers were eager to keep the jukebox playing and do their own share of dancing. Everyone seemed to feel they were stars in their own right, dressed in their trendy outfits and showing off their sexy moves on the floor. This idea of translating the mood of stage dancers to the paying customers was new, and we were all committed to making the next night more exciting than the last.

Music was now a driving force in choices about sex and lifestyle. Beatlemania, along with the music of other bands from across the pond, was sweeping the land and grabbing the attention, hearts, and money of young Americans. As the British were "invading" America and Elvis had to temporarily retreat, there were some American pop artists, such as Johnny Rivers, who were making a name and reputation for themselves. Rivers helped his cause by recording a number of rousing and poignant songs, and by being known as a badass biker who rode his motorcycle through the front doors of clubs. One of his most popular hits—and a personal favorite of mine—was "Mountain of Love," which got more than its share of playtime on our jukebox.

Parents and some sociologists predicted that the music of the day would lead to the moral collapse of society. And the music, along with the dancing styles it engendered, was definitely creating an environment of free and open eroticism that no other music had. But the message was delivered in a package filled with fun and energy. Music was reflecting the frame of mind of the country and being translated into lifestyle. My California go-go club, an upgraded version of what I had designed in Korea, captured that very mood.

My daylight hours were spent prepping for the club's action each night, and then I would slip out to keep an eye on any bars that might become competition. As I visited local joints, I was keenly aware that the price of a song had risen from a dime to a quarter. It seemed inevitable the public would eventually pull back on how much they fed into a jukebox throughout an evening. In fact, I could see that with the cost of feeding it and its passive nature, my beloved jukebox was already losing some of its allure.

I remembered back to the Whisky a Go Go and how the couples had responded with significantly more energy and excitement to the live music of Johnny Rivers' band. To stay on top of the game, I knew I needed to act quickly and jump on this feverish craze I saw developing for live, passionate music, and create that same fervid atmosphere of sexual energy in my club. With that in mind, I began searching for groups that would stir up the interest and emotions of the club's customers.

Sure enough, bringing in live bands generated even more enthusiasm, and the club's popularity increased. The lines to get in grew. We were sold out every weekend and nearly packed on weeknights. All the while, Don manned the door and was living in the glow of his newfound prestige.

But I knew it still wasn't enough. I wanted a bigger club and a name I could hang my hat on. "Girls" wasn't doing it for me. I had an itch for something bigger and better.

Late one night, on my drive home, I grumbled at catching what I knew to be a long red light. While waiting, I gazed out my window and spotted a shop I'd never noticed before: a hair salon that also sold lingerie. *A nice twist*, I thought. My eyes were drawn to the shop's window sign. I sat in total silence and fixated on the sign's words: "Girls, Come to Play."

Girls at play. What a statement! My mind imagined all ages of women having fun, celebrating their feminine attributes, and preparing to satisfy the eyes and needs of their men.

Girls playing. Playgirls. That was it! PLAYGIRL! The magical name I'd been searching for: Playgirl Club! I could hardly keep from laughing out loud.

The light turned green, but with my mind full of the potential of my discovery, I barely inched my way through the intersection. I knew instantly that my new club name was a winner. "Playgirl" conjured up what females wanted in today's world: independence, freedom from the old mores, fun, options, playfulness, and personal decisions based on their terms.

For guys, the name told them that when they walked through our doors, they would find girls who, to put it bluntly, might (or might not) be considering a sexual experience—*but on their terms*. The message was that females were in the lead. Being female was a great thing, and males were poised to enjoy the benefits of these new attitudes.

Later that week, "PLAYGIRL CLUB" signage was set ablaze to replace the old sign, and I prepared to expand and open my second club—a club that would have all the amenities of a Las Vegas showroom.

I was successfully scratching my itch for more.

Hell on Wheels

As it so often goes when things are moving smoothly along, trouble shows up to remind us to stay on our toes.

I arrived at the club around six one evening, where the afterwork crowd was enjoying a beer and one of the twins was yet again dancing to "Mountain of Love" as it blared from the jukebox. I greeted my customers and stepped into my office to tend to the mountain of mundane paperwork I faced nearly every day.

Don had taken a bathroom break, so his bouncer post was vacant. That was when I heard what sounded like the roar of an airplane landing in our parking lot outside. Thunder filled the entire building, rattling the lights and damn near every tooth in my mouth!

Then, other than the Johnny Rivers song still playing, an eerie quiet settled over the club. Seconds later, the problem presented itself.

In walked a dozen motorcycle gang members from eastern California. Although operating under various names, they were all equally terrifying in both appearance and reputation. They were bearded, tattooed, muscular, dressed in dirty jeans, cut up vests, and the skulls and other suggestive symbols emblazoned everywhere complemented the chains hanging from their belts and pockets in the most untoward of ways.

They moved into the club with a collective swagger that oozed intimidation. From the moment they set foot inside my place, they were loud, rowdy, and uncaring about anyone beyond their group. My pulse quickened and I could feel sweat coming out of every pore. Even though there was plenty of law enforcement in El Monte, I had no way of knowing just how much damage these guys might do before the cavalry could get there.

In the short time it took for Don to reappear, several of our customers quickly paid their tabs and vacated the premises. I wasn't happy about it, but I didn't blame them. By then, the bikers had dragged several tables together and started demanding drinks. The wisecracking and shoving between them had already started, and it looked far from playful to me. My gut feeling was that if they stayed and drank long enough, things would not end well. For anyone.

I felt I had no choice but to protect my customers, my establishment, and myself.

I stepped back into my office to retrieve the .38 revolver I'd kept in my desk drawer since Danny's disappearance and slipped it into my coat pocket. Then I eyed Don, and together we approached the biker who appeared to be the leader of the circus. His jacket read "Hells Angels," and his shoulder tattoo said "Berdoo," which was his particular chapter. I later found out that Berdoo was the original charter club of the Hells Angels gang. In my mind, that made him even more dangerous.

I tightened my grip on my revolver still in my pocket. "Good evening gentlemen," I said with less conviction than I would have liked. "My name is Doug Lambert, and I'm the owner of this club. Not sure you noticed, but you're scaring my customers straight outta' here. So I'm going to have to ask you to finish up your beers, then leave."

Everyone fell pin-drop quiet. The leader stared me dead in the eyes, glanced down at my hand in my pocket, then without a word, turned his attention back to his buddies.

Don and I retreated to my office to regroup. But to my surprise, the bikers prepared to leave. Granted, they took their sweet-ass time in doing so, including laughing raucously, pouring a pitcher of beer out all over the table and floor, and kicking aside tables and chairs as they went. It was all an attempt to further intimidate us and make their departure as dramatic as possible...and it worked. All I could do was wait out their big, bad bluff.

Finally, as they slowly swaggered back out the entrance the same way they had swaggered in, I loosened my grip on my gun. I never had to take it out of my coat, but I sure as hell never took my finger off the trigger either.

Outside, they mounted their Harleys, revved up their engines with another deafening clap of thunder, and circled our parking lot a few times before finally roaring off and out of sight.

In my office, neither Don nor I spoke for a full minute. But Don was first to break the silence.

"Damn Doug, I nearly peed my pants."

I almost laughed out loud at the prospect of this 350-pound teddy bear being even more scared than me. "I learned a long time ago that if you don't want a confrontation to escalate, you have to stand your ground," I told him. "You speak your piece, walk away, and wait."

"And what would you have done if they *had* wanted things to escalate?"

I finally pulled the .38 from my pocket, just enough for Don to see. His eyes widened. "I honestly don't know. Nothing I would have enjoyed, though," I said. And that was the truth. Things could have gone much worse than they did, and I was thanking my stars they hadn't.

Few lessons in life are more valuable than the ones that present themselves in the most terrifying of ways. And I would remember this particularly terrifying lesson about standing my ground for years to come.

Standing *My* Ground

Jenny: My life was continuing in the wrong direction. Work was becoming more and more frustrating. Bram was now seeking custody of Michael yet again. Poppi's overbearing and abusive behavior toward Mommi was worsening. And I was lonelier than ever.

In an effort to compensate, I found myself spending more and more time dancing at the clubs. It was such a release of emotion and pent-up energy and frustration. But it didn't solve any of my problems.

Michael was staying with my parents most of the time, although I was increasingly uncomfortable with him there because of my father's erratic behavior. Strict in their religious beliefs, neither Poppi nor Mommi approved of the clubs, the popular music, the new style of dancing, or the way I dressed. Poppi was openly critical and hurtful about it. Mommi just struggled to understand the changes I was going through.

Fortunately, Michael was too young at that time to be affected by all that went on with my parents. But I knew that would eventually change, especially if he were to become a target of Poppi's behavior. And I was sure he would. It was only a matter of time.

By now, Mommi had finally shared with us the mystery about why my father had remained in Jakarta when the rest of our family moved to Holland: Poppi had been secretly keeping a second family there since shortly after returning from the war. It was a devastating blow to my mother when she first discovered this indefensible deception all those many years ago. And it was an indescribable hurt to us all when we found out. It shattered what little trust and respect for our father we had left.

We also questioned why Mommi would have allowed our father to reenter our lives when he finally came to Holland, and why she had not shared this secret with us sooner. But most of all we questioned, given the circumstances, why Mommi would put up with Poppi's continued abusive behavior. We loved, admired, and respected our mother dearly, but this issue was very hard to reconcile in our minds and hearts.

Missing Michael and wanting to spend as much time with him as possible, I would pick him up on weekends and we'd do fun things together: eat his favorite fast foods, play in the park, stay home and watch TV, or occasionally do a big day at Disneyland. Still, I felt like a parent who only had visiting rights, though I knew that living in one place during the week was best for him. Michael and his Oma loved each other dearly, and she provided the consistent home structure and security of her presence that I seemed unable to provide. So, I settled for a while for just being the "fun" person in his life and hoped for the day when we could live together again.

More than ever, I was experiencing the dilemmas faced by single working moms. I wanted to have Michael home with me all the time, but I also had to work. Regardless, I was growing increasingly worried about the effect of my parents' problems on Michael. I didn't have enough money to hire someone to be home with him or to put him in a daycare facility, nor would Mommi have stood for that. Part of the solution seemed to be a better paying job with a schedule that allowed me to spend more of Michael's waking hours with him—and one in which I'd be happier and less frustrated. There had to be such a job for me.

One day when picking up Michael, I found Mommi crying profusely. Michael, still just a toddler, was also unsettled. It turned out that my father had been particularly abusive and threatening to Mommi that day. And for some reason, after all this time, that was the breaking point for me. I knew Mommi, for whatever reason, was not going to take steps to put an end to this herself. So after putting Michael in my car, I raced back into the house. In a rage, I got in my father's face and screamed at him. "If you ever speak or act violently toward Mommi again, I will kill you, Poppi. I will get a gun, find you, and blow your head off!" I put my index finger to his forehead and snapped my thumb down, pulling an invisible trigger.

My father, not used to anyone challenging him, began backing away. But I wasn't done. "You had better believe what I'm saying. I'll find out, and I'll come and kill you. You will not do this to Mommi ever again."

Mommi was pulling my arm and pleading with me to leave the house. Poppi, completely stunned, said nothing.

I turned to leave, begging Mommi to come with me. But still she would not. I stopped again at the front door, pointed my finger at Poppi, and repeated as menacingly as I could, "Never. Again."

I sat in the car with Michael for several minutes, still enraged and trembling with emotion. After regaining enough composure to keep my hands from shaking, I finally drove away, regretting absolutely nothing I'd said. I meant every word. And my father knew it.

After that, it was many years before I heard of any aggression toward my mother by my father. Either he had gotten the message, or great effort was made to keep his behavior from me. And in time, Mommi did finally take action to free herself from his abuse. It didn't come soon enough, but I was thankful it came at all.

After standing up to my father, I was full of conviction. It was time for me to become more proactive in putting my life on a positive course. And as I saw it, the first step was to find that new job.

Table service at the Playgirl Club

Live music and dancing at the Playgirl Club

Jenny in her Playgirl Club costume

Chapter 6

"Wipeout"

1965

Doug: "Gross!?" I challenged the building owners standing in front of me. "If you make me pay you from my gross intake, then that means five percent of my total income off the top before I pay any bills. Hell, even before I pay you rent, I'll have to sell a whole lotta beer to even think about making a profit." I slouched back into my chair. "That dog won't hunt."

The three city slickers must have fallen for my country drawl and chalked me up to a dummy or a fool. "Beer? You plan to only sell beer?" they asked.

No, I certainly did not. But I saw no gain in reminding them that I was only *initially* licensed to sell beer. The three men knew you could buy a beer at a dozen places within walking distance of this location, which in their minds automatically reduced the volume of beer I could sell. I had positioned them to underestimate my revenue and had them exactly where I wanted them.

"Sure, lots of beer. But paying you guys from my gross puts me out of business before I start. Tell you what. I'll give you four-hundred dollars more a month on the rent than you're asking instead."

They looked at each other with slick smiles and quick nods. A long-term contract was agreed upon. We shook hands. Having no faith in my ability to sell more beer than my competitors, the three landlords were smug, thinking they were walking away with the better end of the bargain. As for me, it was a good ol' fashioned "horse trade" my daddy would be proud of.

They all laughed as they went out the door. I laughed all the way to the bank.

Having a sale pending on the lease, furniture, and fixtures of my original club in El Monte, I began the process of moving into the more spacious new location on Harbor Boulevard in Garden Grove. My plans included my good friend the jukebox, but I had decided recorded music would only be used to fill downtime when the bands weren't playing. Experience had taught me you had to keep the action moving, so I developed "Doug's Protocols," which were my rules for success:

1. *Keep customers from thinking by keeping them drinking.*
2. *No slow music until closing time.*
3. *Control lights, angles, and seating to enhance what dancers reveal.*
4. *Schedule songs to build excitement.*
5. *Always keep employees moving.*

Our Las Vegas showroom style bar was designed so that when our customers were served drinks, they were looking at the bare midriff of gorgeous girls. Guys brought their wives and girlfriends; singles mixed it up, some wanting to just enjoy the music and dance all night, and others pairing off when the lights finally went down. No one was complaining. In fact, we enjoyed a constant line of ladies auditioning for coveted dance slots on our stage.

Our emphasis was on making the experience at the club as enjoyable for women as it was for men. This meant that by identifying with the ladies on the stage and the sexuality they were exhibiting, women of all ages, shapes, and sizes could more readily embrace their own sexuality without embarrassment or shame. From our perspective, this was far different than seeing women put out there as mere "playthings" solely for the enjoyment of men.

Some have asked why, if our focus was on women having as much fun as men, didn't we have male dancers? The reality was that the idea was actually on our drawing board, and would have been worked into the acts eventually. However, the time at that moment wasn't right. We wanted women to first relax and embrace their own sexuality by giving them the sense that female bodies, including their own, were beautiful and to be celebrated. In the eyes of most women at that time, that still meant being admired first and foremost by men. Therefore, we felt that by providing a venue where both men and women could enjoy a respectful, uninhibited, fun-for-all atmosphere showing off women's sexuality together, we would achieve our objective.

Even without the addition of male performers, dancing at the Playgirl Club was a popular job. Women patrons knew from word of mouth and from observation that our dancers and waitresses were treated well and were highly valued by all. It was a standard we upheld adamantly and were proud of.

And lucky for me, those facts would end up being a draw for one very important woman in particular.

Hit Me Like a Thunderbolt

At one of our audition sessions, I got word that a strikingly beautiful young lady was in the showroom. As I walked out of my office, she was easy to immediately spot amid the group of other girls on stage. She drew my eyes to her like a magnet. And my eyes were more than happy to stay right there and feast on that optic perfection.

While the other girls giggled and chatted nervously, she was the picture of quiet calm and poise. With lustrous black bouffant hair high on her head, dark, alive eyes, classically high cheek bones, silky light olive skin, and a body that should have been the mold for all other women, her stunning presence added grace and beauty to our stage—in fact, to the whole room. She hit me like a thunderbolt!

JENNY: With my top priority now being to find the right job and have Michael with me full time, I began an all-out search by following up on newspaper ads, registering with employment agencies, and grilling my friends about possibilities.

But looking for a better job was discouraging, since the only thing I seemed qualified for was office work, and I'd had a belly full of working my butt off while others got credit for it. And to be frank, the confinement of a nine-to-five job trapped inside a building often felt like being imprisoned.

Driving home from a girl's night out at the popular Playgirl Club one Friday, my friend Karen asked if I had noticed the sign out front advertising for dancers.

"I sure didn't," I admitted.

"Well, it said 'Vegas Showroom Dancer Position Open. Auditions Monday at 1:00 PM,'" she told me enthusiastically.

I peeked away from the road to see her watching me expectantly. "And?"

"And...I bet it's a nice place to work."

I nodded. "I'm sure they'll have a bunch of girls show up. Even the waitresses seem to love working there." I focused back on the road, now thinking about my time with Michael the next day and all I had planned for just the two of us to do together. I was paying little attention to what Karen was clearly trying to get through to me.

But she wasn't to be hushed. "Jenny, hello! You're gorgeous, you'd look fantastic in those outfits they wear, *and* you dance worlds better than any of the girls we saw tonight. Why don't you try out?"

I actually guffawed as my self-conscious side immediately took charge. "Yeah right. They would never hire me! Besides, I don't have time to take on an extra job. I'd never get to see Michael."

"But Jenny, this would be *instead* of your day job. I hear the Playgirl Club pays really well on top of putting their dancers on a pedestal."

I'd heard that too. I was now admittedly intrigued. But still, it seemed too good to be true. "Then why don't *you* go and try out, Karen?"

She chortled. "If I looked and danced like you, I'd be first in line." Then she clasped her hands together and practically bounced in her seat. "Just think about it, okay? Promise?"

Even though I never agreed to think about it, I did—all weekend. Could I actually be paid to dance? To do the thing I'd so dearly loved since childhood? Could I make enough money working those few hours at night to support Michael and myself? Would it enable me to spend days with him and hire a babysitter at night? Or even let him spend the nights I worked with Mommi?

By Monday morning, I had not only made my decision, but I had put together a sexy, fringed miniskirt with a plunging top to enhance my decision. And, feeling the need for moral support, I lined Karen up to go with me to the audition. Since it was her wild idea in the first place.

There were six of us taken in at a time. As part of the audition, we were asked a bit about our backgrounds and our pictures were taken. Always having more than my share of pride while also being fairly shy, I was feeling uncomfortable with the process—more intimidated than embarrassed, though.

There was nothing cheap about the Playgirl Club's environment. In fact, although I hadn't been to Las Vegas, the setting reminded me of pictures I'd seen in magazines and images portrayed in movies. And Karen said one of the dancers told her there were no drugs, prostitution, or anything else illegal allowed in the club or on its premises. Everything about this place was clear-cut business. And that was intimidating. But I was determined to see this through, so I stayed focused on my reasons for being there.

Now, standing in the middle of the Playgirl Club stage, I answered a few more questions from the owner and his team about my early ballet training, my family's journey from Indonesia to Holland to Toledo to California, and ended the interview by saying, "Coming to America, especially California, was my dream. Dancing is my passion, and I hope my future."

DOUG: My fascination with Jenny began with her extraordinary looks and grew with each new thing I learned about her. She had a passionate love for music and dancing, excelled in her early ballet training, spoke four languages, and was enormously proud to be an American. From her brief remarks, it appeared Jenny and her family were courageously emigrating from Indonesia to Holland at about the same time I was making my way from the Appalachian Mountains to Southern California.

Even before she began dancing, I was already thinking (and hoping) that Miss Sersansie might be a part of my future somehow. I was pouring thousands of dollars and hours into my dream of creating a swanky, deluxe club that would be franchised around the world, and this young lady personified the image I hoped to project: chic and classy, elegant beauty, and top-of-the-line dancing talent that accentuated the music of the day. It all came together to create an addictive sensual environment people couldn't stay away from.

But I was not used to this strange feeling I was experiencing; this instant and near overwhelming attraction to someone. And I was afraid of it. So, as I always did when I found myself more affected by my emotions than my head, I decided to play it "cool."

Big mistake.

JENNY: For my group's audition, someone chose the song "She's About a Mover," which had a solid but not overly demanding beat. I would have preferred something faster and more interesting, but thought I was doing very well interpreting the song nevertheless.

Then, about halfway through, the music abruptly stopped. Mr. Lambert, the owner of the club, leaned toward me and said something I could barely make out. But I did, and I couldn't believe my ears.

I was instantly cut to the core, but tried not to let it show. I quickly regrouped my pride and anger to override the hurt in my voice, and made sure what I said next was for the ears of everyone there. "Too bad you didn't choose a song that was fast enough for me to show you what I can really do." With that, I turned as gracefully as I could and walked out of the room with my head high, but my pride and heart wounded.

Karen, not knowing what had been said to me, followed with her hands up and a bewildered expression on her face. But I couldn't bring myself to tell her what he'd said. All the way home, my emotions fluttered between anger and hurt.

DOUG: The couple of minutes I saw Jenny dancing put an exclamation on my original thoughts about her. But not wanting to play my hand right away, I stopped the music, and in a voice only she could hear, said, "Your outfit looks like crap and you move like a turtle."

Jenny responded instantly with fire in her eyes and yielded no ground. She then did an elegant dancer's pivot, turned her back to me, and walked right out of the room, giving us all a fantastic look at the most magnificent posterior I had ever seen. I was too distracted to think to stop her before she was gone.

I had expected that she would defend herself. In fact, I wanted to see exactly how she handled the pressure of being scrutinized. But I had not expected her to walk away from the audition, and when I finally snapped out of it, that realization concerned me. I turned to Don. "Hire her right away." But upon coming back from the parking lot a minute later, he told me she was already gone.

For two weeks, Don called the number on Jenny's application. For two weeks, there was no answer. She flashed through my mind regularly, delightful memories of her face, her body, her dance moves, and her furious departure. I didn't want to lose her, and I was not at all accustomed to being ignored. So I devised a devilish plan that I thought would assure her return.

JENNY: For two weeks, my phone rang day and night, but I refused to take calls from anyone at the club. I wasn't used to having derogatory remarks made about my looks or my dancing, and I never wanted to think about the Playgirl Club again. And I most certainly did not want to think about that bastard Doug Lambert.

But I soon noticed people at the bank staring at me strangely, with quirky little smiles on their faces. Some of the men even began whistling when I'd walk past them. I had gotten plenty of attention before, but nothing like this. I began dressing as inconspicuously as I could, but it seemed to make no difference.

Then some friends told me about a large picture of a woman behind the bandstand at the Playgirl Club that "looks exactly like you." Karen finally banged on my door late one night, and I opened it to find her nearly falling down with excitement. "Jenny, there's a six-foot picture of you in your audition outfit on top of the Playgirl Club! With a spotlight on it!"

DOUG: Not long after the pictures went up, Jenny Sersansie stormed into my club madder than a hen whose eggs had just been stolen. And she was clearly ready to do some serious flogging.

Don intercepted her as she headed for my office. "I want to see Mr. Lambert!" she demanded.

"He's...uh, not available."

But she didn't slow down. Instead, she caught Don off guard by pushing both hands into his big belly and shouting so everyone in the building could hear. "The hell he isn't! He's going to see me right now!" Then she simply sidestepped a dumbstruck Don and made it through my open door before he could regain his senses.

Jenny stood before me with that same fire in her eyes. Before I could speak, she whipped open her coat to reveal the two-piece costume she had worn for her audition. "Looks like crap, huh? That why you have a six-foot tall picture of me wearing it on top of your building?" She took a breath and slapped her hand down on my desk. "Hire me and turn those pictures into an honest advertisement. Or take my pictures down completely. If you don't do one or the other, I will sue you for anything I can make stick, Mr. Lambert."

Somehow, I kept myself from smiling as I looked deep into her brilliant eyes. "Miss Sersansie, you make an excellent point. And I like that you came prepared to dance. Let's give this another shot, shall we?" I said calmly. Taking her by the elbow and graciously escorting her into the interior of the club, I guided her up to the stage. Then I dropped a coin in the jukebox and pushed A-12. "Wipe Out" was the fastest song in the entire selection.

The song, first recorded by The Surfaris, personifies the dramatic crash a surfer feels wiping out on a major ocean wave. It opens with a male voice cackling an offensive taunt. His cruel laugh mocks the imaginary surfer before he bellows, "WIPE...OUT!" The rest of the song is an instrumental of a frantic, unforgettable, triple-beat tune that's impossible to get out of your head.

Jenny, alone on the stage and with patrons watching, took charge immediately. Her body's rhythmic movements began a slow introduction that punched every other beat in a sexy, seductive opening to her dance. The slow movement was clearly mocking my turtle reference. Then she smiled at me briefly before shifting into a wild, fringe shaking, mind blowing pace. The customers and other dancers began clapping to the beat, encouraging Jenny with their approval. Her arms and body were moving at an incredibly rapid speed. She carried the crowd into a frenzy, matching every drumbeat with a body move. The customers were clapping, lights were flashing, music was blaring, and everyone was cheering. She had total command of my club...damnit!

Taking back control, I hit a button to shut down the music. Jenny didn't miss a beat in hitting a finishing pose, and the crowd cheered wildly. I walked to the stage and Jenny went to one knee in a ballerina style bow. I whispered in her ear, and she gave me a wink and a confident, "Yes," before she departed the stage to applause picking up again.

Jenny started work the very next night. I gave her a top billing and put her name next to the life-sized photograph on top of my building. It was indeed an honest advertisement now—just like she wanted.

JENNY: I was ecstatic! I was going to be dancing professionally! It wasn't with the Bolshoi Ballet as I had dreamed about as a child, but I would be making money doing something I loved more than anything else.

I gave a week's notice at the bank the next morning and readied myself to start at the club that night. I figured I could handle doing both jobs for a week.

Walking away from the club after my second audition, I had an entirely different image of Douglas. And once my employment started, I continued to be impressed with his treatment of not only me but the other girls as well. In fact, I came more and more to like and respect him. I was to find out firsthand that the nightclub business was a tough one, and to keep it first class—meaning, keep all the bad stuff out of it—he had to be tough himself.

I fell seamlessly into my new life. The opportunity to dance nearly every night felt incredible. And better yet, that meant I had my days free to take care of Michael and bring him back into my life for good. It was a win-win for both of us.

The only downside to my rapidly growing role at the Playgirl Club was the necessity to hide it from Mommi. I knew she would never approve of my shaking it up on a stage for all to see. So I told her I had gotten an overnight job doing paperwork in an office, because I needed her help with Michael at night. Miraculously, the fib worked.

In addition to my role as a dancer, Douglas was appreciative of my insights and work ethic, and so began involving me more and more in certain business aspects of the club. I was learning all about Playgirl's operations and discovered it was an intricate and exciting business from all sides of the table. Even though I began as a stranger, an outsider graciously given access to the inner circle, I felt as deeply passionate about seeing the club succeed as Douglas did.

I was friendly to all of our customers and employees, but learned quickly it was best to not socialize with anyone outside the club. Douglas seemed to have learned the same thing, because it didn't appear the boss was dating any girls from the club. And I turned down any interest tossed my way from staff and customers too. We were both so determined to put our heads down and make the Playgirl Club the best spot in town that any thoughts of life beyond the here and now were just that—thoughts.

Before I knew it, the next few years sped blissfully by.

Eventually, however, I did start paying closer attention to the natural chemistry Douglas and I had when working together. I could tell he liked me. And I had grown to like him too. When all our hard work together caused the club to start operating like a well-oiled machine, I finally found room in my brain to start wondering if he'd ever ask me out.

After three years, he finally did.

LIKE A PRECIOUS GEM

Doug: I watched Jenny with interest and intrigue. She was my star performer, the favorite among our customers by a mile. She was friendly but not overly cozy with the other employees, and while she was always polite, she kept her distance with the customers.

Jenny was special, independent, self-confident, and incredibly beautiful. She was different from anyone I had ever known. Though I rarely showed it, I found myself thinking of her as I would a precious gem. In fact, to ensure she was kept safe, I had Don escort her to her car every night.

After several years of hard work and total focus on the business, I surprised even myself when I approached Jenny backstage as she was waiting for her time in front of the crowd. I suddenly felt nervous—a rare emotion for me. "Would you like to have dinner with me one night?" I asked shyly. Another rare characteristic.

She put her perfect leg on a stool top, adjusted her shoe, and called me out. "I'm not sure. You and I don't seem to have much of a life outside the club. How would we know what to do?"

Breathing in her hint of perfume and taking a good close-up peek at her majestic cleavage, my shyness gave way to something more along the lines of pure lust. "How about we figure that out together?"

She dropped her leg and crossed her arms. "I dunno. What would the other girls say?" Her voice was teasing now. So I gave it right back.

"I don't much care about 'other girls' at the moment."

Then Jenny smiled that radiant smile I'd come to admire so much. "Dinner sounds wonderful."

I smiled back as triumph swelled in my chest.

But I realized she was right. What would the rest of the club staff think? I certainly didn't want to start any undue tension or drama. "Maybe we should keep it between us, though. For professional reasons, of course," I told her, smoothing my hair for lack of anything else to do.

Jenny nodded. "Of course. For...professional reasons." Then she casually made her way past me and to the stage.

Professional or not, I found myself quite liking the idea of Jenny and me having our own little secret to share. And I got the inkling that she did too.

Wakeup Calls

Wanting to make a big impression on our first date, I took Jenny to the exclusive Playboy Club atop a skyscraper on Sunset Boulevard. The Playboy "bunnies" were decked out in satin, one-piece suits molded to fit each individual girl perfectly. Cut high on the bottom and low on the top, they were accessorized with a big fluffy tail and a hair band of bunny ears. Much like my Playgirl Club go-go dancers, these women were treated like gold.

I had been a semi-regular customer at the club, and now I watched to measure Jenny's reaction to being in this internationally famous setting. The environment intimidated many women. It did, after all, cater to men and their desires. But she wasn't giving anything away.

Halfway through the evening, Jenny said she was going to the ladies' room. A few minutes later, she returned to our table with a big smile on her face. "Everything okay?" I inquired.

"Oh, yes. A poor little bunny was in a rush, so I let her cut in front of me. She gave me a big hug and said, 'You are precious.' Those bunnies are just such sweet girls."

And that was the end of any possibility of intimidation. Jenny had not only found a way to embrace the "bunny-ness," but even viewed the bunnies simply as the "sweet girls" they truly were. The rest of the evening went smoothly, and Jenny's bunny friend even popped over to say good evening to us.

That night, we shared a tender but passionate kiss, and I knew I was hooked on Jenny. I made myself a promise to not be so busy that weeks would pass before I took her out again.

But it was summer, and the California heat drove our patronage numbers higher than ever. We got so busy that Jenny was asked to work both day and night shifts, and she stepped up admirably. We were together every hour except when sleeping in separate places, and had become very close friends—even partners, in essence. I came to trust her opinions and value her input immensely. Jenny had a way of telling me her thoughts and ideas without offending me.

The truth is, if you had looked up the words "egocentric" and "arrogant" in the dictionary, you would have found my picture next to them. I was self-centered, selfish, opinionated, and full of myself. Yet with Jenny, I found myself interested in and respecting her feelings, thoughts, and opinions like I had for no one before. We developed an easy way with each other, working hard and laughing often. With Jenny by my side, the club was humming along better than even I had expected it to.

Johnny, the bookie and partner in the auto shop in El Monte, was not only my investor, but he also oversaw the early club shift while I snuck in a few hours of sleep. Our evening shift change was at six and as the routine began, Johnny helped clock employees in and out. And even though we had a very capable club manager named Willie Brown, I was burning the candle at both ends. But the club was continually improving and growing.

It's true what they say, though: The water is calmest before the storm.

Our rip-roaring thunderstorm came in the form of a new customer who every night for nearly a week had gotten drunk and boisterous to the point of being disruptive. On about day seven of this behavior, Willie escorted him to the door and suggested he go home and sleep it off. Once outside, though, Willie made it clear to the man he was not to return, or the police would be called. He was permanently banned from the Playgirl Club.

An hour later, we were filling up with evening customers escaping the heat and winding down after work. Suddenly, the unmistakable sound of bullets rang out. I immediately grabbed my trusty .38 from my office and bolted for the stage. The huge bar back mirror was shattered, and shards of glass were falling to the floor. I dove to my hands and knees and tried to maneuver without getting my head blown off. I was making my way to the front of the building where the shots had come from. They seemed to have stopped, but I couldn't be sure.

The next thing I saw was Jenny, also on her hands and knees, bravely guiding people to safety toward the back of the building. From a distance we made eye contact, and my mind and body instantly flooded with relief. It was like being shot with a tranquilizer—unexpected and all-consuming. I knew at that moment that I loved Jenny without reservation, and never wanted to be without her.

Thankfully, the shooter, none other than the raucous drunk who had been kicked out, had emptied his gun by now, and having done so, staggered back to his car. But he was too drunk and probably too stunned by his own actions to even attempt a getaway.

Unthankfully, Willie had been hit. Seeing the blood, Johnny called an ambulance and the police, and within minutes we heard their sirens. Johnny tended to Willie, who miraculously had only minor wounds and actually wanted to go back into the club to finish his shift. We of course insisted he be taken to the hospital. After Willie was tended to, I watched the police arrest the dazed drunk and take him away. Then I turned to my terrified customers.

Jenny fell right in step with me, calming and reassuring patrons and employees alike. The police questioned everyone about the incident then left, leaving us to our own devices once again. As the night settled back into some state of normalcy, everyone began sharing stories of what had happened, and a near-tragedy morphed into a great tale.

The next day, the news was all over town that our customers had saved themselves and the Playgirl Club with their brave actions. Everyone was a hero! While I was glad everything had turned out mostly okay, all my mind could focus on was the memory of Jenny bravely crawling alongside the people in her charge, leading them to safety, and my feeling of utter relief and thankfulness that she was alive.

I knew I couldn't wait any longer. I asked her out for our second date.

Exotic Evenings

"Do you always have to mix in business with pleasure?" Johnny queried me. "Especially when you leave so little time for pleasure in the first place?" He knew that one of my hidden motives behind my second date with Jenny was to check out a local club. I just couldn't help myself.

I had booked a prominent table at a restaurant and lounge called Oasis that offered dinner and a musical show for a hefty price tag. They boasted a distinct Middle Eastern menu and an exotic Arabian atmosphere. Naturally, I was curious as to how they were selling out most nights.

Jenny and I settled into a private booth that made for a very romantic setting. She allowed me a few kisses mid-dinner, and let me know very directly that she was enjoying the physical contact. I was again impressed by this bold message from such a ladylike young woman. These were the type of surprises a man responds to well, and so far, Jenny had never disappointed in her ability to catch me off guard—in the most pleasant and arousing of ways.

After a satisfying meal and plenty of good wine, we moved to the lounge for after-dinner drinks and the show. The house lights went dark, and as the drums and bells began pounding out a seductive beat, I put my arm around her bare shoulder. A well-placed spotlight captured a line of belly dancers stepping onto the stage. They rotated their breasts and hips, and sashayed their scantily clad golden bodies within reach of our table. I was beaming as one dancer plopped herself into my lap and then bounded back to the stage.

That's when Jenny stood up. Her spiked heel dug hard into my foot as she stormed away from our table. One shoe even came off, but she continued her determined departure. She wasn't making a scene, but was certainly leaving me in the lurch.

I followed her outside, where she threw her other high heel at me with uncanny precision. I barely managed to catch up with her as she sat inside my car. "What happened?" I asked as I got in next to her.

"Douglas." No one ever called me by my formal name other than my parents and my sister Nell. "Your idea of a date is for me to watch other women prance around you? The Playboy bunnies strutting around were mildly tolerable, but this? Gee, how romantic to watch another woman sit in your lap. You know, you can be a real chauvinist pig, Mr. Lambert!"

As her words hit my brain, the light bulb lit up and I realized I had been unbelievably dense about our dates. "You're right. That was incredibly stupid of me. I'm sorry." I reached for her hand and was relieved she didn't resist. "Please believe me, nothing about tonight or the first date was intentionally done to embarrass, disrespect, or hurt you in any way. It was just plain thoughtless. Please, can we start over?" I gently took her in my arms for what I hoped was the most passionate kiss of my life.

After, we looked into each other's eyes and the world suddenly seemed different. Taking a deep breath, I started the car and silently began the drive home. After a few minutes, I couldn't take the silence anymore. "Next time though, will you please wear sneakers?" We both burst out laughing, and it seemed at that moment, Jenny was radiating every flavor of emotion I felt myself: love, desire, respect, trust, and the deep contentment of knowing your soul at last has found its mate.

She leaned her head against my arm. "Okay. But next time, I get to pick the place."

True to her word, a few days later, Jenny asked me to reserve dinner and a show at the Kona Hawaiian Club, a themed restaurant not far from the Playgirl Club.

The food was mouthwatering, a flow of perfectly spiced small dishes and entrées. Each was a treat to the palate without overfilling the belly. "Do you mind if I select a wine?" Jenny asked. Mind? I knew nothing about wine other than making it available in the club for those who did. I loved being with a woman who knew fine wine and wasn't shy about making a choice for us to share. She explained that red wine is best with red meat, and white is best with fish and poultry. And when the dessert tray came around, she described the delicacy of each, and again chose for us both. All in all, it was quite an interesting education for a guy from honky tonks and go-go clubs, whose eating habits rarely included a sit-down meal.

Before our meal had even ended, I found myself desiring this woman in a way I had never experienced before. I wanted her body, yes, but I also wanted her mind, thoughts, and her invaluable life experiences. It was then I remembered Nell's laughing admonition: "Mark my words, Douglas, one day you'll meet your match, and that'll be the woman you'll fall the hardest for."

I knew without a doubt that Jenny was my match, and that I had indeed fallen hard. I was happily guilty on both counts.

Dinner was ending and it was showtime. I had sensed Jenny's choice of restaurant had a deeper purpose than just good food and wine. She was always full of surprises, so I prepared myself for whatever came next. The house lights went dark and the thundering drums began a pulsating Hawaiian beat that I felt deep within my bones. I risked a glance at Jenny, who was wearing a sweet smile.

That's when women, and to my utter surprise, *men*, gyrated their way onto the stage. The men wore Hawaiian style briefs only, and instead of my go-go girl fringe, the women's costumes created mystery by covering their legs with long, soft, brown grassy fabric and matching bra tops. Their bodies moved in ways even I had never seen. The dance was more than just sexual; it was sensual in the way it stimulated both the heart and the hormones. It was as though the dancers were telling us a story of love and sex. The beautiful movement of their hands referenced their hearts and each other. They danced separately, yet they were connected in the most personal way. It was the most beautiful dance I'd ever witnessed. I couldn't decide between watching the women or the men, because it was a completely whole and sensuous experience where both were equally important.

JENNY: I was extremely pleased to see that Douglas did not appear to shy away from watching the male dancers as much as he watched the female dancers. It was a relief, really, and showed me that he could be the kind of open-minded person I wanted in my life.

As he continued watching, Douglas leaned into my ear. "So, do you like watching the men dance?" he asked.

I smiled up at him and couldn't resist the urge to nuzzle into his neck. "Yes, Douglas. Women like a little standup foreplay too. We enjoy being turned on by what we're seeing and hearing. It doesn't have to be physical all the time. Did you think we were so different from men in that way?"

He finally tore his eyes away from the stage long enough to give me a look of sheer wonder and amazement. I don't think anyone had ever looked at me like that before. I could tell he was registering my words carefully, taking them to heart, memorizing them. And I sensed it was because he was ready to implement this knowledge not only for his own personal use, but perhaps for his business acumen as well. And I think that would have benefitted both quite nicely.

After the show, it seemed that word got out around the Kona Club that the owner of the Playgirl Club was seated at table one. A mix of dancers introduced themselves to us both and sat with us for drinks after the show. A few of them said they frequented our club after hours, and we shared laughs, drinks, and stories about the business. I'll admit it was mostly Doug doing the talking, as I was quite content to let it appear that he was the big hero for booking our spectacular evening. We both knew it had all been my doing, and that was good enough for me.

I realized on the short drive home what an incredible and important night it had actually been for us. I snuggled into his shoulder once again and said, "You surprised me tonight."

"How so?"

"You weren't turned off by the male dancers, and really gave them a chance to impress you. And you seemed to understand how communication can make a sexual experience truly great—even when that communication is wordless. I like that in my man. I like it very much."

Yes, I had just called him *my man*. By the way he lit up, I could tell those words were music to his ears, and they sure felt like a song coming out of my mouth. At just about the time the rest of the country was embracing open sex and promiscuity, Douglas and I were finally beginning to feel settled in with just one person. And it felt completely right.

The rest of that night was a truly great experience, with plenty of "communicating" to accompany it.

And so, Douglas and I settled into our life together. Our minds and bodies were perfectly matched to bring mutual gratification on all fronts. Our days were filled with club business, our nights with unimaginable pleasure.

Though we had only reached this point of pure connection now, the moment I knew I loved Douglas beyond a shadow of a doubt occurred while crawling on the floor through shattered glass trying to get everyone out the back door to safety following the shooting inside the club. Upon hearing the shots, my first terrified thoughts went to Douglas. *Where was he? Was he hurt?* And then I saw him on his hands and knees making his way to the front door. I wanted to cry with relief. Our eyes briefly met, and he gave a reassuring smile and nod. It was in those few seconds I knew this was the man I had been searching for all my life. Despite all the temporary chaos and fear around me, I felt a surge of joy I'd never experienced before.

Now, for the first time in my life, I felt that a man appreciated me not only for my body, but for the totality of my being. And for the first time in my life, I knew the indescribable bliss that only comes when physical love is melded so completely with the mind and heart.

With Doug's continued openness to my input, the club was enjoying a new level of success. We stepped up our shows, increased customer count, and raised the price for a coveted seat inside the Playgirl Club. We were experiencing a new level of status, offering *the* place to see and be seen. It was a wondrous time that I wouldn't have traded for the world.

Grazing in the Grass

Doug: "Three days of peace & music." That was the slogan for the event now known as Woodstock.

On a mid-August weekend in 1969, four-hundred thousand young people converged on a six-hundred-acre muddy field for a free concert performed by the most revered musicians of the day. Although people attended because of the music, the event evolved into something a great deal more meaningful. It became a symbol of peaceful protest and resistance regarding those societal wrongs musicians sang about and the people marched against. At the same time, it became a message of peace and love to a country at war with itself. And of course, it became a mecca for unrestrained drug use and sex.

The timing of the event was perfect. Much of America's youth was angry and discouraged about our military involvement in Vietnam, as well as the social injustices and civil rights violations going on throughout the country. To support their cause, be it the Vietnam War, civil rights, women's rights, gay rights, or something else entirely, many marched in parades, participated in demonstrations, or simply "dropped out" of conventional society. Some used their social, financial, and political clout to avoid the draft; many fled to Canada to avoid serving; others joined the freedom fighters in the south. And no matter what people chose or how they reacted to unfolding events, nearly all of them turned to the music.

A group of music promoters and investors funded Woodstock. They booked acts that used music to reflect and interpret the increasing anger and rebellion that were quickly festering in a growing counterculture. Rumor was that Creedence Clearwater Revival was the first act confirmed to perform at Woodstock. Their social conscience was evidenced in the lyrics to songs that were anti-war. The already legendary Bob Dylan declined, but Janis Joplin, Santana, John Fogerty, Arlo Guthrie, Joan Baez, Joe Cocker, Blood, Sweat & Tears, Jefferson Airplane, Grateful Dead and Crosby, Stills, Nash & Young had the wisdom to accept helicopter rides into the venue.

Woodstock marked the time that drugs were affirmed in the lifestyle of sex and rock and roll. Hippies became bohemians and attendees showed the rest of the world that their culture would dominate the music scene. The last artist to make history with his participation was Jimi Hendrix, who performed his iconic version of "The Star-Spangled Banner," which segued into "Purple Haze."

At home in California, Jenny and I watched the news coverage of Woodstock with our eyes on a changing culture and a revolutionary music scene. Jenny literally jumped up and down on the bed when the news included footage of a group called Canned Heat performing a song Jenny and I already knew well. We had recently booked Canned Heat at the Playgirl Club, and they were a big hit. After their show, we visited with the band as they packed up their instruments. They shared their excitement about the following morning, when they'd be heading to a Los Angeles studio to record the song "On the Road Again."

By the summer of 1969, Jenny and I had openly merged our professional and personal lives. We were a team, respected by our management staff and envied by our friends. We knew we had found what so many are searching for: a shared life with your best and most trusted friend, an incredible lover, and an astute business partner.

Knowing that Johnny and Willie were very capable of holding down the fort for short periods of time, we made frequent trips to Las Vegas to scout out singers and bands that would be great acts for the Playgirl Club. Attending parties in New York, Vegas, and at home in California was part of our job description, and we easily balanced hard work with fun. Together we played, we laughed, and with our minds in total concert, we completed each other's sentences and verbalized each other's thoughts. And in between, we made incredible love on a level that can only be fantasized about.

Jenny and I were about as compatible as two people can be, and enjoyed each other in every way a man and woman can enjoy each other. All in all, it resulted in a time of supreme happiness, success, and growing wealth. It seemed a perfect world.

Doug and Jenny's first date

Jenny's Playgirl Key Club ad

The Playgirl Key Club membership card

Chapter 7

"Misirlou"

1969

Doug: The atmosphere in the newly renovated club was magical. I'd invested plenty of money, but what made the place so special was our constant attention to every detail; things that a customer would never deliberately notice. I had designed the room to feature live bands and performers who provided the music the girls danced to. The lighting made everyone look spectacular, and the pacing of the show bands and dancing girls was a journey through an evening of entertainment and fun.

I thought about and carefully implemented lessons from the days when I watched the carnival bosses carefully set up tents, booths, rides, and concessions all to lure the customer from A to Z and to spend money at each stop.

There were valuable lessons from my Korean go-go club too. I'd had so little to work with, but I knew even a used jukebox could be cleaned and polished to a sparkling, useful shine, and cheap lighting could still accent specific areas of a room.

And, of course, there was the music. Always the music. From day one, I selected songs that got the room up and moving, inserted a few slow dances for the lovers, and then whipped the customers into a frenzy just before the last dance. For me, the key to choosing songs began with the beat. I found that my customers were happy with a mix of themes. Druggie songs, such as "White Rabbit" by Jefferson Airplane were filled with lyrics most likely lost on parents, whereas Jimi Hendrix's "Purple

Haze" got a bit more blatant in its message. Sexual themes were equally popular. Robert Plant of Led Zeppelin moaned his way through "Whole Lotta Love," and The Doors upped the game with sexual references in "Light My Fire."

Surf music was also growing bolder. The heavy-handed rock drums and bass were replaced with a pumping adrenaline beat and the taunting power of untamed water, commonly associated with sexuality. Surf music commanded respect, as it was connected to surf champions whose thrilling footage flashed on big screens in bars, theaters, and venues around the world. These water cowboys balanced their nearly bare bodies on a slim piece of fiberglass and competed to ride the hugest waves possible. It required incredible courage and skill, and never mind that they were shark bait!

Dick Dale was unchallenged as the king of instrumental surf music. His most famous hit "Misirlou" was one of Jenny's all-time favorites to dance to, and our customers always went wild over her performance. And they went even *more* wild when I actually managed to book Dick to perform in our club. It was an unforgettable night.

With the right atmosphere and music choices, the Playgirl Club was officially on the map of places that guaranteed a great experience. Even as we raised our cover and drink prices, the customers clamored for more. Many nights we were at capacity, with people standing and waiting for a table to open. Hard work had paid off, and with Jenny by my side, I felt unstoppable.

Now it was time for me to take steps to protect my club name and my future success.

DAVID VS. GOLIATH

Hugh Hefner felt he had a monopoly on the word "playgirl" because in his mind, he owned all the rights to sexuality and its part in entertainment. I knew that he had successfully shut down other businesses that made moves to enhance their image and sales through an association (even a loose one) with any reference he thought threatened his Playboy franchise.

He focused on his magazine sales internationally, which further helped expand views about sexuality. He set the tone for what was acceptable to growing numbers of consumers willing to spend big for their own piece of sexual beauty: a Playmate calendar, bunny cufflinks in 14 karat gold, a flashy cigarette lighter, and plenty more.

I acknowledged that Hugh Hefner was a trailblazer, but I didn't buy the attitude that if there was an Elvis, there couldn't be a Buddy Holly. There was room in the world for more than one great artist or writer, more than one great comic and, for sure, more than one sexual lifestyle business. Jenny and I had ideas that Hef hadn't thought of, and I wasn't going to be limited because one guy wanted it all.

I needed my best strategy to secure and protect my Playgirl brand. Of course, Hefner would fight with everything he had if he thought anyone was threatening his domain. He had declared himself the king of sexuality, and so far, no one had knocked him off his soft porn pedestal.

I ultimately decided I had to make Hefner sue me for using "Playgirl," and then I absolutely had to win the case and declare the name as mine. Taking on a legend was never easy, but I was beginning to think a David vs. Goliath story would win me some popular opinion—and possibly a judge's decision in my favor.

Late one night, to clear my head, I took a ride up the Sunset Strip, as I often did. Other than Times Square and the Las Vegas Strip, there was no place more alive at all hours. Billboards flashed larger-than-life movie promotions, and neon signs as big as the buildings they adorned touted the latest rock singers, newest model cars, and advertisements for bestselling fashions, hotels, and restaurants.

I kept my speed low, enjoying the color and bright lights. About a block from the Playboy Club, I caught the light and glanced up at the bunny logo at the top of the high rise. I grinned as I remembered my first date with Jenny and how crafty she had been to make a buddy out of a scantily clad bunny. Then the billboard across the street from the club caught my eye, and when the light turned green, I pulled into a parking space to get a better look at it.

The enormous billboard was a catchy advertisement for one of our local stations, KCOP Channel 13 TV News. It read "Today's News Today...Hollywood News Every Day and Night." Son of a gun. Here was the second time a great idea came to me while waiting out a red stoplight.

My scheme to take on Goliath came together in my mind on the ride home.

Trapper Instinct

That week, I arranged to meet with Robert Hitchcock. He was an attorney at Richards, Watson & Dreyfuss, a firm specializing in copyright law. We spent a few minutes getting to know each other, progressed to a first name basis, and Bob appeared to be an upstanding guy. At least I figured he was bound by his law degree to be mostly ethical.

I placed my check for a retainer in front of him to indicate that anything I said was held in complete confidence. He eyed it appreciatively, then simply waited.

I laid out my plan to goad Hefner into suing me by getting right in his face. And I'd do so by plastering advertisements for the Playgirl Club all over the town's most popular entertainment TV station. "I intend to force Hugh Hefner to sue me for the rights to the name Playgirl, and then I expect you to win my case. I don't want to namby-pamby around this issue, Bob. I need a lawyer who has balls bigger than Hefner's."

His laugh was genuine; he was amused by my plan, but he wasn't mocking me. "Are you full blown crazy, Doug? Hugh Hefner is a steamroller taking control of most anything with the word 'play' in it. Playboy...playmate...playpen...he's impossible to beat. You'd be wasting your money and my good reputation." He lit a cigarette and leaned back in his chair.

"My understanding is that there are two things necessary to secure a trademark," I said, having done my legal homework. "One is 'use,' or using the name for a business. Hefner has never used Playgirl, and I have. With great success, I might add. The second thing is 'confusion.' The question is, will my area of business be confusing to his customers?" I shook my head. "Hell, Bob, there ain't any confusion between boys and girls. Ask your secretary to step in here and we'll all pull our pants down to prove it." Bob slapped his desk and roared with laughter.

But I got serious. "I know I need to expand my circle of ownership beyond just a location. I've formed a corporation called Playgirl Key Club, which is the operating company for the club. It'll draw Hefner's attention." I showed him my artist's mockup of my logo. "I've proven for sure that men will knock doors down to watch beautiful, talented, classy women entertain. And I was as surprised as anyone to find that women gladly come to the club with their husbands, dates, and even on their own. This feminism deal and women's lib thing is more than burning bras. It's women who are tired of missing out on the fun." Jenny's face and words flashed into my mind. "Women are becoming bold, outspoken, and confident in their choices to live their lives. It's a new time, Bob."

He considered all I had just told him. "It'll take a big effort to get Hefner's attention. You can't play your hand until you're ready," he finally said.

I grinned. "I've got that big effort in the works." I leaned into our conversation. "My TV commercial will be ready in six weeks. I only need to get the attention of one man. And his name is Hugh Hefner."

Bob grinned at me. He sensed that I had trapper instinct in me, and he was ready to get onboard for the big catch.

The Playgirl Key Club

Over the next four weeks, I had two major deals to put together. First, I had to make my Playgirl Key Club a reality, so I introduced it through an exclusive and limited pre-sales program for the girls in the club to sell to our customers. I mounted excitement over it by announcing that the girl who sold the most memberships would win an all-expense trip (with a guest) to the beautiful islands of Hawaii.

Meanwhile, Jenny was the only person who knew about my second, outside project. After weeks of research and interviews, I signed off on an advertising plan with KCOP TV. Then I contracted with a Hollywood advertising agency and hired them to produce a thirty-second TV commercial that would show the glamour, sex, fun, and prestigious party lifestyle attainable through membership in the Playgirl Key Club.

The advertising team presented us with storyboards and drawings of each detail of every scene that would be in the commercial. I added in more sex and Jenny added in more class. We were a team that respected the other's creative ideas, and we complemented and balanced each other to create an impressive outcome in everything we did. And I do mean everything.

The editors needed two weeks to put together a finished commercial: color corrections, flash editing that was seamless, perfect music to punctuate each second of footage, and all other final touches. We agreed to meet again in two weeks to see the first completed video cut.

Jenny and I were silent during the first part of the drive back to the club after that meeting. Our minds were busy questioning if we had missed anything, wondering if there was any one change or suggestion to improve our commercial. As I navigated the car away from Sunset Boulevard and into the more peaceful Coldwater Canyon, I pulled over to the side of the road and reached for Jenny's hand. "Think it'll work? Will Hef take my bait?"

My angel put her head on my shoulder. "Baby, you're offering them the most delicious bait ever. My bet is he'll take a nice juicy bite." She seductively ran a hand through my hair. "Now I need you to nibble on my bait," she whispered. We kissed deeply, practically making out in the car like two teenagers.

Two nights later, the winner of the Playgirl Key Club contest was announced. Most of our dancers and waitresses had been very enthusiastic about the competition, soliciting memberships both inside and outside the club. We even enjoyed an increase in business as new customers poured in. This was the first in-house promotion I'd ever created, and I was already thinking of new ways to leverage our business.

I was paying all the expenses for the winner to enjoy Hawaii for four days, but I'll never know if the contest was all on the up and up, or if Johnny and Willie had tweaked the fishbowl. However it happened, when Jenny's name was pulled, the crowd went absolutely wild with excitement for her. Confetti fell, balloons and champagne popped, and every person was cheering for our winner. It was like midnight on New Year's Eve at my prized Playgirl Club.

Several hours later, the celebration began to wind down. Jenny had danced one of the most memorable performances of her career while wearing a faux Hawaiian lei around her neck. We finally had a few minutes alone and I teased her. "So, who're you bringing along as your guest for your big trip?"

She narrowed her eyes. "Oh, Douglas, if you tell me you don't have a ticket to join me, you better believe I won't be going."

She knew me too well. During the celebration, I had indeed snuck off to upgrade the two tickets to first-class and put our names down for Hawaiian paradise. "Well it's a good thing I figured that might be the case," I told her, watching her magnificent eyes sparkle.

Close Your Eyes

Jenny: The flight from Los Angeles to Honolulu was smooth, but Douglas didn't put his work down for a single second. To give him a taste of his own medicine, I stuck my nose in a book and didn't look up either. But it didn't work. I had to give him my signature sigh just to get his attention.

Finally, he put down his paperwork. "I'd think you'd be happy, Jenny. We're headed for a great getaway. Just the two of us."

I snapped my book shut. "Just the two of us? You've been working this entire flight. I might as well be sitting somewhere else so you can put that damn briefcase in my seat. Do you even know how to relax? To let go of what we're flying away from and adjust to what's ahead?"

But I already knew that Douglas had never been one to relax. He'd tell me stories of how his mother and sister would try to get him to just...sit. But he always felt like he'd be wasting time. I'd witnessed the same behavior myself nearly every day I'd known him. I suppose it was what made him such a great businessman, but at the same time, he needed to learn that relaxing and rejuvenating can bring about a great burst of productivity on the other end. And I intended to make that the case for him with this trip.

To my surprise, he conceded easily when I told him how I really felt. He placed his paperwork in a folder, tucked it all into his briefcase, and slid it under the seat. "Okay. I'm going to try things your way. I'll do my best to relax."

I laughed and whacked him with my book. "Geez, Douglas. You make it sound like some terrible punishment!" And if punishment was what he wanted, then my "special punishment" he would get.

I pushed the button to recline his seat. "Close your eyes. Take a deep breath." Then I reclined my own seat and turned my entire body to face him. I made sure my breath was right on his ear. "I'm going to tell you a story. This story is about a handsome prince who was going on a wonderful journey with the princess of his dreams. They were going to have time together without any phones ringing or unwanted knocks on the door. They would have time to hold each other all day if they wanted. And the princess had a few surprises for her prince. Very small things that she had hidden in her travel case." I moved even closer to his ear and began softly running my fingers through his hair. "These little gifts are very soft and silky. There's a black one, and another one in shimmering gold. They cover very little, but still fit perfectly in all the right places. It's up to the prince to remove these—"

"Jenny!" he croaked my name. "This is *not* relaxing me! How long until this damn thing lands?" We both doubled over in laughter.

I don't know if he was exactly relaxed, but I was pretty sure he wasn't thinking about work anymore.

Doug: For the next few days, I found what Jenny called "balance." I did check in by phone with the ad agency, and if I had an idea, I'd scribble it down, knowing I could return to it when we departed paradise. But this was still the most relaxed I'd ever been.

Jenny and I slept until we naturally awoke to the smell of fresh air and florals blooming outside our window. We enjoyed leisurely breakfasts gazing at the ocean, and took long walks along the beach collecting shells as the tide rolled in and out. We watched boats of all sizes come and go, and Jenny said, "Douglas, let's get a boat one day. I want to be surrounded by water and looking back at the world." She wasn't looking for an agreement, but I vowed to myself at that moment that I'd one day buy her the grandest boat I could find.

We took turns making dinner reservations, both equally curious about the kind of shows and food we'd find each night. We enjoyed the mega-hotels' showrooms, but later in the night we'd have our driver take us to local pubs and bars. We found some truly talented singers and discussed the pros and cons of adding comics to our lineup. Without a schedule, I found new energy in my creativity, and discovered how possible it is to mix business and pleasure.

On our last night, we sat by the pool holding hands. It was deliciously warm out, with a perfectly balmy ocean breeze. Jenny was in a dress that formed and flowed around her body. She was always amazing me with a simple but spectacular outfit. "So, remember that story you told me on the plane?" I asked her.

"The story we've lived out every single day here? Except for the days there was no skimpy lingerie at all?" she teased.

"Yes. Well, the prince has a surprise, too." From my shirt pocket I pulled out a key on a chain with a single key and an address attached to the key ring. "This is the key to a place of our own. So we can be together every night."

"Douglas..." For once, my princess was speechless.

"I don't want to spend another day or night without you, Jenny." She put her arms around my neck and kissed me with both gentleness and passion. It was a kiss that communicated the deepest corners of her love. I made sure to return it with the same fervor.

Then we took each other's hands, jumped in the pool, and laughed and splashed, completely unaware of anyone else in the world.

Taking the Bait

While Jenny got us settled into our new home, I was refocused on claiming Playgirl as my own by baiting Hugh Hefner. If I won his eventual lawsuit, I would be the one and only owner of the Playgirl name. Once that was official, I could move forward with creating my own sexual entertainment empire.

To make sure Hefner (or at least his team of people) took notice of my commercial for the Playgirl Key Club, I mounted my media strategy.

Hefner was known to be a night owl, famous for working in his silk pajamas and robe. I could imagine meetings in his office or boardroom, where a television would be broadcasting entertainment news capped off by my commercials for the Playgirl Key Club. I figured that even if Hefner didn't personally see my advertisement, someone on his team would.

The commercial ran over a Friday, Saturday, and Sunday. On Monday afternoon, a caller to the TV station was looking to find "the Playgirl people." We could only imagine the conversations among Hefner's team. We had not only forced them into immediate action, but we had done it right in their own front yard.

Jenny and I carried on with our work, but we were reveling in the likelihood that customers at the Playboy Club were innocently asking Hef if he was launching the Playgirl Key Club. I hoped he was fuming in his silk slippers, as furious as I would have been.

Our plan was officially working. There was no turning back now.

Chapel at the Coco Palms Resort in Hawaii

Doug and Jenny marry in 1971 with Della in attendance

Chapter 8

"Blue Hawaii"

1970

Jenny: The courtroom was quiet. The early morning sun set the polished wood aglow and the serious mood in the room was palpable. Doug, Bob Hitchcock, and I sat behind the defendant's table. I was already unusually nervous while waiting to begin when Hefner's team arrived, consisting of no less than six glowering attorneys. We were in the Court of Los Angeles, with the Honorable Manuel L. Real presiding.

The sound of a gavel crashing down was our notification to stand for the judge's entrance into the courtroom. He filed in, and then we followed his lead to be seated as he planted his body in his huge leather chair. The clerk called our case into the record, and there was not a sound other than Judge Real sorting through papers. Doug had mentioned the judge was the son of a fisherman; he had come a long way from his humble beginnings. I liked the sound of that.

"I have read both briefs submitted to this court, and I'd like to start by hearing from Playboy on its points and authorities," Judge Real finally said. Doug and I exchanged a look of hope, relaxing us both just a bit.

Hefner's lawyers began taking us through the entire history of Playboy. Each attorney took a section of the business. Lawyer number one went on and on about the magazine. Lawyer number two had a huge stack of numbers regarding Playboy's holdings. Lawyer number three covered all the nightclubs. And lawyer number four covered the entertainment division, detail after detail.

It was quite a presentation, but it became repetitive. Even I could tell that much, namely because Doug's eyes were starting to gloss over. And he loves to hear a good story. Now, if only the judge were starting to feel the same way...

Doug: I had purposely manipulated the lawsuit filed by the plaintiff, Hugh Hefner and Playboy Clubs International. Considering that my entire business was at stake, I felt my anxiety growing.

The brief that Bob's team had filed was anything but brief. It was an elegantly bound document that contained all the legal jargon of our position. In my opinion, that document said it all and included every important detail the judge needed to know.

The running theme put on by the lawyers was that Playboy was a huge empire created by the one and only Hugh Hefner, and all Hef was asking was for Douglas Lambert to stop using the name Playgirl. An especially big push went into all the previous cases Hefner had won.

After an hour with no end in sight, Judge Real raised his hand and nodded to the Playboy table. "Thank you, gentlemen. Now I'd like to hear Playgirl state its case. Mr. Hitchcock?" He looked to Bob.

"Yes. Yes, your honor." Out of the corner of his mouth Bob whispered to me, "You just won the case!" Jenny and I stared at him in utter disbelief, not at all sure what he was getting at. He made a few quick notes on a pad, then stood up and cleared his throat.

"Judge, the Playboy company, for all its effort to challenge the name Playgirl, has never used the Playgirl name for any purpose, business or otherwise. Mr. Lambert's effort to conduct his own business in no way infringes on Playboy." Bob turned to the table of lawyers. "Meanwhile, they attempt to hold a monopoly; particularly on certain words."

At that point, Bob began to hem and haw a bit. He repeated my story about the difference between boys and girls, and while no one scowled, it didn't get the laugh he wanted.

Bob cleared his throat yet again and returned to the facts. "Your Honor, Mr. Lambert has invested his own money and sweat effort into building his club. He's been using the Playgirl name for years without any notice by Mr. Hefner. And now that Mr. Lambert wants to expand his business, the sharks begin circling." With that, he sat down, and I looked at him blankly, wondering how in the hell he assumed we'd already won.

"You just sold me out, Bob," I whispered to him. "Their guys had an hour of facts, and you present maybe one full paragraph on my behalf?" I was frustrated, mad, and most of all, worried. Bad feelings washed over me, but I made myself sit calmly while Hefner's team filed out of the room. I felt that the Playboy lawyers had dominated the court session and Bob was in over his head.

When the last of the paperwork with the clerk had been completed, Jenny, Bob, and I were alone. "Doug," Bob started before I could say a word. "You are the best damn producer and director I've ever met. You've built your success from your creative abilities, and no one can beat you in the entertainment world." I blinked at him. Well, that was true. The man understood that my Playgirl Club wasn't some fluke; it was the result of talent and hard work.

"But I know courtroom law," Bob continued. "Those guys oversold their case. They didn't know when the hell to shut up, and it came off as borderline insulting to the judge. They talked like he'd never heard of Playboy, and that was just plain dumb."

"So, what happens now?" I asked.

"Go back to work. Do what you do. It may take six months to get a decision from the judge. He'll give this case due consideration. Sit tight until you hear from me." Bob smiled, shook my hand, then Jenny's, and left.

With Jenny's encouragement, I did my very best to take Bob's advice. My entire future was hanging in the breeze, but there was no further action I could take. So I kept my ambitions high for my business.

As Bob had mentioned in court about expanding, we had begun to discuss other business projects under the name Playgirl. The nightclub business was changing quickly to make room for the newest trend, "disco," where jukeboxes and bands were replaced by a "disc jockey" that would spin records for a minimal fee. So I needed to start thinking about the bigger picture. I opened an office on Wilshire Boulevard and while my investor and partner Johnny oversaw the club's daytime business, I pondered my next move; one that would make Playgirl an international brand.

In the meantime, Jenny and I still visited Vegas regularly to sign acts for the club. I began to think that one day, I might like to get in on the action of these big-time casinos and hotels, and all the entertainment possibilities that came with them. On our visits, I scheduled meetings to quietly learn about which casinos might be available for sale. It was all just research for now, but you never know.

At this time, I had so many balls in the air I felt like a one-man Vegas show myself. I'd put in ten or twelve hours at our office, then make the drive to the club, where I'd always have what seemed like a million fires to put out.

We continued advertising the club and developed a few promotions that were sneaky but successful. At least twice a week, Jenny and I headed out to a restaurant or bar in our area. Our plan was simple: We'd order a drink and I'd play a slow song on the jukebox. As the mood turned quiet, Jenny would excuse herself and head to the ladies' room. I'd had fake five-dollar bills printed which looked like a real bill on one side, but on the other side was the Playgirl Club's location and a "First Drink Free" coupon. Jenny would drop a few for girls to find, and I'd do the same in the men's room. Sometimes we'd finish our drinks and watch people return from the bathrooms, amused that they thought they had picked up a fiver, when in fact they had scored a free drink waiting just down the road.

While our personal life was somewhat neglected, we knew that we had to maintain the best image possible for the Playgirl Club and name, at least until the lawsuit was decided.

The reality was several unexpected, sordid, or untimely events could have brought everything crashing down. With me burning the candle at both ends, Johnny was asked to step up and assume more responsibilities.

Jenny and I talked privately about the day that was surely looming: the day we'd agree to sell the club to Johnny. Again, it was speculative for now, but like I felt about a Las Vegas casino at the time, it was something that would surely happen one way or another. Jenny and I had already started moving physically and emotionally away from our jewel of a club. We were just biding time until the judge handed us his verdict, which would either result in heartbreak and disappointment, or be the well-deserved gift of our lives: ownership of the Playgirl name, and freedom to do whatever we wanted with it.

JENNY: I had known Douglas Lambert for five years by this point. For over a year now, we had shared a relationship filled with highs and lows. I witnessed his brilliant mind, integrity, and unmatched work ethic daily. I knew I was deeply in love with him.

I also knew that Doug was walking around with a creative itch he couldn't scratch. It was a restlessness that I didn't necessarily understand, but knew was real for him. So I waited for the right time to approach him with an idea I thought might help.

We were watching the magnificent California sunset. Doug had already been to the club for his daily meeting with our staff, and he would return again before nine to stay until closing. Fourteen-hour days were typical during this time, as he rarely slowed down. But I needed him to now, so I took his hand. "Everyone deserves happiness, Douglas. What is the one thing that would make you happy?"

He looked at me with a serious expression, because he knew *I* was serious. I really did want to know what he wanted. "Okay, Jenny," he started. "When you look at an artist's painting, you're not just looking at the finished masterpiece. You're seeing all the versions that led up to that painting. The viewer might not, but the artist judges their final work on all the sketches, the drawings, the endless mixing and blending of oils for the perfect shade of a color. For the artist, at every crucial step, it's always the *next* step that's driving them forward, striving for perfection. Never satisfied until a true masterpiece is achieved."

I let that settle on me before responding. "I take it you're the artist in this scenario? Trying to create a masterpiece?" He nodded slowly. "That's quite a standard to set for yourself," I said. This wasn't quite the direction I had intended the question to lead, but I kept my tone gentle, wanting him to feel free to talk to me about these important feelings. "It's an admirable standard for your business, Douglas. I understand it. But what about..." my words caught in my throat. "What about the standards you set for your personal life? And for the people in it?" I waited for an answer, but he stayed quiet. *He* may not have gotten the point I was trying to make, but I understood that to run with him, you had to always measure up. Always be the next step he wanted to take. Always keep him satisfied that things were leading to that masterpiece.

At this point in time, Doug had lost focus on everything except business. Between the lawsuit and the club, he seemed to be as frustrated as I'd ever seen a person. This waiting game was a huge distraction from us and our relationship.

I felt he had been taking for granted that I was at the club when needed, maintaining our home, raising my son (with some major help from Mommi), and still standing by his side during everything we were both going through. Staying together and loving each other was my most important goal, but I had needs too. And now, I could see that it was up to me to get them met.

I knew what worked on Doug, and I sure as hell wasn't afraid to use it. I silently decided to redirect some of his attention toward our relationship. It would be a necessity for both of us.

Upping the Ante

A few weeks had passed since my brief talk with Doug, and nothing had changed.

I had just zipped up my new dress, a pale yellow strapless piece that showed off my tan with just the right amount of bare shoulders and legs. I was at my vanity mirror putting the finishing touches on my makeup when Doug came storming into the house. He only missed the evening staff prep when he was traveling, so my surprise was obvious.

His veins were actually popping out of his neck. "What in the hell is this, Jenny?" he said, punching his finger into a page of the daily newspaper.

I took the paper from him and tried not to smile when I looked at it. It was a lovely photo of me on the beach in a bikini...with a very handsome young man who was *not* Doug. We were sharing a box of chocolates from a heart shaped box as two glasses of champagne balanced in the sand.

Understandably, Doug started ranting, growing angrier as he yelled at me.

But now it was my turn to do some yelling. "Douglas Lambert, I am an unmarried woman who is free to make her own choices, and I've done nothing I'm not proud of. And to be honest, I'm surprised you even noticed something I've done lately! You're so damn caught up in making money that everything else is a blur. Do you notice that I always do my job and more? Do you notice that I'm always here for you? Do you? You have some nerve, Mr. Lambert! I'm making myself a drink." And I brushed right by him.

Doug sat on the bed. He appeared to be trying to calm himself as I exited the room. Pouring a glass of wine, I considered telling him how the photo had come to be, but decided he could stew over it a bit longer.

The week before, Lorna, Doug's secretary at the club, took me aside. "Jenny, I got a call from a reporter at the *Orange County Register*. She comes into the club with her husband, and she's seen you dance. She's asking if you would pose for a tribute photo to run on Valentine's Day."

I took the paper with the reporter's name and phone number from Lorna with curiosity. "It sounds pretty simple," she continued. "She'll bring the props, a beach blanket, a box of chocolates, maybe a glass of champagne, and they have a male model booked to pose with you."

"Sounds interesting." I kept my tone serious, but inside I was smiling like the Cheshire Cat.

"Great," Lorna replied. "I'll call her to confirm. She and her photographer will meet you and the other model at the steps to Breeze Beach at eleven tomorrow morning. And don't forget to wear your cutest bikini."

"Will do. Oh, and Lorna, keep this our little secret, would you? If they don't end up using the photo, I don't want to create a fuss over it."

"Sure thing, honey." She winked at me.

The photo session took about an hour by the time they set up the props and touched up our hair and makeup. The male model was very sweet, and we had some good laughs about who could eat the most chocolate. He asked for my phone number and I politely declined, explaining I was seeing someone. It was an entirely innocent and incredibly fun event.

Of course, the eventual newspaper photo told a different story. As Doug always told me, a picture is worth a thousand words. And there we were: an attractive young couple, scantily clothed, gazing into each other's eyes, celebrating a day meant for lovers.

Lorna had phoned me earlier that day to rave about the photo, and someone in the club obviously couldn't wait to show it to Doug. Which had brought him stomping into our house now.

I finally walked back into our bedroom, set my wineglass down, and stood in front of him. He continued to huff, unable to stop looking at the photo. "I can't stand to see you with another man. It's the worst feeling in the world." He stood up and put his arms around me. "Damn it, Jenny. I love you. I want to marry you. Will you marry me?"

Finally, there it was. The spark our relationship had been so desperately needing. It was also the assurance I had been seeking that Doug envisioned me as part of the masterpiece of his life.

"Yes I will, Mr. Lambert," I said, smiling widely. We kissed passionately, and my new yellow dress was on the floor in minutes.

A Mother's Love

I was high on life and love. We were newly engaged, I was utterly glowing, and everyone at the club and in our lives seemed just as happy for us as we felt.

But it didn't occur to me that people outside the club had also seen the newspaper photo.

One evening while covering shifts for two of my dancers who had gotten the flu, the main door opened and the bright sunlight poured in, revealing a woman standing in the doorway. She took another step inside, obviously having trouble adjusting her eyes to the dark room.

"Jenny?" I heard an incredulous voice ring out. Oh my God, I knew that voice. I ducked into the reception area and threw a raincoat over my skimpy costume.

"Mommi? What are you doing here?" Holding the coat closed, I hugged her and guided her to the table furthest away from the bar. "What a surprise! Is everything okay?" My voice had gone up to pure soprano; a sign of guilt whenever I was caught fibbing.

She took my hand in hers. "So, this is your 'paperwork' job?" She tipped her head to one side as if to say, "Really?" She didn't even give me a chance to come up with a story. "Young lady, I saw your picture in the paper and showed it to my friend. She told me she'd also seen you on a big billboard on top of the Playgirl Club. So here I am. It's time to talk."

I felt so guilty that tears began flowing down my cheeks. I couldn't even look my sweet Mommi in the eyes. But she took my chin in her hand and forced my eyes upward. "Jenny, I raised you. I know what a good girl and great person you are. I know you have good reasons for your choices." She paused, choosing her next words carefully. "You should have more faith in me to understand and accept the choices you make for yourself." Then she smiled softly.

I finally smiled in return, tears still rolling. "I love you, Mommi. I'm so sorry I didn't tell you sooner." Then I spilled everything. I took her through the last few years: the impetuous idea to audition, gaining top billing at the club, meeting my crazy boss, and learning that a dance club could be a great place to earn a living. Then I shared with her my feelings for Doug. "Oh, Mommi, he's so damn complicated, but he keeps me interested, and we love being together. He's asked me to marry him. And I've said yes."

She handed me a napkin from the table. "Jenny, that's *wonderful*. I'm so proud of the young lady you are. Your happiness is all that matters to me." We hugged again. Now both of us were bawling. "In fact, I was always worried you would never marry again, that no man would ever be good enough for you." Then she deadpanned me. "I was worried you'd end up living off me forever!" We broke out in laughter, relieved that the truth was on the table and our love was still intact. The tears had finally stopped.

"I'll walk you to your car," I told her. I pulled the raincoat around me. "I'm working tonight, but let's have a long lunch tomorrow so I can catch you up on wedding plans."

Back in the sunshine, Mommi opened her car door and tossed the newspaper with my picture onto the seat. "I love you my precious flower." We hugged for the umpteenth time. As she climbed into her car, she glanced up at the enormous photo of me on the club roof. "Though it'd be nice if we could throw a coat over her too," she added with a wink.

I laughed as she drove away, my heart feeling even lighter than it already did just minutes earlier.

Slice of Paradise

Doug and I discussed wedding plans, and we agreed that if we got married at home, the guest list would be unmanageable. Between friends, employees, customers, vendors, and lawyers, it would turn into a circus. Besides, we realized all we really wanted was a private, intimate ceremony.

We invited both our mothers to join us in Hawaii for our wedding day. My mom suggested that she instead stay with Michael so she could get him to school each day while we were gone. She pointed out that a young boy wouldn't find a wedding nearly as much fun as a trip to the Los Angeles Zoo, which she planned enthusiastically. Although I was deeply disappointed they wouldn't be coming, I accepted Mommi's suggestion and was grateful to her for making my absence fun for Michael.

But Doug's mother, Della, gladly accepted the invitation. I had spoken with her many times by phone and had come to feel like I knew her well. She shared recipes with me, and I treasured her warm acceptance. Like Mommi, she wanted her child to be happy. Who couldn't love a woman like that?

Doug: I was somewhat surprised my mother accepted our invitation. But nonetheless, she arrived from Tennessee, and we allowed a few days for her to rest up before leaving for Hawaii. Jenny, her mom, and my mother even did some shopping for a honeymoon wardrobe before we left. I never mentioned that all Jenny wore in Hawaii were bikinis and lingerie.

The night before our flight, Jenny and both our moms prepared dinner together, and I was struck by how much I enjoyed this family setting. I had been single for thirty-seven years, but I knew there wasn't one thing I would miss out on by being married to Jenny.

JENNY: Our wedding trip was perfect. The glorious Hawaiian setting encompassed us in beauty. We reveled in the delicious fragrances and listened to gentle rain and roaring ocean waves. We ducked between raindrops and basked in the incredible sunshine. We savored every ripe piece of fruit and asked the chef to surprise us with the fresh catch of the day. Douglas was delighted each time I selected the perfect wine, and his mother happily sipped on virgin Mai Tais with her meals. She saved every little umbrella that adorned each drink, and would later take them home to show off to her friends.

Including Doug's mother made our wedding day all the more special. I saw that they had an easy way with each other; they didn't need an abundance of words. The two were cut from the same cloth, as they say. I admired it so.

DOUG: We chose the famous Coco Palms Resort in Waialua, Kauai. It's well known that Elvis Presley filmed his movie *Blue Hawaii* there. Lesser known is that Elvis first arrived in Hawaii in 1957, and that his music was immediately influenced by the surf culture. The final scene in the film is when Elvis sings "The Hawaiian Wedding Song" to actress Joan Blackman as their characters approach a pretty little church. That church happened to be the first church in Hawaii, called the Chapel of the Palms. It was the very church where Jenny and I pledged our wedding vows.

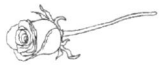

JENNY: After the wedding, we put Doug's mother on a plane home and began a proper honeymoon. Well, maybe not as proper as we would have liked. Two weeks would have been nicer than five days, but business was calling.

On the plane ride home, Doug slept, looking very content. I reflected on the beautiful beginning to our marriage and wondered what my crazy husband was planning next. Whatever it was, I was along for the ride. Now and forever.

Playgirl Club opens for after-hours service

Jenny shooting pool in the Playgirl Club

Chapter 9

"Money"

1972

Doug: Jenny was lying on her tummy on our bed, wearing one of my shirts and kicking her legs back and forth above her like a proper Hollywood movie mistress. She tucked a pencil behind her ear as she scanned our project list. "A Vegas casino would sure be a huge commitment, Douglas."

I inhaled deeply. "Yeah, and every other business I've ever started was fully funded before I opened the doors. I've never carried any debt, and a casino would need plenty of loans. I don't like it—at least not for now."

Jenny scratched the casino off the list and looked up at me. "Where do we stand with securing an after-hours license for the Playgirl Club?"

I knew I had to keep the club busy, and constantly growing our customer base wasn't easy because as the city grew, so did the competition. That being the case, I had done the groundwork to solicit the local city council to obtain a license that would allow us to keep the club open twenty-four hours a day. My plan was to temporarily close at 2:00 AM (per the regular city code), then reopen quickly with food, nonalcoholic drinks, live entertainment, and dancing.

Council people were not fond of all-night businesses, but I had nothing to lose by asking to be the exception. With the after-hours license being a key part of the continued growth of the club, I had run the city council meeting scenario through my mind a thousand times, each time thinking about all the objections the members would have to granting me the license. I had a plan for how I would overcome each objection and make it clear that granting the club the license would make sense for everyone. I felt confident with my plan and couldn't help but think about my first "council" presentation back in Korea to get girls and live bands into that ol' Quonset hut. I'd done the impossible then. Surely, I could do it again.

Playgirl After Hours

Jenny and I were all suited up to meet the city council women and men. They had approved standard licenses and permits for us in the past, but this particular permit was not a mere formality. It would take persuasion.

When our club's name was called, I stepped forward. "Mr. Lambert," the councilwoman acknowledged me. "What do you have in mind today?" I presented copies of my request to everyone at the table to read, saving myself from saying the words "all night" out loud.

The councilwoman glanced at the bottom-line request, allowing time for the others to read it too. "Mr. Lambert, late night hours are nothing but trouble. Intoxicated people fresh off 'last call' are not always the best citizens."

"I appreciate your point, ma'am, but I'd like to offer a few details." I geared up to say the speech I'd rehearsed a thousand times.

"I grew up in the Appalachian Mountain Range of southwest Virginia with my family, who was in the dry goods business. I'm an eighth grade dropout, and have worked in the honky tonk business since I was twelve years old. I began running moonshine before I was a teenager. I know the bad effects late-night boozing can have on a community.

"So what I'm proposing is briefly closing and then readmitting my customers. We'll serve food, nonalcoholic drinks, and plenty of hot coffee. And the music and dancing will continue. I believe everyone on this honorable council will agree that staying at the Playgirl Club to sober up with friends and neighbors is better than hitting the streets intoxicated."

Then I closed out my speech by flashing them them my signature smile, which I had also practiced a thousand times just that week. Not to mention, all the weeks of my life leading up to that moment.

Lo and behold, I had an after-hours license in hand before the end of the day.

Wolfman

In addition to the late-night license, I also had a new trick up my sleeve for making a big splash at the club.

Listening to radio performers and jockeys in your home, car, or business was like listening to the voice of a friend. Cousin Brucie and Murray the K were among the most popular, but the king of them all was a man with a larger-than-life personality. Wolfman Jack had developed his talent to include a wolfman-like beard and a raspy voice. In his pursuit of on-air freedom, he started working for XERB, a radio station just south of the border in Rosarito Beach, Mexico.

XERB was known as a "border blaster," with a broadcast signal that was five times stronger than was allowed in the U.S. The Mighty 1090 reached most of the continental U.S., and on a clear night, could be picked up as far away as the Soviet Union.

American radio stations had to adhere to strict FCC guidelines of broadcast power, as well as on-air moral conduct. But on-air standards were far more relaxed in Mexico, and this freedom allowed Wolfman to develop his late-night persona. In the true spirit of a wolfman, he used his signature growling, howling, and other antics to urge his listeners to "get naked, lay your hand on the radio, and squeeze my knobs." The U.S. audience loved it.

Looking to grow his Wolfman persona, he moved back to the U.S., recorded his shows, and sent them into the stations to be broadcast. It was at this time that Wolfman met Don Kelley, who had his own popular band. They had played on *The Ed Sullivan Show* and in the Playgirl Club many times. Don was now looking to do other things and grow as well. It was his idea to introduce me to Wolfman Jack, and it was that particular meeting that led to Don becoming Wolfman's personal manager and business partner of twenty years.

Over the course of a few meetings with them and running various scenarios through my head, a clear plan emerged. I'd book Wolfman as the emcee for the after-hours crowd and mix up the entertainment with Wolfman as the star. He knew of the Playgirl Club and certainly realized this in-person exposure would be a big career boost that fit his style perfectly. It was a win-win.

Just as I had planned, over the next few weeks, customers from other clubs began coming in, many of them earlier in the evening. Crowds at the door grew; the Wolfman and the late-night bands were popular. Most customers stayed until their stomachs were full of food and coffee, then went homeward bound sober and without incident. Revenue was up. After hours was a success!

Meanwhile, however, I had another issue to deal with. Don Taylor, my first employee, had been given more responsibilities as head of security. And over time, Don became a friend. So naturally, I was stunned to learn that his behavior had become problematic. He was drinking on the job, was often moody, and had been neglecting his duties in the club. But there was no indication of what the problem was. I gave him several warnings, and one night I finally confronted him, telling him to get some coffee and sober up. Soon after, Don walked out of the club when he was supposed to be working. An hour later, I found him at a local bar playing the piano, drunk as a skunk.

"What the hell are you doing, Don?"

He could barely talk, but managed to slur, "Whassit look like? I'm playin' the piano!"

I had no choice—I fired him on the spot. But I neglected to get his keys to the club, and late that night, as I was closing the bookkeeping, he showed up in even worse condition. He unlocked the door to my office and used his huge stature to block me from leaving. Once again, I found myself hoping like hell I wouldn't actually have to use my .38 for its intended purpose.

But just like that day with the Hells Angels, I managed to remain calm and speak my part. I also made sure to be as kind as possible, considering he was a physical threat wrapped up in a horrible mental state. Thankfully, after a few words from me, he left the club. I never saw him again.

I just never had any way of knowing what the comings and goings of a business like that were going to be. For every up, there always seemed to be some kind of down.

And then, the day after Don's abrupt absence from the club, Bob Hitchcock's secretary called and asked us to meet with him.

The Verdict

Jenny and I arrived at Bob's office nervous as hell, and neither of us could read his mood as we sat down in front of his desk. He just opened a folder and with a straight face said, "Judge Real was fairly brief in setting forward his decision." Then he paused, and the anticipation in the room was palpable. "He ruled in favor of the Playgirl Key Club and one Douglas Lambert." Finally, a big smile covered his face. "We did it. You took down Goliath."

The king of sexuality had suffered possibly his first loss ever, and I was relieved beyond belief! My thoughts suddenly went to the reaction of the losers on the other side. Hefner was not accustomed to dealing with defeat. I smiled as I wondered which lawyer would draw the short straw and have to break the news that the pedestal he was standing on had been cracked. I could imagine the wrath he would unleash upon attorneys and advisors who had smugly (and incorrectly) assumed victory was inevitable, as it always had been.

"He'll appeal the case, won't he? That's what I would do," I remembered to ask.

"Yeah," Bob replied. "But let's deal with that when it comes. Right now is a time for celebration."

I allowed the news to sink in, but I wasn't celebrating. Hefner and I had very different beginnings, but we were similar in many ways. If I were in his shoes, I'd take immediate further action. I had awakened a sleeping lion that was now functioning with a bruised ego. This was a huge loss for his team, and suddenly, I was a proven competitor.

JENNY: On the ride home, my head was positively spinning. "Douglas, can you believe it? We won! The club and the name are ours. Now we can expand." I was nearly jumping out of my body with excitement.

"I have some ideas. Now hear me out." I took a deep breath. This is something I had been sitting on for a while, and now felt like the right time to finally let it fly. "Let's open a club with *male* go-go dancers. The ladies will *love* it." My thoughts were practically tumbling out of my mouth. "I'm not talking about anything lewd or tacky…not ever. We should dress the guys in cleverly themed costumes. Each dancer would have two or three costume changes, making it seem like a big production. We could have a cowboy with sexy chaps, maybe a hunky construction worker with a hard hat, or what about a policeman? I think women would just love something like this. Maybe we could make it exclusive; a ladies-only club!"

He was smiling, and that was a good sign. But then he reached for my hand gently, and I knew what was coming. "Jenny, I like the idea, but I've got to put my nose back to the grindstone and work with Bob to win the appeal that Hefner's sure to file. He'll come in loaded for bears this round."

I knew the fight with Hefner likely wasn't completely over, but I hadn't considered things might get more challenging from here. The club we had fought so hard for was free from bondage, at least for now—wasn't it? But hearing the seriousness in Doug's voice, I better understood the tasks that still lay ahead of us. And of course, I wanted to help him focus on them as best I could.

He was right, after all. Within days, Hefner's team filed their appeal to the 9th Circuit Court. That meant the legal wheel went back into motion.

LOVE INSPIRES EROTICA

DOUG: Even as I continued to feed my lawyer's money meter, we kept our pulse on the changing times and how they might affect the club.

On one of our trips to Vegas, we caught a few shows and stopped in to hear several lounge acts. Music was going through yet another interesting transition. Woodstock had led millions of fans in several different directions. The hippie movement's peace and love message was popularized by groups like The Byrds, Peter, Paul and Mary, and The Lovin' Spoonful. These were the marijuana smoking, mellowed out portion of our population. Then there were the psychedelic fans, dropping acid and other concoctions to complement the hard rock music experience.

I was also watching the funk scene closely, as my prediction was that live bands would eventually fully succumb to disco. Jenny was alert to these trends, and her current favorite was the song "Money (That's What I Want)." Originally recorded in 1959 by Barrett Strong, the driving beat had catchy lyrics written by Berry Gordy, who was the legendary founder of Motown Records and the Motown sound. Jenny couldn't get the lyric about "wanting, needing, and loving money" out of her head, and it seemed to be the only song she sang in the shower, car, kitchen, and club. I teased her about it, but she was simply relating to the message, as many others did. "Money" would become a favorite cover song recorded by such super stars as Rod Stewart.

Magazines were also all the rage at this time. Jenny and I had spent nearly two hours browsing a Vegas newsstand that had to have been a block long. You could find a magazine on virtually any topic, from music to fashion to boats to nude women, and Jenny had plopped down twenty dollars to cover her selection, including *Playboy*. "For you, for the plane ride home," she said, grinning at me as she made the purchase.

That night, I was having a drink at the bar with one of the lounge managers while Jenny was still making herself beautiful for a night on the town. A man a few seats down greeted me by my first name. I recognized him as a semi-regular at the Playgirl Club, and we struck up a conversation. I remembered that he worked in publishing, so I asked him about the magazine business. "I can tell you, that business is booming with no end in sight," he said enthusiastically. I asked him to tell me more, and without seeming too eager, I listened to his education on the basics of producing a monthly publication. He explained many of the details, including how the numbers worked. The risks were high, but when you found a winner, you could hit it big. Product makers loved having their glossy advertisements on a page next to a beautiful movie star or a magnificent yacht.

That's when I also remembered that one night, in my club, he had mentioned a title he owned that I found interesting. But I wanted to go about it casually. "So, what are you working on now?"

He noted a few ideas for magazines, ending with the one that had already caught my attention: *Millionaire*. I could easily envision the content, as well as the kinds of advertisers that would be attracted to the topic of making and spending millions of dollars. Our country's economy was promising, and everyone loves to dream of their "first million."

As we exchanged business cards I casually remarked, "If you're ever interested in selling that title, give me a call." Of course, he wasn't interested at the time, so our conversation moved away from magazines and on to how he was doing at the poker tables. Even so, I had already gathered a lot of useful information from him.

When Jenny walked up, I could tell I moved up about ten notches in Mr. Magazine's approval rating. She was always sexy yet classy, seductive yet soft and feminine. And she was certainly dressed to impress. We left for dinner at a five-star restaurant off the beaten path of the Las Vegas Strip, and Jenny left Mr. Magazine's mouth hanging open.

During dinner, I told Jenny about my conversation with him, and I found myself enthused about a monthly publication where lucrative five-year advertising contracts were as good as money in the bank. I told her about the opportunities to sell magazines regionally or nationally. "Being national means you create one advertisement for a client, but you charge a national rate. So for the same amount of work, you've increased your profit tremendously. The challenge is finding a theme that's exciting and new." Jenny was listening intently, glass of wine in hand. "There's already a damn magazine on everything in the world," I lamented.

"The man you met. What's he working on?" she asked. Her instincts were scary.

"He owns the title *Millionaire*, which I really like. I think there are plenty of people who dream about being rich, many who are working on it, and plenty who are already millionaires. The advertising for a publication with that kind of title could attract big ticket spenders: airlines, resort destinations, exclusive fashion designers, and high-end products." I tossed my napkin onto the table. "The thing is, I know a lot more about entertainment, music, and sex than I do about jet setting."

Jenny laughed. "The jet setting will come in time. Let's go to back to our hotel and focus on the sex for now."

We returned to our hotel on the Strip and stood out front for a minute, taking in the majesty of the incredible fountains at the entrance. I put my arms around my wife, ready for a kiss. Instead, Jenny tucked her head and faced me with a conviction in her eyes I hadn't seen for a long time.

JENNY: The idea came to fruition somewhere between leaving the restaurant and standing there, staring into the crisp fountain waters. I couldn't shake the idea of starting a magazine, and only partially because I could already tell Doug was having a hard time shaking it too.

"I've been thinking," I said, dodging his kiss and attempting to make it clear I was serious. "You said you would only publish a magazine if you knew the topic well, right?" I stared deep into his eyes as he nodded slowly. "Well, judging by the success of the club, you clearly know a lot about making bodies look beautiful. You do it every day with our dancers." He cocked his head at me ever so slightly. "Okay, yes, I help them with their dance routines, but you're the genius behind the music choices, the lighting, even their placement in the club. You truly know how to make women look and feel their most beautiful."

"So, a magazine filled with beautiful women? Jenny, those already exist. You haven' forgotten about *Playboy*, have you? I'm telling you, there are no new ideas when it comes to magazines."

I smiled as I shook my head at him. "Yes there are. Because no one's doing a magazine filled with beautiful *men*." I continued staring, willing him to see what I was seeing. "Why don't we create a magazine that features a different nude male centerfold every month? Just like *Playboy* does with women?" He narrowed his eyes at me, so it was time to push the point home. "We already own the title: Playgirl."

DOUG: She said it so casually and confidently that it made her idea seem simple and almost obvious. I couldn't keep my jaw from dropping open, and could already feel the wheels in my head turning.

"Jenny, that's...brilliant. A magazine all about men, meant for women." I stared back at the fountain, trying to wrangle my suddenly rapid thoughts. "But do you really think women would buy a magazine filled with naked men? You don't think the idea, I dunno...assumes too much?"

She nodded eagerly. "That's the point! The world needs to start assuming women like looking at those kinds of things the same way men do. I *know* women will buy this magazine. They will because they've already started making it clear they're ready for unabashed access to sex, in all the same ways men have it."

I took her hands now, trying to make sure we both first followed a path of logic. "I get what you're saying, but how sexual are we talking here? The topic might be beyond us. I mean, we're anything but prudes, but I wouldn't call our lovemaking wild or kinky. Would you?"

She laughed. "No, we're not exactly into all the stuff I hear people at the club talk about. But that's not the point. This magazine wouldn't have to be all about sex necessarily. It would be about giving women a way to find the confidence they need to fully explore themselves and their desires. It would be an outlet for free and equal thinking, *including* when it comes to sex. Because, in its most basic form, it would clearly let men know that we do, in fact, get turned on by a picture of a sexy man's naked body."

I could see her point. Even just talking about it for a few minutes was suddenly bringing to light some new ideas about women for me. I could only imagine what an entire magazine would have the power to do.

"Women are just as curious and eager to sexually explore as men are. Let's give them that opportunity," Jenny continued. "Besides, one of the domino effects of doing so could be that men benefit in some very gratifying ways." She intertwined her fingers with mine.

JENNY: That certainly seemed to grab his full attention. But at the same time, a look of embarrassment crossed his face that I didn't expect. And then it donned on me: Douglas wasn't used to talking about these kinds of things out loud. We rarely discussed details about our sex life, and certainly not the details of how other people enjoyed sex. But if we were going to produce a magazine about it, then I wanted him to realize just how important it was to talk about all this.

I quickly put his fingertips to my lips and kissed each one. "It's okay, Douglas. What we do and how we do it is an expression of our love. That's why it's called lovemaking. The same is true for any two people who share romantic love. People do what their love and passion lead them to do." I looked into his eyes and waited to see if he understood the truth of what I was saying, and was pleased to see that the connection seemed to be there. "How you make love to me may be different than how you made love to someone else. And how you'd like me to make love to you could be different than what you've wanted from anyone before me. Sometimes, lovers can feel shy about going all-out with their sexual preferences—even husbands and wives. They may be afraid that what they want would be strange or unacceptable to their partner. Women especially are inclined to feel this way. So, both partners hide how they really feel. But sex should be about open, free, and comfortable communication. Because first and foremost, it's an expression of emotion."

I knew Douglas had never been excellent about expressing his deepest feelings or desires, especially when it came to the bedroom. And I knew the same was true for others, both men and women. The type of magazine I envisioned could finally open that communication up.

"Thankfully, that's starting to change," I continued. "The sexual train is pulling out of the station. Women are ready and willing to sexually express themselves in every way they feel like it. And society needs to be brought along for that change! A magazine like *Playgirl* would go a long way in bringing that acceptance about. So, we can either jump on the train and ride it to its destination, or we can wave goodbye as it pulls away."

I let that statement breathe as I decided what to say next. The truth was, I was toning down what I was hearing from our Playgirl Club dancers and conversations between our female customers. They freely talked about oral and anal sex, vibrators, food in the bedroom, multiple orgasms, triads, and even sexual sadism. There were times I had to work to control my look of surprise and even incredulousness at some of their descriptions. As the head dancer and their supervisor, I didn't want to appear naïve or judgmental. But no matter what I heard, my next thought was always, *Hell, if two people agree to that, then who am I to say it's good or bad?*

There was even one night in the dressing room when Sara, one of our dancers, pulled a dildo out of her tote bag. When we all looked at her with surprise, she laughed. "Hey, I love my man, but he's not always around when I need him. This man-friend goes with me anywhere." We all burst out laughing, aware that a beautiful thing about our blossoming sexuality was that we had the personal choice to "vibrate or not."

I knew that the world of women's repressed sexuality was quickly coming to an end. And I determined that was a good thing. I knew Douglas didn't need convincing that was a good thing too, but he would need to feel like this endeavor was possible, and that the timing was right.

"I realize that a male go-go club would be very time consuming right now, and maybe it's not the best moment for it. But what we *can* do is get *Playgirl Magazine* up and running, and make sure it includes erotica for women, as well as sexual fantasy stories that appeal to women. These erotic stories could be sold as independent magazines or books as we introduce them to our readers," I explained. Then I smiled seductively, making sure to use the one that that always overcame any resistance he might have left.

I took the collar of his suit into my hands. "Douglas. We want to make money. If you put nude men in a centerfold magazine, I guarantee you we will make a lot of money." Then I stood on my toes, pulled him into me, and went in for the most passionate kiss of my life. I could hear the hotel fountain roaring behind me, matching the exploding triumph I felt inside at that moment.

I just needed to seal the deal.

"Let's think about it," I cooed into his ear. "But not tonight." I pulled our hotel key out of my handbag. "We have some unfinished—and maybe some brand new—business to take care of up in our room."

Without pause, Doug grabbed my hand and called out, "Hold that elevator!"

Neither of us could imagine at that moment that my crazy idea would become one of the bestselling magazines in the world, and that we would be part of shaping the women's sexual revolution.

Neither of us knew that our lives were about to change forever.

Doug and Jenny attend a Hollywood event

Playgirl Club dancers on the bandstand

Chapter 10

"Superfly"

1971

Doug: Jenny was sleeping soundly in our hotel bed. More than wide awake, I moved to the living room of our suite. Could Jenny be onto something? She had been very confident in her statements. But would women *really* want to see naked men in a centerfold? Even if they were handsome, appealing and, yes, sexy? More importantly, would they buy the magazine regularly, continuously plopping down money to see the man of the month?

The word "Playgirl" certainly conjured up many visions. One person might see a woman out painting the town red. Another might envision a confident, successful, somewhat serious woman getting her own needs met. Some might see it as a combination of both. But the real question remained: Would a fold out of a naked man appeal to women?

The floor to ceiling windows in our suite offered a striking view of Las Vegas in all its lit up, nighttime glory. It was almost a shame the sun ever rose on this desert city. In the glare of day, it lost much of its magic and allure as the relentless sun obliterated the flashing neon lights that screamed out fun, glamour, big jackpots, and high times.

Now, sitting in the dark looking out at the bejeweled city, there was a growing excitement within me as I indulged thoughts of what might be possible with a magazine called *Playgirl*. The idea definitely created an itch that demanded attention. However, it wasn't any easy one to scratch—at least not yet.

To this point, life for me had never been humdrum or predictable. Living on the edge was what got all my creative juices flowing and made me feel fully alive. So I wasn't about to let the easy life that can come with success take the fire out of my belly and suffocate the drive and originality I had always relied on to be ahead of the curve. And implementing Jenny's idea of exposing women to the "full monty" in a monthly nationwide magazine would not only put us ahead—it would give us ownership of this particular curve.

From the go-go club in the DMZ to the brightly painted cars in L.A. County to the most successful nightclub west of the Mississippi, I had created attractions that were unique and desirable—goods and entertainment that people paid top dollar for. Was Jenny's crazy idea the next creation?

If anything, it sure made me excited in that moment.

Slipping into bed with my adrenaline still running high, I reached out for my wife, giving in to the temptation of waking this incredibly beautiful creature lying next to me. Her immediate and unbelievable responsiveness thrilled me beyond description, as it always did!

The Thinker

Jenny: Doug and I spent the rest of our Vegas trip huddled together, evaluating the pros and cons of a centerfold magazine for women. Like a couple of kids, we whispered in case some kind of magazine spy was lurking in the shadows to steal our plan.

I couldn't think of a time I'd enjoyed Douglas more. Without the distractions of the club, he spun his ideas like the carnies of his youth spun cotton candy. But would they hold up, or quickly melt away as they were put to the test?

We began to create a structure for *Playgirl Magazine*. What would be out slant, our platform? Over the last few years at the club, we watched both men and women, but especially women, free themselves from the social and sexual taboos set in concrete by previous generations. And with this change, they became more fun loving, generous, confident, and open to new experiences.

Our customer base had evolved from men being the majority of people looking at dancing girls (nothing wrong with that), to women being nearly fifty percent of our regular crowd. It seemed women liked that the dancers got the guys interested and aroused, but left the field open for our lady customers to close their night with a "ripe" man...or not. It was their choice. But undoubtedly, women were growing increasingly more comfortable stepping up and showing their stuff both on and off the dance floor. They were clearly beginning to take charge of themselves and their relationships with men. And the men seemed all too happy to let it be so.

During that time, Doug and I didn't yet fully realize what was happening. However, we sensed it was something bigger than just a trend, and we realized whatever "it" was, the Playgirl Club was playing a significant role in moving it forward. And that gave us a wildly useful advantage in dreaming up how to approach our magazine.

Also during this time, music was changing right along with everything else. The era of rock and roll finally gave way to disco and soul-funk hit songs like "Superfly." American soul-funk musician Curtis Mayfield released the theme of the movie of the same name. In the end, this progression was not a true revolution, but more a continuance of the music of the time. The trend was more interesting than it was exciting, and the main benefit was that disc jockeys were a lot more affordable and less trouble than live bands. The downside of this trend was that it didn't bode well for the specific style of our club—even as groundbreaking as it was in other ways.

Doug: The exciting changes in our customers unfortunately didn't translate into *more* customers for the club. Discos were thriving and our business was hurting. Since getting into the nightclub arena, all I had experienced was ongoing growth and rip-roaring success. This was new, and it was troubling. We were worried. And to make matters worse, I was still burning the candle at both ends—spending days working on the magazine concept at our office in Hollywood and running the club at night. It was clear we had to put more time and effort into converting the club to meet the changing times, or we had to move ahead with the magazine at a faster pace. But we couldn't do both.

It was time for one of those life-altering decisions. Jenny and I agreed to take Johnny into our confidence and tell him about our plans for *Playgirl Magazine*. Early on, he had invested good money in the club, and over time had come to trust my business instincts. Seeing right away the potential for success with the magazine, Johnny was willing to work out an agreement: He would take responsibility for the club, Jenny and I would retain fifty percent ownership, and Johnny would receive fifty percent of the magazine revenue. It was a tough decision, and looking back, maybe not the smartest business deal on our part. But the club at that point was still a cash cow, and we needed the money to launch a first-class magazine. Johnny was the only person we knew who could keep the club going in the quality manner it had always been operated. The deal seemed to be the most logical to achieve our goal.

Now able to shift our focus fully to the magazine, we began in earnest the exciting and fun process of creating something new and on the cutting edge of publishing—a business we knew nothing about! Hell, we didn't even know how much we didn't know. But we soon found out.

There were starts, stops, back-tracking, and restarts. But this kind of challenge was just what I fed on, thrived on, and, fact be known, couldn't live without. And most importantly, Jenny was right there on that roller coaster ride with me, making every high more exhilarating and every low more tolerable.

The first all-important step was to decide the image we wanted the magazine to project; the message it would give. At this point in our relationship, after sharing with one another our lives from childhood on, Jenny and I both felt strongly about upholding women. From my male, still somewhat chauvinistic perspective, upholding meant "protecting and defending." However, Jenny had a much broader and more in-depth view. And she explained this, much to my wonder, by asking one question: "Why do women need protecting?"

Then, with a heated passion I rarely saw, she also answered that question with a gushing, emotional barrage: "Because they get so little respect from men. They're not accepted as equal human beings. They have no power. They don't even have control over their own bodies and sexuality. Society doesn't even believe women have a right to feel and look sexy or enjoy sex without being labelled a whore. A man can knock his woman around, rape her, screw every other woman in town, come home drunk every night, and she's *still* expected to be the perfect wife, mother, cook, and toilet cleaner. Businesses don't recognize women as having sense enough to do anything but type and run errands. And when they *are* allowed to do something more responsible, they're not paid for it!" Tears had started running down her cheeks.

I was speechless. But my mind conjured images of my mother so beaten down by the very circumstances Jenny was describing, and my sister who time and again was betrayed by men she loved, and the near obsession I had with protecting the girls at the club who were so vulnerable to being taken advantage of. Also, I remembered all Jenny had told me about the hard and repressed lives of her mother and grandmother. Wiping her tears with my hand and holding her close, I began to get a grip on what Jenny was saying and why it fueled such emotion in her. At that moment, it became crystal clear to me what the message of our magazine needed to be: elevating women to their equal and rightful position in society. Jenny had known that all along; it just took some doing to bring me into the loop.

From that point on, our excitement about a new business venture was not just about us making money, though we sure hoped to do that. We now had a purpose far more important than ourselves, and one dear to both our hearts. This added a whole new dimension to our work and our lives. Sure, we knew that any impact we would have on women's issues might be very little, especially when the focus would be on the novelty of naked men appearing in the magazine. However, we also figured that very novelty would sell the magazine and, thereby, provide the opportunity to get our messages regarding women's issues out to a large number of readers, especially women.

Most people would likely find it hard to understand how putting pictures of naked men in a magazine would help the feminist cause. But experience taught me that getting people's attention had to come before you could sell anything. And what better way of selling the message that women are extraordinary beings who don't have to accept second class citizenship than by demystifying the very "thing" that makes men feel so powerful? And where better to start helping women feel more empowered themselves than by putting them on equal footing sexually? One other lesson experience had taught me: Never underestimate the power and influence of sex, be it in the marital bedroom, the business office, the workings of politics, or the local honky tonk.

Maybe it wouldn't make a difference to the larger movement of women to gain equality, but it became important to us to do something. And this is what we could do.

Two of the first important details to work on were assembling examples of content and identifying potential advertisers. In considering the content, there was an endless array of topics of interest to women, ranging from beauty and fashion to lifestyle and careers to abortion and the pill. These articles were to go on our feature pages spread throughout the magazine. And, of course, we had to consider how to present the male nude and near-nude pictures, including who would be in the pictures, how much to expose, and in what manner. Without question this would be critical not only to the success of sales, but of paramount importance to Jenny and me, to the artistic quality of the magazine, and to how well these pictures fit into the overall "pro-woman" message we wanted to project.

JENNY: After weeks of discussion, brainstorming, and even a few arguments over the direction of our magazine, we agreed that our spectacular difference in a centerfold would be to feature celebrities. *Playboy Magazine* was known for finding unknown girls often from small towns. We felt that men, especially those with a healthy sense of humor, would be more interesting to women when the ladies already watched these "hunks" in movies or on TV. It added a new level to the centerfold idea—famous faces (and other body parts) of singers, actors, and sports figures. I knew that women already felt a kinship with these men. Now we would show women the *rest* of the story. We knew it would be a controversial gamble; the theme of a celebrity centerfold would either be embraced or not—a major hit or a total bomb. But it was just a risk we felt necessary to take.

A few weeks later, Doug showed me a photo mock-up of an idea for the first *Playgirl* cover, that all-important first impression you have to make on a possible customer. I stared at it for what seemed an eternity. "Well, what do you think?" he asked enthusiastically.

I wasn't sure *what* I was supposed to think. "Douglas...you know that's the famous nude statue 'The Thinker,' right? By Rodin?"

"Yeah," he acknowledged, very animated. "What do you think?"

I paused, choosing my words carefully. "Why would you want our first cover to showcase a huge statue of a nude man, looked troubled, and with his balls hanging between his legs?"

He started laughing. "Because that's me! I'm thinking. I'm trying to figure out what the hell I'm doing!" We laughed together now, falling onto the bed. He knew what he was doing all right.

One morning that week, out of nowhere Doug blurted, "Jenny, I'm convinced we have a good shot at making *Playgirl Magazine* a success." Then he frowned. "If we win Hefner's appeal, that is. If we win, we're really going to do this thing."

"No, Douglas," I said, staring him down. "Not 'if' we win. *When* we win."

SEEN BUT NOT HEARD

DOUG: Jenny and I had agreed that our male centerfolds should be celebrities, but it was a bold idea because "stars" are always concerned about their image and the publicity they generate. Yet, famous faces willing to show off in their nakedness would guarantee us sales. We needed to connect with people who did regular business with stars, people who were trusted by their famous clients, people who could convince male celebrities that posing nude for a centerfold in a new magazine for women was a good idea. I knew that once we got the first issue in the hands of the public, most every actor on the planet would want to have a month of glory and fame. But securing that first face (and body) would be a huge hurdle to overcome.

A customer who worked as a Los Angeles talent agent for kids had referred me to a lady who was a writer at *The Hollywood Reporter*, one of the two major trade publications exclusively about the entertainment industry at the time. *The Reporter* covered news about the business of show business. Everyone who was anyone in the entertainment industry read the daily publication first thing every morning.

Hearing that I needed a contact who had solid connections with Hollywood's elite, and preferably someone who could write editorials, my customer, the agent, immediately said, "You need Marveen Jones." He wrote the number on a napkin. "Her specialty is interviewing celebrities for *The Reporter*, and she knows every agent and manager in town."

I made the call the next day and got through to Marveen by dropping the talent agent's name. I told Marveen I was publishing a magazine for women that would feature celebrities. I didn't tell her the rest of the story. Marveen suggested we include an associate of hers at our meeting, a man named Phil Paladino. She explained that Phil was a public relations whiz who represented some of the town's top actors and musicians, and that he was one of the top publicists who had given her access to his A-list for interviews. Marveen then proposed we all meet at the famous Polo Lounge, the "in" place for celebrities to dine.

Jenny and I knew we were about to encounter the movers and shakers who made things happen in Hollywood. Neither of us had been to the Polo before, not because we couldn't afford the pricey cost of a meal there, but because we'd never had a reason to schmooze with the Hollywood elite. Now we did.

We checked in with the maître d' and were escorted to our table. Jenny was dressed in a snug fitting, low cut silk top and slacks that revealed a figure most women would die for, and most men pant for. Her regally confident poise and incredible Indonesian beauty turned every head in the room as she walked through the restaurant.

The Polo Lounge was the place to be seen. If you wanted privacy, you picked a Mexican restaurant in The Valley. But if you wanted to send the message that your meeting was important, the Polo Lounge was the place. And Jenny dripped with importance. She was definitely my greatest asset!

We were escorted to a prime table. The restaurant, nestled inside the famous pink Beverly Hills Hotel, is known for its Irish green, leaf-patterned wallpaper and booths, allowing customers to be seen but not heard. Marveen and Phil were already there and rose to greet us.

My talent agent friend had told Marveen as little about me as possible, so after the typical greetings and conversation about L.A. traffic, I quickly got to the point. My method of operation was to not spend a lot of time on socializing. Jenny followed my lead and, as she often did, assumed the role of intent listener, which along with her exotic looks made her seem mysterious and aloof. She would let me know her own observations and opinions later.

Providing some background about my experience in honky tonks, the Korean go-go club, and building a business from a beer bar to a highly successful Vegas-style nightclub, I sensed their disappointment that Jenny and I were not in their league of superstardom. Then I showed them the mock-up of our magazine with the statue of "The Thinker" and the title "Playgirl" on the cover. They studied it intently.

"But what about Playboy?" Phil asked.

"I legally own the name Playgirl. We won a court battle that Hefner filed, but of course, he's appealed. We're still waiting on the outcome."

Marveen was flipping through our pages filled with mocked-up editorial stories about women's issues, dating, marriage, birth control, the workplace, and fashion. We had also used print advertisements to show the kinds of products we planned to display: cosmetics, fashion, and skin care. She seemed genuinely interested. "If you lose the appeal, then what? Would all this work be for nothing?" she asked. Both of them looked worried.

I took no time to answer. "I've been through controversy and faced many a challenge. I'm very confident we'll retain ownership of the Playgirl name. But the important thing is not what we think; it's what *you* think you can do to make this magazine happen. Let's start with our need to get some Hollywood actors to pose in our centerfold."

I knew from my research that Marveen and Phil were pros. They worked daily with a nice stable of TV and film actors, musicians, show hosts, and singers who toured solo and with bands. They ate dinner with these people, entertained them in their homes, and knew their secrets. But their body language and faces told me they'd never seen anything like our magazine mock-up with a nude, male center foldout for women. They were dumbfounded.

Jenny decided this was the moment to break her silence. "Marveen, we women are liberated now. We're following our needs and desires, and we certainly have the same right to entertainment as men. Don't you agree?" She had them cornered. If they ended the meeting now, they'd appear to be unsophisticated buffoons. So Jenny and I just waited.

"So," Phil stumbled over his words, "their...um...everything...would be on display?"

Jenny answered. "If girls can pose nude, why shouldn't guys? We're all adults after all. And as a female, I am not offended by the nude body of a man. In fact, I happen to find the male body interesting, and I have no doubt plenty of other females feel the same way. If not, why would 'The Thinker' be one of the most celebrated sculptures ever known?"

The silence continued as Marveen and Phil looked uncomfortably back and forth between the mock-up and each other. Phil finally spoke again. "Well, as I think more about it, getting men to pose wouldn't be the problem. Some of them would come running. After all, there are a lot of exhibitionists here in Hollywood. We might be the capitol of exhibitionism." Phil let out a nervous laugh the rest of us didn't echo.

That's when he rose and said he was going to the men's room. Marveen apologized and followed right behind him.

After a few seconds, I stood up. "This isn't a bathroom break. They're having a powwow," I told Jenny. I turned down the hall, and while I couldn't hear them, I could see them having a very animated conversation, which included Phil twirling his pointer finger next to his temple—the classic motion for "this guy's loony."

I slipped back into our booth, and the look on Jenny's face told me she already knew. "They think we're wacky country clucks with a crazy idea," she whispered worriedly.

Marveen and Phil returned to the table, and over the rest of lunch, they instigated some very general talk about the magazine. They were both using terms like "evaluate the timing," "research teams to identify our target market," and "focus groups to test the water." We were being tossed back and forth between them like a beachball. They were patronizing us.

We quickly finished our meals and once the dishes were cleared, I sat back and narrowed my eyes. "Marveen, Phil, I bet I can read your minds. You didn't go to the restroom earlier. In fact, you had a little discussion about these two hayseeds from The Valley and how they're just plain crazy."

Phil and Marveen looked embarrassed and avoided glancing at each other.

"Look," Phil took the lead. "We do both think you have a wild idea here, even revolutionary. Will this be easy to do? Hell no. But most great ideas seem impossible until some 'crazy' person like you makes it happen." He made the loony gesture again but laughed sincerely this time.

Marveen followed up. "In fairness, I did think you were nuts. But the more you present the plan, the more it seems like you could have a real winner here. It's got beauty, sex, glamour, controversy, and it's never been done before."

Phil added, "But a huge issue is that my agency can't be involved in any litigation before the fact. You have to understand that we can only work on projects that have been cleared by lawyers and the courts, especially for something this controversial. There are plenty of hoops to jump through without a legal judgment hanging over our heads."

At least now he was making sense.

Phil attempted to conclude the meeting. "It was very nice to meet you both. If you make more headway, call me."

I fired my last shot. "How about you two take one night to visit our club and see what we're all about? All expenses paid. If nothing else, you'll have a great time. And if you don't think *Playgirl Magazine* is a winner after that, we part company. You'll go your way, and we'll go ours. But before that happens, we invite you to do some of that research you talked about."

Marveen politely declined, which I respected, as club life wasn't everyone's cup of tea. But Phil heartily agreed, so we set a date and shook hands. Phil paid the bill, and before Jenny and I left, I made my final statement. "One day, someone is going to do this. That's a fact. I just want it to be us."

THAT PLAYGIRL MAGIC

A week later, Phil looked like a kid at the circus. Settled in the largest and finest booth in the club, it would have taken a bulldozer to wipe the grin off his face.

The club was in full swing. Waitresses delivered opulent champagne to the table, and hors d'oeuvres prepared to perfection kept Phil's hands busy.

Over the next four hours, he lived out a great fantasy we called "The Playgirl Experience." He was mesmerized by the classy, sexy dancers popping on and off the stage with dramatic lighting to accent their moves. And when the dancers stopped by to say hello, they were welcoming but not aggressive—first class all the way. Johnny asked a few of our regular customers, who were single ladies and knew we were putting on a show, to coax Phil onto the dance floor when the jukebox played. Then Phil and his partners cheered and whooped with the rest of the customers when the band rolled out hit after hit. It was one climactic moment after another, and you could feel the fun and excitement this Hollywood Man was experiencing right there in my paradise.

In the midst of it all, Phil pulled me aside. "I guess I was expecting a dark strip club," he admitted. "But your Playgirl Club is exciting for men and women. It makes sex acceptable...and fun!"

Hallelujah! my mind celebrated.

Hours later, Jenny and I escorted Phil to his limo, and he was practically hugging me—and for sure hugging Jenny. "Man!" Phil roared. "That was just amazing, Doug! Jenny, your dancers are the best I've ever seen, and the band was on fire! Who would have known you could do this out here in the sticks? And I'll bet you're making a shit load of money. Sorry Jenny. But without the overhead in my overpriced neighborhood, you must be doing quite well." Then he actually *winked* at me. I laughed out loud.

Then everyone was laughing, and we all took a collective deep breath to compose ourselves. Phil turned to me. "Doug, thank you for inviting me. It was an eye opener to see firsthand the quality of what you do and your professionalism. Marveen and I could never have imagined what the two of you are capable of. I have no doubt that you would deliver this quality in everything you and Jenny would do. I'm pretty sure my agency would love to do business with you, and if they don't, I'll work with you personally. Let me set up a meeting with our department executives to get you all signed up with us."

Phil was probably waiting for my thank you, but I didn't want to waste an opportunity. "I need a publisher and distributor, Phil. I need the biggest."

He smiled at my business acumen. "I have a friend in the publishing business. I'll connect you two. You have a lot in common."

Phil left me wondering who this person could be as he rolled into his limo, laughing and thanking Jenny for the thermos of hot coffee, warm croissants, and jam for the ride home. The last thing Jenny and I heard was Phil satisfactorily demand, "Driver, work that radio and find us some of that great Playgirl music for the ride home." Jenny and I laughed so hard that we fell into each other's arms.

It's a Deal

True to his word, the next week, Phil introduced me by phone to Fred Klein, Executive Vice President of Printing and Distribution for Fawcett Publications in New York.

I had done my homework and learned that Fawcett Publications had a rich and fascinating history. "Captain Billy" Fawcett was a colorful character who at age sixteen had joined the army and served in the Philippines during the Spanish-American War. He worked for the army publication *Stars and Stripes Magazine* before returning home and eventually founding his powerhouse firm in 1919 in Robbinsdale, Minnesota. They published his bawdy cartoon and joke magazine, choosing the catchy title *Captain Billy's Whiz Bang*. It was both irreverent and hilarious, and ultimately became the launch project of a publishing empire of magazines, comic books, and paperbacks.

Captain Billy was bold and unafraid in his choice of material, such as with pieces that explained the term AWOL (Absent Without Leave) from a military post as "After Women or Liquor." Men and women serving in the military or retired from armed services found that Billy's deeply intentional humor lightened up the seriousness of tough days and unthinkable memories of war. For many, *Whiz Bang*, a one-of-a-kind magazine containing off-color jokes and naughty poetry and puns, represented open mindedness and social advancement. It shook up the status quo, and for most of the 1920s, Captain Billy's was the most popular comic magazine in the U.S.

I related in a number of ways to Captain Billy, the primary one being he had chosen to publish material that in its day was held up as one reason for America's decline of morality. Ol' Captain Billy was an ace at flaunting sexual immodesty. I knew we were also headed for huge controversy with our nude male centerfold, and like Billy, I imagined myself willing and ready to take on the challenge. It seemed to me our nation was ready for another shake up, and I had the recipe. Frankly, I felt the folks at Fawcett would feel right at home with *Playgirl* and me.

Sitting together in his office, Phil put us on speakerphone with Fred Klein, and after introductions, I let Phil lay out the scenario. I didn't know what Phil had meant that night at the club when he said that Fred and I had many things in common, but I held an unexpressed affinity for Fred's company founder. So I imagined good things would come.

I listened intently as Phil happily yet carefully walked Fred through the series of events where I had goaded Hefner into a lawsuit with my TV advertising campaign, which got a big laugh from Fred. Phil established that in addition to having a first-of-a-kind publication concept, I was also skilled in business, particularly in manipulating my enemies. He was upfront about my current situation, stating clearly that while I had won the Playboy suit, Hefner had filed a subsequent appeal that was pending. Fred obviously understood the situation and said he was comfortable that I had and could handle my business and myself.

Phil held Fred's attention for a full ten minutes, and when he wrapped up, he took a big breath and sat back in his chair, pleased with his pitch.

Fred asked his first question. "Phil, are you confident that you can get male celebrities to pose nude?"

"Yes I am."

Fred then began speaking to me. He asked for a bit of background, so I took him through the short version with all the hillbilly charm I could muster. I concluded with a statement about my wife's input. "Jenny is a woman with her pulse on the American woman's temperature. In fact, on the world's temperature. She's lived in several countries, speaks many languages, has an international point of view, and an understanding of why sex sells. She brings the most important mind and experience of all to our magazine: that of a worldly, vibrant, exciting woman who has overcome hardships and found success. She can relate to the difficulties and barriers women experience, and is a model for women who long for equality and sexual freedom." I paused, but Fred didn't jump in. "Granted, this concept is a first, which makes it exciting. And it's edgy for sure. But Jenny, more than anyone, is one hundred percent confident that women, and some men, will find this magazine more than fascinating. It's a winner, Fred."

Fred's next question was to the point. "What do you think your chances are on Hefner's appellate case?"

"I'm going to win," I said without skipping a beat.

Phil and I looked at each other, both knowing there was no more to say. So we waited for Fred. "Well, Doug, since we don't know when that ruling will come down, and the chances of winning any appeal seem to have at least even odds, can you come to New York to develop this project? In the case that you do win?"

"You bet I can. When?"

Fred leaned away from the phone and rustled around on his desk. Phil and I took the opportunity to exchange congratulatory looks. "Be here next Wednesday morning at eight. I gotta run. Looking forward to meeting you, Doug. Thanks, Phil. I'll speak with you soon."

Phil and I shook hands and embraced like two players who had just coordinated a touchdown. Phil had brought in the whale, and I had delivered the bait.

I made one more call. "Jenny, I'll meet you at home. Put some champagne on to chill."

The Red Eye

The airlines were working hard to become better at first class service. They understood and catered to their business customers. Flights known as "red eyes" departed Los Angeles around midnight, and with the three-hour time difference between L.A. and New York, a passenger could sleep for four or five hours and land in New York in time to make an eight o'clock business meeting the next morning. And I indeed managed to snooze during most of my red eye flight.

After shaving and freshening up in the airport men's room, I hailed a taxi and arrived at Fawcett Publications just before our scheduled meeting. I had been in opulent buildings before, but I wasn't prepared for the lavish, almost palatial appearance of this structure. Located on Seventh Avenue in the heart of the publishing world, it climbed nearly one hundred floors and was built to be exciting and intimidating all at the same time. Well, mission accomplished!

An attendant escorted me to the Fawcett floor of the building. A lovely young lady ushered me into an enormous conference room where orange juice, water, hot coffee, tea, and warm Danish pastries were waiting. Just as I had put my jaw back into place and told myself to relax,

Fred and his team entered. The group consisted of the heads of layout, editorial, printing, and world distribution. Did I hear that correctly? World distribution was here...all because of a magazine mock-up with "The Thinker" on the cover. Fred also included his personal secretary and two female assistants from various divisions. Smart man.

We went through introductions and brief social talk as the group served themselves from the buffet. How was the flight? Are you enjoying New York? Oh, the red eye. Very efficient. You're going back tonight? What a shame. You live in California? How wonderful!

Finally, with everyone seated, Fred asked me to show what I had brought to the meeting. I pulled the mock-up from my briefcase and set it on the table to my right. Then I placed an oversized artist's case on the center of the table and turned it toward the team. An artist's case is a costly item; a huge leather zip binder with cellophane pages that allow you to insert whatever pictures you need to support your message. Supermodels use these "books" to show their prized photos, magazine layouts, and covers.

I had hired an artist to create storyboards similar to what they had used to plan my TV commercial. But for the magazine, we had color drawings of the content Jenny and I had decided on. In addition, there was an index page listing the topics in each issue, and then a kind of demo page for each section, to show the regular and ongoing columns we would include each month: fashion, relationships, the workplace, beauty, interior design, and the like. I explained that what was missing, by choice, was any reference to recipes or homemaking. We were confident that stay at home moms would read *Playgirl*, but we wanted them to find a kind of escape or fantasy within our pages, including information that would advance their dream of living beyond the humdrum role of their life as wife and mother.

Before reaching the middle of the magazine, which everyone was anticipating, I wanted these people to know that our readers would enjoy this publication for its editorial substance as well as its eroticism, and that our target market was women who were looking to live life at its finest. But the room went silent as necks stretched for a better look at the artist's rendering of our nude male at the center of everything.

As I turned the page for the big reveal, I carefully watched the faces of the Fawcett employees. I saw looks of surprise but not shock. I saw that the women, more than men, moved in for a closer look. I couldn't have choreographed their reactions for a better outcome.

My two-fold centerfold drawing was of a masculine guy, not overly buff, but in good shape, handsome, and showing a suggestion of his private parts. He looked approachable, and not at all threatening. The rendering was artistic, with no hint of pornography. It definitely grabbed attention without being shocking.

Once the group had seen proof that we would deliver solid, professional content and, as promised, a male centerfold, I moved on to the advertising. With this, I was preaching to the choir, because these people knew the magazine business better than I did. But it was important for them to know that we had carefully planned which advertisers would be a great match for *Playgirl*. "We will appeal to products for women who are confident, smart, curious, and sexy."

Sitting back in my chair, again I carefully watched as a few of the employees flipped through more pages, waiting for their leader to...well, take the lead. At last, Fred spoke. "We would want a ten-year contract for print and distribution rights worldwide."

Managing to conceal the excitement making my heart pound and my head swim, I put my mind on track. "How many magazines would you publish on the first printing?"

Fred didn't hesitate. "Two hundred and fifty thousand. That's as large an amount you'd ever do on a start-up."

"No," escaped my lips before I could stop it. Did I really just say that? I knew I was shaking my head no, but I wasn't certain the word had actually come out of my mouth. "No." This time I knew it was my voice. "We should print one million, and we'll sell out the first week."

"You're crazy," Fred said with no emotion.

There was that word again. Crazy? I hoped so! Because it was the same kind of crazy I'd been all the times before when people threw that word at me. I folded my book, stood up, and was about to head for the door when Fred stopped me. "Doug, let's discuss this." I slowly sat back down, not moving and maybe not even breathing.

Fred thought for a minute and made some notes on the pad in front of him. "Tell you what. We'll do four hundred thousand, which has never, ever been done."

Already packed up, I stood again and headed for the door. "Hold on, hold on. Sit down." I took my seat once again. "I'm making my final offer. We'll print six hundred thousand first printing and increase it to one million *if* we sell out. You'll never get a better deal anywhere, Doug. I promise you. No one ever has." The group nodded and grumbled their affirmation.

I finally believed him. We shook hands as he said, "If you win the appeal, you will have a deal with Fawcett for worldwide printing and distribution. We'll set the deal for six hundred thousand on your next trip here. If you win." He smiled sincerely. "Okay, *when* you win," he added generously.

I checked in for my return flight and called Jenny to share the news. She was elated, but we were both having a reality check. This was huge. And it was seemingly happening. She immediately caught wind of my pause on the other end of the line. "Are you having second thoughts?" she asked.

"No...I just have a million questions running through my head. I know society has changed, and women have freedoms they couldn't have dreamed of ten years ago, but we can't really know if they're ready for naked men in a magazine, can we?"

"Women will love it. This is a once in a lifetime opportunity, and we are the perfect people to make it a hit. I know it." And that was that.

While waiting for a legal decision, Jenny and I knew that we'd be fools not to prepare for a ruling in our favor. We had been told it took a full year to get a start-up monthly magazine ready for market. And it would take months to meet and hire people who were perfect for each job. There was no official contract from Fawcett yet, so we knew the cost of everything and everyone was on us for now. But it was a risk we had to take.

Since we were still largely swinging in the dark, our most immediate task was to research exactly what was involved in every aspect of operating a highly visible magazine. And we began that education in earnest.

CREATING A DREAM TEAM

JENNY: My faith in our future never wavered. That being the case, I convinced Doug to begin looking for a more impressive office space. We'd need a prestigious location to impress stars for the centerfold, advertisers, and the quality professionals we wanted to attract to work on the magazine. There would need to be enough space to house an editor, journalists, photographers, artists, an advertising sales team, as well as handpicked professional office staff that could be trusted to keep our project confidential until it was launched. It was a lot to undertake, so we needed to get moving.

Taking this big step was not only a practical move, but also a huge psychological boost for us both. It declared loudly, clearly, and as often as I could that we were now beyond the drawing board. Turning back would not be an option—even if we didn't get a favorable judgment on the appeal. But now, there was plenty to distract us from that prospect!

First, there were so may choices for office spaces: older, private brick buildings, secluded offices with security, enormous high-rise offices where the elevator opened right into the reception area and windows offered spectacular views of the mountains. On a clear day, in some high-rises, you could even see a slice of the Pacific Ocean. They were all so different, but they were all similarly costly.

We settled on a high-rise office suite in the Century City District of L.A. The upscale area was originally owned and used as a ranch by cowboy actor Tom Mix, and it later became the backlot for 20th Century Fox's movies. In fact, Fox's headquarters were still located down the street. It was the perfect setting for our purpose, sure to impress. When we were up there, Doug simply referred to it as "living high off the hog." I often reminded him to refrain from saying that in front of any visitors we had.

As a publicist, Phil Paladino knew everyone in Hollywood, so he was our choice to approach agents, managers, and stars directly about being a *Playgirl* centerfold. And Marveen Jones came on board as a contributing writer. But the main person to be found was our editor-in-chief, the person who, next to Doug and me, would need to understand the brains and the heart of our publication.

"Our editor has to be a woman," I adamantly told Douglas. "We're creating this magazine specifically for women, so it will take a very special woman to identify and communicate exactly what women need and like, and how they think, feel, and behave. Not to mention," I giggled, "You've still got some male chauvinist pig in you, and a great female editor will 'whup' that right out."

"Hey, if anyone gets to 'whup' me, it's you," Doug responded with a smile. "Our editor-in-chief will just have to find other ways to teach me. But that means I'm onboard. A female editor-in-chief it will be."

Phil set us up for meetings with many of the people who do the hard work that makes a publication happen. We never, ever shared our title with them, but we were clear with everyone that we were going to produce a national, full color, glossy magazine. A judge was still holding our future hostage, so we couldn't take the chance of being unprepared if we won. *When* we won. So we kept plowing ahead, staying busy.

But the waiting was agonizing. That nagging fear in the back of our minds that we might lose did make us hesitate at times, especially when it came to spending the big bucks.

Hot Dog!

Doug: I was in my office signing checks when the phone rang. "Hello?"

"Mr. *Playgirl Magazine*?" I recognized Bob Hitchcock's voice, but I didn't know him to be much of a joker.

"What's up, Bob?"

"You're up, my friend. Hefner lost his appeal. The Playgirl name is all yours."

"Holy crap," I barely muttered. "Wow. Geez." I was standing now, trying to contain myself.

"I'll give you the details when you can speak in full sentences," Bob laughed. "We need to let Fawcett know, and New York has already closed for business today. Come to my office at ten o'clock tomorrow so we can phone Fred with the news. In the meantime, you have yourself a fantastic night." I could practically hear his smile through the phone.

Spinning out of the office parking lot, I risked life, limb, and a ticket to get to Jenny as quickly as possible. I practically dragged her from the club to the car. Bewildered, began questioning me with every step. "What is it? Tell me! What happened?"

I paused before opening the car door for her. "Jenny, we are the proud parents of soon-to-be-born *Playgirl Magazine*!"

"It's ours? We won the appeal? Oh, Douglas, you did it!"

"*We* did it. Now there's nothing but a mountain of work in front of us. But tonight, I'm taking you out for a steak dinner and a bottle of Dom."

As we headed away from the club, Jenny sighed contentedly. "Douglas, let's just go to that little hot dog stand and eat in the car. That way I can keep screaming with joy. Besides," she reminded me, "'HOT DOGS' was your very first business lesson from your dad. Now that lesson is about to make you known all over the world."

I couldn't have agreed with her celebratory dinner decision more.

Jenny modeling for the Playgirl Club

Jenny modeling for a Playgirl Magazine ad

Chapter 11

"I Heard it Through the Grapevine"

1972

Doug: We initially settled into our Century City office with only a small, trusted group, including Phil Paladino and Marveen Jones. But we had plenty of space to grow into as our staff increased. Since it was imperative that we keep our brand a secret for as long as possible, the Playgirl name was not posted on any doors or parking spaces. We even spoke amongst ourselves in hushed voices, as if the walls had ears. Someone commented that the Manhattan Project was less secretive than us. What the hell was the Manhattan Project?

We had only been in the office about a month when my secretary tapped on my office door and entered. She was visibly shaken and white as a ghost, and didn't wait to blurt out, "I just took a phone call. The man spoke slow, and gruffly said that he'd heard it through the grapevine that Helen Gurley Brown is going to scoop our big idea in *Cosmo*. Then he just...hung up."

My mind began racing. Could that be true? Was he being serious about "hearing it through the grapevine"? Because in my mind, that meant word would have had to travel from our team and out into the open. Had someone betrayed us by talking about *Playgirl Magazine* boasting the first nude male centerfold? How else could it be considered a "scoop" by *Cosmopolitan*? Would they run a nude male ahead of our hugely strategized premier issue? And, if true, what would this mean for the success of *Playgirl?*

These thoughts were like plunging at top speed down a steep roller coaster track. I felt sick.

SEX AND THE SINGLE GIRL

JENNY: The caller's reference was, of course, to *Cosmopolitan Magazine*, one of the most successful women's magazines in history. The publication, founded as a family magazine in 1886, had reached a peak in their U.S. distribution of two million copies per month. Then in the mid-1960s, a forty-year-old author named Helen Gurley Brown signed on as their editor-in-chief.

Two years earlier, Gurley Brown had written the bestselling book *Sex and the Single Girl*. The book's premise was essentially a "how to" guide with the purpose of advising women on seeking and enjoying, without guilt, sexual gratification, in or out of marriage, and seeking an independent work life and financial freedom. She presented the concept that women should not be viewed as "answering" to a man. Rather, Helen declared men and women should share a more equal relationship in the bedroom, office, and boardroom. The book was one of the early factors that helped chip away at the glass ceiling for women.

Starting her career as a secretary for talent and music agencies, the highly ambitious Gurley Brown moved up the career and social ladders. She was married to movie producer David Brown (*The Sting, Jaws, Driving Miss Daisy*), and they were one of the biggest power couples of their time. *Sex and the Single Girl* made Gurley Brown, in the minds of many, *the* advocate and expert on women's social and sexual issues.

Helen Gurly Brown was hired and given the task of reversing the flatline of *Cosmo's* sales. With her credentials and in her position, she was an ideal person to introduce male nudity to the public. We had good reason to be worried.

So the first thing we did was round up Phil to tell him about the alarming phone call. He was silent as he took in the impact that if there was, in fact, a scoop, it could well have a dramatic and negative outcome for our magazine and his financial future.

"The caller's use of the phrase 'heard it through the grapevine' should worry us," Doug said as he began nervously pacing around the office. "Someone on the inside is sharing information, and Helen Gurley Brown obviously sees a golden opportunity to get out in front of us. She'll ruin our big premiere and completely take the wind out of our sails. She'll fucking sink our ship, Phil."

My nerves were too rattled to not chime in. "I have to agree with Douglas. *If* this is true, and she knows our plans for a nude male centerfold, then it's most likely that someone on our team is in on it. And whoever that is may continue to share our ideas and plans with *Cosmo* as we go forward." That implication added to the grim possibilities the phone call conjured up. And it didn't help that Phil stayed noticeably quiet throughout much of the call.

No Rumor at All

Doug: Fred Klein at Fawcett took the news of the phone call with a surprising sense of calm. "Doug," he began when I finished my recap, "we've kept your magazine as under wraps as much as is humanly possible. My team is made up of people who have been with us a long time, and I have a hard time thinking any of them would have leaked the news." I waited for the shoe to drop. "Could it be someone on your side? You barely know Phil and Marveen."

Fred and I bantered our suspicions back and forth, and he vowed to find out anything and everything he could about *Cosmo's* upcoming editorial, including a centerfold. True to his word, Fred phoned me the next morning. The rumor was no rumor at all. In fact, the situation was much worse than we could have imagined. Gurley Brown not only had a centerfold already in production, but she had also landed superstar film actor Burt Reynolds, fresh off the success of the mega movie hit *Deliverance*, for her foldout.

Scheduled to hit newsstands in April of 1972, with our first edition not due out until June of 1973, she not only had a huge jump on us, she had a major star as her prize! Every ounce of my oversized competitive spirit was riled up, and my blood would boil whenever I thought about the *Cosmo* team celebrating their scoop and beating us to the punch.

Equally disturbing was that my mind could not resolve this grand coincidence. Developing the magazine concept was a very personal undertaking to us. It was created from mine and Jenny's years of experience at the Playgirl Club, watching our customers evolve as both men and women came around to embrace Helen Reddy's "I Am Woman" message. We had invested our hearts, minds, creativity, finances, time, and a big part of our future in the concept that women would happily and freely welcome the magazine. In so doing, they would normalize the public display of male nudity.

Now you mean to tell me that suddenly, Helen Gurley Brown had the exact same idea? All on her own? I didn't think so. Something was up, and Jenny and I tried hard to find some perspective on the situation.

Marveen, we believed, was a close-mouthed person who kept her nose to the grindstone and focused on turning out pages of good written material. It was a daunting task, since there were so few of us within the inner circle. It seemed unlikely she had let the news slip.

Phil Paladino, on the other hand, was a non-stop socializer, a true people-person who spent his life talking on the phone, in meetings, at parties, lunches, and dinners. His mind was always whirling as he glad-handed and rubbed elbows with one and all, eager to please and give off the image of being a "hail fellow well met." It was all a part of his immense talent. However, Phil's "talent" could also be a weakness, as he chatted people up and shared gossip, rumors, and innuendo. It was certainly possible he had inadvertently shared something about the magazine project.

Hollywood was and still is a news town. People get together daily to discuss the weekend's movie ticket sales, the overnight ratings on a new TV show, and who's sleeping with whom. It was all considered the "light" side of the community news churned out daily. Privacy for superstars was disappearing. The days of Rock Hudson, Elizabeth Taylor, and Cary Grant keeping sexual secrets was fading as a new breed of reporters was hatched: "Stringers." These were freelance "reporters," production crewmembers, agents, and deliverers of dinner meals who were paid to spy on stars.

The magazine business was huge and still growing because in America, we thought of film, television, and music stars as our "royalty." Oh, how we loved to build them up and watch them fall! Yellow page papers, as they were known, brought these picture-perfect idols down to a human level where they suffered through the same ordinary and tragic problems as the rest of us. America's love-hate relationship with stardom was in its early stages, but the train had definitely left the station. Rumors, and rumors *of* rumors, kept the engine going full speed ahead. Considering all of this, it was easy to imagine how our plans had spread like kudzu in the south; just one vine planted in the wrong place and an entire mountainside was soon covered.

Keeping my eye on Phil over the next few weeks, I mulled over what I wanted to say to him, if anything. Wrongly accusing a person of something was not my style, but the issue needed to at least be brought to the table.

Finally, one day, as we were finishing an update meeting, I found my moment. "Phil, I want to be candid with you," I began. He seemed to stiffen a bit. "You and Burt Reynolds were roommates for a while, and you still see him at parties and such."

Phil looked me in the eye, already knowing what was coming. "I have not told Burt about your project, Doug. Not directly anyway."

We both knew that Phil attended a party or get together with the Hollywood crowd at least three or four times a week. His job for our magazine was to scout out famous, young, and handsome men who might be willing to show their "all" in our centerfold. As such, I had always known the dangers of some talk getting around. But I hadn't imagined another magazine getting ahold of enough specific information to actually scoop us.

"It doesn't take a rocket scientist to connect the dots, Phil. You see Burt at parties, and much of your talk is about finding men for our magazine. Plus, Burt seems to be dating Dinah Shore." Dinah was an all-American singer and personality who starred in her own music and variety TV shows in the 1950s and early 60s. Her TV talk show back then was very popular, and top tier stars used her friendly format to promote a new movie, book, TV show, or record release. Although Dinah was about twenty years older than Burt, they were inseparable at that time. "Dinah Shore and Helen Gurley Brown are good friends. It's not so hard to make a connection there."

Without being defensive, Phil calmly added, "Yeah, and Hefner is friends with all of them. There are so many damn ways your idea could have gotten out, Doug."

"True," I relented. I could easily blame Phil for this fiasco, but I knew the scenario; the people involved and their relationships with one another were complicated. These people thrived in a community where the lines between business and social talk were often blurred. Without concrete evidence, I really didn't have any choice but to let Phil off the hook. "We'll have to let this play out, but now more than ever I need you to get high profile guys to pose for us," I told him sternly.

In the end, I had no choice but to force myself to let go of the whole *Cosmo* issue, and deal with the facts at hand as well as the towering tasks before us.

Fred agreed to still move forward with our magazine, which was a relief. And when I was finally able to put the negative news out of my head, I realized I was actually as happy as I'd ever been.

Every letter, every word, every sentence of a magazine must be perfect. Once it's printed, there's no do-over, no going back. I thrived on this level of challenge, and my attitude about the scoop was evolving.

"Let Helen put our idea out there," I told Jenny one night as we were falling into a much-needed sleep. "She'll pave the way for us, and *Playgirl* will embarrass *Cosmo* by being fresh and exciting. We'll make this work to our advantage." We both slept well that night for the first time since the hoopla began.

Burt's "Big" Cover-Up

JENNY: The April 1972 issue of *Cosmopolitan Magazine* was a huge sensation. Doug and I spent some time flipping pages of other magazines at our corner newsstand so we could observe women hot to get their hands on a copy. Many bought two or three copies, likely picking up extras for friends or as keepsakes. Most of them also seemed to be in a jovial mood—nothing like anticipating a nude Burt Reynolds to brighten a girl's day! I didn't hesitate to pay my money for one.

But the photo was surprisingly disappointing. Burt had wisely posed with a big smile on his face, typical of his self-deprecating good sense of humor, which set a positive tone. With a cigar hanging from his mouth, he lay on his side on a bearskin rug, propping up his head with one hand and the other conspicuously covering his genitals. The picture reflected a very warm, friendly, and non-threatening environment. But it certainly left people wondering what he had to hide.

The press went wild though, and the more Burt did (or didn't) comment about his nudity (or lack of), the better the sales; and it soon sold out. Burt handled the relentless media questions quite well. "I have big hands," he'd explain while laughing when asked about his cover-up.

Amidst our group's gloom and doom, we were all aware that the celebrity male nude centerfold had been tested and, as I had known it would be, the idea was an enormous success. Such a success that if *Cosmo* continued to include centerfolds, we'd be out of a business we'd never gotten into.

But I maintained a decidedly strong position on the future of *Playgirl Magazine*. "One thing is for sure. Helen is no one's fool, and if she found our concept worth giving to the center pages of *Cosmo*, then she knows the idea is a huge winner," I told our staff over lunch one day. That was true, but if we were to be competitive, we needed to up our game and not just be a player, but also be on the cutting edge of the new sexual frontier. To do that, we needed to set a standard for how far women would be ready and willing to go to fully embrace their sexuality and the Playgirl Identity.

Many nights, Doug and I would head back to the office to put ideas into action. Taking the existing and proposed editorial and columns page by page, we added in content that would titillate, inform, and excite women. We featured a serious and positive photo layout on toe fetishes, the fun of having a bedroom mirror on the ceiling, facts on both vaginal and clitoral masturbation, and sex toys.

We included columns ranging from how to prevent sexually transmitted diseases to how to defend against the increasing incidence of rape to the rise in women's breast cancer cases. Our fictional section was expanded to include sexual fantasies of women, including titles like "Crisis: Copulation." We scheduled interviews with superstars such as the legendary Richard Harris, and included sex-related humor in cartoons and articles like "What Do You Say to a Nude Skydiver?" And they all had photos, of course. Reviews of provocative films and music and a healthy dish of celebrity gossip were regular offerings as well. It turned out that Helen Gurley Brown had unwittingly presented us with a challenge that only improved every aspect of *Playgirl Magazine*.

Helen's Center *Folds*

Not long after we started revamping our ideas, some incredible news broke that I had to share with Doug right away. I bounded into his office, jumping up and down and shouting. "Douglas! Helen pulled out! It's over! I heard it on the radio on the way here. She's out!"

He looked at me like he wasn't quite sure if he could believe it was true. He took me by the shoulders and attempted to tamp down my rising excitement long enough to grab my attention. Slowly, he asked, "Jenny, are you telling me *Cosmo* isn't doing another centerfold?"

"Yes, yes!" I yelled again as I hugged and kissed him. Okay, enough celebrating—time for the facts. I caught my breath and explained. "Hearst Publishing got very negative feedback from their advertisers. They don't want male nudity, and Gurley Brown has been told no more centerfolds."

The news had reported that Helen had threatened to quit if the centerfold was pulled, and the Hearst spokesperson called her bluff. The publisher had said, in so many words, "If Mrs. Gurley Brown wishes to step down over this issue, we are still prepared to go forward." The Hearst representative was sending a message to advertisers in *Cosmo* and to their other dozen publications: "If necessary, we'll find another editor." The combined millions of advertising dollars could not and would not be ignored. The advertisers had won this battle. Now Doug and I were signing up to win the war.

Doug: With Helen and Hearst in a very public feud, I was weighing the pros and cons of possibly hiring Helen Gurley Brown, should she actually leave her beloved *Cosmo*. I would gain an experienced, very pro-woman, successful editor—albeit one who probably had stolen our idea. But she had implemented it with clever, even humorous style. Of course, I reminded myself, there was always the chance that Hearst and Helen had waged their "battle" just to attract media attention and boost circulation. But I couldn't afford to let my mind go wandering down those kinds of rabbit holes at this point.

I worried that the *Cosmo* backdown would put the concept of a male nude centerfold in a negative light. The issue of women's sexual freedom had been tested, and the response had been phenomenal, but the buzz had quickly died out since there was no follow up centerfold in the magazine for future issues. Likely everyone except Jenny thought *Playgirl Magazine's* chance of success had been, at the least, diminished. Gurley Brown had planted her flagpole in this particular planet of publishing first. Being second was not something I swallowed easily, and the indigestion that followed was... unpleasant.

Seeing past the glitz of *Cosmo's* one-time issue, in my mind, Gurley Brown had insulted the importance of women's sexuality. Burt's jokes about penis size distracted from the real point. Jenny and I saw the nudity in our magazine as just one part of a much larger and more important message. We were meticulously sourcing content that would support and elevate women in an authentic way.

In our first issue, we wanted to make clear to women the contrast between *Playgirl Magazine's* commitment to the woman's cause, and *Cosmo's* one-time lip service with a nude photo. We had so much more to say than *Cosmo* ever did or would. And we wanted to push forward with proving that.

Striptease

While Fawcett Publishing didn't desert us, they too had closely followed the *Cosmo* centerfold release. As a result, Fred and his team were having cold feet about full-frontal nudity in our upcoming centerfolds.

Although I understood his perspective, I knew Fred came into this deal, in part, because of my audacity and plain ol' chutzpah. Now was not the time to back off that image. I needed him to fight our battles in New York.

"Fred, have you reminded your New York guys that the Supreme Court, the highest court in our country, declared that male frontal nudity is legal? I can cite you the ruling that allows distribution of adult nudity through the United States Postal Service, for God's sake. Jenny and I believe the liberated woman, the 'Playgirl,' will be on fire for our magazine, and then your advertisers will become heroes who had the foresight, empathy, and balls to affiliate early with the women's cause, despite all the controversy," I told him candidly on a call.

Fred and his bosses admitted that Burt Reynold's picture was a huge sensation and a big hit. However, they were not budging on the "Do *Not* Go Fully Nude" campaign. Jenny and I had no choice but to find a middle ground.

Always the optimist, Jenny calmed the storm in my head. "Douglas, think of it like this: We'll give ladies a well-planned striptease. Rather than giving them full exposure the first time out, we'll progressively slip in a few more millimeters over the first three editions. It'll tease curiosity, create anticipation, and be a reason to check out the new issue each month."

There she went again. Smart and sensual as ever.

Editor-in-Chief

We had increased our staff to include a marketing team. They were experienced, detailed, and confident we had a huge success on our hands. As they proved they could design and deliver a solid marketing plan, I began to delegate some of the endless challenges on my list so that I could focus on delivering a quality product each month.

The hole in our donut was the position of editor-in-chief; the person who carries forward the mission of the publisher. With the magazine's point of view being the advocacy for and advancement of women in society, Jenny and I had already agreed that we needed a qualified female for this job who had or could quickly get her finger on the pulse of the surge for women's rights and equality.

Phil introduced us to a possible candidate named Marcia Borie. She was the producer and writer of Hollywood's Golden Apple Awards, an event that ran from 1941 to 2001. The Golden Apple Awards recognized actors and actresses for their positive, cooperative behavior with the press. Sometimes they presented The Sour Apple Award for being uncooperative and difficult. Bob Hope and Mae West won Golden Apples while Elvis and Frank Sinatra were awarded Sour Apples for their reluctance to work with the press.

Jenny and I were invited to attend the glamorous, red carpet Golden Apple Awards that year. Rock Hudson sat at the table next to us, and like every other woman in the room, Jenny could hardly take her eyes off him. We were both thinking the same thing: Centerfold? Dare we ask?

We also had an excellent view of Marcia in action as she worked the room and everyone in it. "She's impressive," Jenny whispered to me. "She makes business look like fun. Let's meet with her."

Ultimately, however, Marcia was hired as our features writer. We were considering her for editor-in-chief, but felt the position should first be earned. In addition to Marcia, we brought in Toni Holt, another talented editorial writer, to coordinate every detail of our centerfolds.

But Marcia began her campaign for the job of editor-in-chief from day one. While I appreciated her passion and ambition, focusing on the total job at hand was my priority, rather than one person's career path. At some point, one of our photographers took me aside to tell me about another candidate for the job. Jenny and I researched this particular candidate's background and discovered she had an impressive resume of writing, editing, and meeting deadlines for television production. In addition, she was both respected and well-liked by her clients and peers. After several interviews, we strongly felt we had found our editor-in-chief.

When Marcia got word of our interest in someone else, she called a meeting with us…and her attorney. I included my lawyer at the meeting, and in short time we learned that Marcia felt the editor's job had been "promised" to her. Although untrue, I was sympathetic to her claim. She had worked diligently in the position she had, after all. However, I learned early in life that sentimentality must move down the list when making decisions about what's best for business. That may have seemed cold hearted to many, but the businesses I was in couldn't be run by the heart alone. So I kept my mouth shut and let our lawyer present our position.

"Ms. Borie, Mr. Lambert certainly appreciates your contribution as a writer, but there's a contract specific to the editor-in-chief's job description. Has he ever presented you with this contract?" There was no response. "Do you have a signed copy of this contract?"

Marcia's lawyer stumbled around trying to explain why Marcia felt she was entitled to the position. Finally, my attorney stood, signaling for me to do the same. "Doug, there's no valid claim here." He turned to Marcia and her lawyer. "If you two have a legitimate lawsuit, then file it, and we'll see you in court. Have a nice day."

And that was that. Marcia continued with story research and writing for a short time, but ultimately left *Playgirl* for "other interests and pursuits," as stated in her resignation letter. We sincerely wished her well and thanked her profusely, for Marcia had made an important contribution to the start-up of the magazine. Even though our relationship ended, we were eternally grateful for it.

IN THE NUDE

JENNY: Our photo test sessions were the best investment we could have made on behalf of *Playgirl Magazine*. Taking pictures of beautiful naked women is fairly easy. You highlight their soft curves and the gentle flow of the ups and downs of their shape, and the sensuality of their expressions. But when men are the sexual focus, it's a totally different challenge.

As we cast and photographed numerous models, we had no idea if our subjects were straight, gay, or both. And we didn't ask, because it didn't matter. Every model was handsome, sexy, and confident. Some were even cocky…until they removed their clothing and began to pose. Without exception, when even the most professional model removed his pants, he became self-conscious, nervous, awkward, uncomfortable, and stiff (but unfortunately, not always where it counted). We thought of anything and everything that would make a photoshoot relaxing, fun, and, at the least, comfortable for our male models. If I was present at the shoot and felt the fellow was really tense, I'd do my cutup routine: make comical faces, cross my eyes, or spin funny comments. Sometimes I would just engage him in friendly chitchat about himself. While we were learning from each of these sessions, we also intended to use these pictures to provide our readers with some adventure and escape.

Soon, a regular column from a personal astrologer and a quiz we called "Are You a Potential Playgirl?" were added. Our male models for our astrology layout were a mix of Caucasian, African American,

Hispanic, and Asian men. To us, they were a natural mix of society, but multicultural layouts were virtually unheard of in the mid-1970s.

Since we had to cover their "peenies" (as we were now calling multiple penises) in every photo, our daily challenge was to find clever and appealing ways to do so. Towels, guitars, hats, roses, hands, pillows, teddy bears...we were exhausted from the mind game of finding new items for our models to straddle or be covered by, while still remaining "manly."

A position we overlooked in the beginning was that of a fashion editor. But our choice to fill that position would turn out to be a grand one. Known only as "Mr. Blackwell," this fashion maven was a peculiar, elfish, yet very dynamic gentleman. His flamboyant personality was both intimidating and endearing. He didn't care what anyone thought, and he spoke with candor and great passion about his beloved field of fashion. Mr. Blackwell brought pizazz, style, and energy to the glamour component of the magazine, which, when coupled with the sensual male poses, further titillated the imagination of our women readers. He was a woman's man in the best of ways.

Doug: If you had told me as a youngster, or when I was in the army, or even when I was hiring dancers for my club, that I would one day be calculating the size of another man's penis to show the world, I would have either stayed in the hills or run back to them. But here I was, a straight, very happily married man, directing nude male photo sessions. At first, I felt I was definitely taking one for the team. But I soon came to understand why some women said, "If you've seen one, you've seen them all."

Jenny was balancing her days between the Playgirl Club, her first love, and *Playgirl Magazine*, her brainchild. I was working almost wholly on the magazine. Under my direction and oversight, the staff had become a well-tuned operation efficiently setting and meeting deadlines. Although we all were working long hours, everyone seemed to have the feeling we were doing something new, different, and important. With that, despite the many differences in our personalities and backgrounds, there was a sense of camaraderie. We all loved and believed in what we did.

MR. COOL

Jenny and I were making final decisions necessary to sign off for printing. On the "boards," we had completed three fully written and photographed issues. Months ago, we had chosen television star Lyle Waggoner as a choice for a centerfold, and now we all agreed he should be our premiere Hollywood celebrity nude male centerfold.

Also inside our first issue were prestigious brands advertising their products: fashion, make-up, cigarettes, liquor, deodorant, vacation cruises, and music albums. Every sponsor was rolling the dice in the hope that women everywhere would embrace *Playgirl Magazine*.

Marcia Borie had put our message into words with the anthem "What is a Playgirl?" The three pages of content laid out our attitude and philosophy. Quoting Jenny, Marcia wrote our love letter to women: "Our foremost aim is to make your life a rewarding one…to love one other person…or many people, and to be loved in return."

JENNY: Exciting things were happening. Our editorial calendar was filled with everything from celebrity interviews to articles that dealt with interracial relationships and unmarried women choosing to have and raise children. I was delighted when Academy Award-winning actress Cloris Leachman, considered to be smart, educated, and funny, came onto the *Playgirl* team. She was a hoot! With her sassy personality, humor, and progressive opinions about a woman's role in society, she joined the magazine in supporting the revealing theories of sex laid down by the expert Alfred Kinsey in the mid-1950s.

In his *Kinsey Reports*, Alfred Kinsey ripped off society's hypocritical façade that masked what was really happening in the minds and bedrooms of women regarding both their fantasy and real sexual lives: unmarried sex and pregnancy, adultery, self-stimulation, sexual fantasizing, and homosexual and bisexual tendencies. His published works brought a certain amount of comfort to women who began to realize that, despite overt disapproval and even laws against certain sexual practices, some of these feelings and behaviors were, in fact, not uncommon among women.

Kinsey was neither approving nor disapproving of what he found, but his revelations simply brought into the light the truth regarding women's sexuality. He helped pave the way for a magazine like *Playgirl*, whose mission, in part, was also to make acceptable the fact that women have as varied and full a sexual life (be it fantasy, real, or a combination) as men.

But at *Playgirl*, we saw our mission as bigger and broader. We wanted to address and celebrate the "whole" woman—yes, certainly our sexuality, but also our minds, hearts, souls, and potential to exert power and influence, thereby changing the world for the better. Sometimes, with us all caught up in the issue of women's sexual freedom and the novelty of the "centerfold," it was easy to put women's other concerns on the back burner. But I remained adamant about the point of addressing *all* aspects of a woman's life, especially our potential to have a huge and positive impact on the world.

One time, disagreeing with Doug about a particular point in an article to appear in the magazine, I began shouting at him out of exasperation and frustration. "With few exceptions in history, women have been a vastly untapped resource on this *man's* earth. And though you guys don't want to admit it, the world would be a whole lot better place if that wasn't true, and women actually had more power and control!"

Startled, Doug threw his hands up defensively and tried to backtrack his argument. "What guys? Not me! I've seen the light. I'm a believer! I've walked the aisle and been converted, thanks to my brilliant wife who proves her point every day."

Well, that was pouring it on a little thick considering he was still evolving, but Douglas knew it never hurt to be on the good side of the woman he adored and lusted after. Still, as he started pulling me close to him, I saw right through it. Shoving him away, I chortled, "Yeah, you've come a long way, baby—but you ain't there yet!"

We had spent a full year living inside *Playgirl's* head and heart. During that time, we changed our views about many important issues. We knew that most men (with Fred at the top of the list) couldn't understand that we were opening windows and doors that would enable women to see themselves in a more clear, fresh, balanced, and liberated way. Our serious article topics included "Compulsions of a Promiscuous Woman," where *Playgirl* writer Jane Willkie observed "It's a smart man who admits he knows nothing about women." Our male staff members had given that statement a thumbs up. And we were also proud of the piece entitled "Do Wives Have Choices, Too?" We had added in fiction, an advice column from a respected psychologist and, at the last minute, several recipes.

As planned, our first celebrity centerfold was Lyle Waggoner. An all-American guy from Kansas, Waggoner had proven himself to be a successful comedic actor. He was a regular on *The Carol Burnett Show*, which was critically acclaimed and enormously popular. Like Burt Reynolds, Lyle had a self-deprecating sense of humor, not taking himself or his extraordinarily good looks seriously. This was a plus. In addition, he was charming, genuinely modest, very likable, and always a gentleman. He agreed, in part, to be our first centerfold because he was not expected to go full monty. His wife, Sharon, accompanied him to the photo session and her lovely presence and great sense of humor resulted in a very enjoyable and successful session.

DOUG: After the Waggoner shoot, Jenny and I were the last to leave the studio, making certain that no Polaroid test pictures had been left behind. Tired, we leisurely walked hand in hand to our convertible. I knew we were having similar thoughts: Between legal battles (and costs), fights with would-be-rivals like Hefner, the drama of the attempted *Cosmopolitan* scoop, waiting for judges' decisions, and the uncertainty of limiting the nude exposure in our first three issues, Jenny and I had been on quite an exciting but exhausting roller coaster ride.

It was a beautiful California evening with the city lights sparkling and the palms swaying in the warm breeze. I put the top down on the ride home, and Jenny dialed in a soft tune on the radio before laying her head on my shoulder. I took her hand and gently placed it on my leg.

"Douglas," she murmured. "Don't you think I've seen enough for one day?"

I could only laugh at this incredible woman. At that moment, it didn't seem possible I could ever love Jenny more. But I was wrong.

The Playgirl Magazine red carpet event. Left to right: Ryan MacDonald, Jenny, Lyle Waggoner

Doug and Jenny with George Maharis at the Playgirl Magazine red carpet event

Chapter 12

"ALSO SPRACH ZARATHUSTRA"

1973

DOUG: Everyone's nerves were at the final breaking point as our premiere edition was scheduled to hit newsstands around the world in late May 1973. Setting an all-time record for a first issue of a magazine release, six hundred thousand copies of our June issue of *Playgirl Magazine*, starring our first celebrity male nude centerfold, were on their way to our customers. The world would now be our judge.

In the magazine business, three issues must be completed, finalized, and ready for print before the first issue can be shipped to stores. That meant Jenny and I led our team in continuing to work like hell on the upcoming content as we awaited results from our first issue. What was coming? Sales? Returns? Hate mail? Love letters? More lawsuits? Regardless, at last we were ready to let real women decide the destiny of *Playgirl*.

THE RED CARPET

JENNY: Our prerelease press party exemplified the term "red carpet." Phil Paladino pulled out every public relations trick in his toolbox and more. After all, when was the last time a completely fresh and provocative concept had been served up on a platter to hungry consumers? We couldn't risk missing any and every opportunity to get word out to the press and consumers.

Phil and our editor-in-chief had meticulously coordinated the press event: the A-name guest list, the classy invitations, flashy atmosphere, and free-flowing champagne. Stars, heavy security, and not just one, but three of our soon-to-be famous centerfolds would be in attendance. In the spotlight was Lyle Waggoner. With his beautiful wife on his arm, he arrived fashionably dressed and beaming from ear to ear. Awed by his fantastically good looks and absolutely charming personality, I whispered to Doug, "I'll take him any day, with or without clothes."

Not to be outdone, Doug replied, "Yeah, well, what does he have that I don't?"

I looked at him from head to toe and smiled. "Not a thing, dear. Not a thing."

Doug: Ryan MacDonald, a very well-known star from the daytime series *Days of Our Lives*, also attended because he was featured in a layout in our first issue. And George Maharis, the dreamy star of the legendary TV series *Route 66*, was there because he was scheduled for our second issue. Our third centerfold was renowned actor Gary Conway, who had starred on the critically acclaimed sci-fi series *Land of the Giants* and in numerous popular western shows.

Even before our exclusive press event, news outlets, talk shows, and lifestyle reporters were beating down our door for interviews, hoping for some kind of scoop that would give them a presence in the media frenzy. At this moment in time, we couldn't yet measure how our magazine customers would react. Would they be shocked and send our centerfold to the trash? Would they share the foldout with friends? Would they show it to the men in their lives? Everything Jenny and I had worked for, fought for, and believed in was now out of our control.

JENNY: While we waited for customer reaction, we were already becoming an overnight sensation with the press. Doug and I thought long and hard about our place in the publicity frenzy. We were both very private people. Neither of us wanted any part of the media mania. We were determined to remain behind the scenes, cherishing this time to watch the results and reactions. As our team reported growing demands from the press for information, photos (of course), and an education about *Playgirl*, we had the perfect face for our brand.

Our editor-in-chief happened to be a stunning brunette who stood well over six feet tall in her glamorous pumps and designer fashions. She had perfected the art of being a Playgirl: self-confident, highly intelligent, insightful about the world around her, a quick sense of humor, contemporary and openminded in her views, articulate, aware of and comfortable with her own sexuality, and able to successfully balance her family life with her career. She was the perfect choice for the limelight, and would ultimately make countless appearances on the most-watched TV talk shows, give hundreds of interviews in magazines and newspapers, and do plenty of guesting on radio shows around the country.

By this point, we had worked for two years to develop *Playgirl*, and we'd invested countless hours in bringing our creative team along to understand and develop our vision for this first-of-its-kind publication. Doug and I had spent many meetings thoroughly educating our executive staff so that everyone was communicating a consistent message: Comfortable in her own skin, a Playgirl can be of any age, shape, or size. She is smart, self-assured, and independent; she loves and respects herself and takes care of her own needs; she radiates passion and is loving, caring, and giving; she freely and unabashedly enjoys sex and all things sensual; while meeting her responsibilities to family and work, she happily seeks out and enjoys a fun lifestyle; she feels personally empowered and is her own best advocate.

But Doug made another excellent point to our team. "Until we turn these words into actions, they remain just that: Words. Every article you experts write, every fashion layout, every tidbit of advice we offer must pass the Playgirl test. Becoming a Playgirl means that you have mentally, emotionally, and physically acknowledged that you are an individual; that you are an authentic version of yourself, and you are free to be outspoken about your ideas, opinions, thoughts, feelings, and core needs. It requires that you open your heart and mind and take advantage of all of the magnificent possibilities life has to offer." Truer words had never been spoken.

Together, Douglas and I had diligently worked behind the scenes to oversee every detail of the magazine's creation. I had kept a finger on columns like "What is a Playgirl?," "Pamper Yourself with Homemade Beauty Formulas," "The Fall and Rise of Virginity," and "Echoes and Vibrations" (which was about music, in case you were thinking of something else). Our publication was about much more than a nude male celebrity centerfold; it was to be entertainment, education, and information for women on all levels.

But naked men were surely our attention getters.

Doug: We continued to do battle with New York over how much nudity we could show—or rather, *not* show. Lyle Waggoner's centerfold was a four-fold layout with his legs strategically crossed to cover the fun. The feature included editorial about Lyle and his life and additional photos of our hunk in his underwear and in slacks standing next to his sports car. His vanity license plate read "Mr. Cool," but the only thing "dangling" in the first issue was the small cigar he held loosely between his lips.

As we finalized upcoming issues, we photographed our centerfolds so that a "suggestion" of the male organ was in play. This slow reveal began with issues two (George Maharis in July) and three (Gary Conway in August). Issue four featured the popular rock and roll singer Fabian, one of those personalities so popular he only needed a first name.

In hindsight, it was wise to reveal the penis slowly; we gave women the opportunity to become comfortable with male nudity in our photos as we offered up healthy doses of editorial that opened their minds to the Playgirl attitudes and lifestyle choices. Jenny and I believed that women would find their way to personal choices about being a Playgirl. Some would aspire to the same self-discovery and sexual freedom that men enjoyed. Some would experiment with specific sexual freedoms, and many would simply introduce our suggestions to their partners, behind the closed bedroom door. And all of those options were just fine with us.

Our New Frontier

JENNY: The more we talked about and began to think in terms of women having wants and needs, the more we believed our readers would follow their natural curiosity.

I also believed that our readers would welcome an element of fantasy in each magazine. I often made this point to our staff: "Most women may not choose or want a complete lifestyle change in their bedrooms, but they will indulge themselves in a bit of sexual fantasy to enhance their sexual experience." At one staff meeting, I read a few paragraphs from one of the proposed articles describing some of those fantasies. There were knowing and eager nods from most of the women, and the men instantly perked up. I could tell they thought this was too good to be true. I was sure I even saw several drooling.

Both the men and women were finally becoming "enlightened," but I often thought how sad it was that women around the world for so many years had repressed their feelings about sex. They often felt guilty enough about their sexual fantasies and yearnings that when they became too strong, they could only escape into their conscious mind, lest they be called a harlot. What would it be like to spend a lifetime believing yourself to be unclean, ungodly, even perverted because you desired and enjoyed uninhibited sex? This was why we dipped our toe, then our foot, and eventually our whole leg into the swirling, hot, erotic waters of women's awakening sexuality.

One of the popular monthly features was our Q&A section that invited women (and men) to ask questions about virtually any topic. We carefully screened what would ultimately end up in this section though, since some of the questions went into territory that was verboten based on the standards we had set for the erotica that would appear in the magazine. We made plans to develop this "Playgirl Advisor" into a separate booklet with stories of passion and pleasure, photographs to depict where a thumb or mouth might go for maximum satisfaction, and storylines that not only aroused, but also educated those who really had no place else to go for this kind of information. I was proud of the sexually enlightened world we were opening up for women and the courage we had to do it, because we knew it would be perceived as scurrilous and repugnant by many.

Sometimes I would read some of this material to Douglas for his help with making approval or censorship decisions and would be rewarded with an extra dose of passion and fun, if you catch my drift. Turns out our readers weren't the only ones being "enlightened"!

THE KING OF ROCK AND ROLL

DOUG: While the press party had been a huge success, we were told not to expect any measurement of accounting sales and results until around the time issue three hit the stands. Our next two issues were completed, and our team was working hard on issues four, five, and six. I decided this would be the ideal time to take my deserving and gorgeous wife on a short vacation.

Jenny and I checked into the Las Vegas Hilton Resort. We had become regulars there, as we still sought out bands for the Playgirl Club. A shop owner greeted Jenny, and they stepped inside to discuss what was new in fashion. When I asked our man Roy at VIP check-in about tickets to Elvis Presley's show, he was genuinely regretful. "I'm so sorry, Mr. Lambert. The show sold out almost immediately. My own mother is furious that I can't get her a seat." I had to laugh, as I should have known this would happen for "The King of Rock and Roll."

But I decided not to say a word to Jenny about it. We relaxed in our suite for a bit, then dressed for Elvis' show. We approached the maître d', and I was more than ready for him. "Evening, Mario."

He smiled "Good to see you, Mr. Lambert. You look lovely as always, Mrs. Lambert."

I pulled Mario aside. "I neglected to call ahead for my tickets," I whispered as I laid a healthy stack of bills in his palm. I knew that any great club manager worth their salt always had a few extra seats for those willing to pay well for them. And I knew Mario to be a great club manager.

"Yes, of course, Mr. Lambert. Right this way." Jenny followed him, gliding past the crowded tables to our front row seats. We ordered champagne and could feel the excitement building in the cavernous show room, which quickly filled to capacity. Just after we received our drinks, the lights dimmed, and Elvis' dramatic opening theme music boomed through the intricately balanced audio system designed exclusively for him. The song, "Also sprach Zarathustra," was actually something called a "tone poem," and was composed in 1896 by Richard Strauss. Once you hear the tune, you'll never forget it. The sounds are as appropriate for the blastoff of a spaceship as they are for the dramatic entrance for the world's one and only King of Rock and Roll.

And there he was, in shimmering white, his thick black hair tousled just so, the diamond studded cape flowing off his broad shoulders. That dimpled smile melted the hearts of the thousands of fans screaming for him, and he hadn't even plucked a guitar string or sung a note yet. He had a distinct way of making what could only be called a sexual connection with every woman in that huge, sold-out room. The sheer magic of his presence flowed like a warm fog. Elvis was, indeed, in the building. And there had never been, nor would there ever be, any entertainer in history who manifested sensuality and aroused it in women more than Elvis Presley.

Like everyone else, Jenny had her eyes glued to Elvis. He was truly an original, a consummate performer who had an obvious camaraderie with his orchestra members. He and the musicians exchanged knowing glances and smiles, probably when a difficult note had been played perfectly. I could hardly take my eyes off this magnetic performer either.

Pulling the audience in as he shook, rattled, and rolled, Elvis eventually slowed his pace to a powerful ballad. He worked the huge stage with confidence, yet there was country boy humility in him as sections of women screamed with enraptured emotion. As he made his way to our area of the room, he paused to look directly at Jenny and serenaded a few notes to her. Jenny somehow managed to appear that this happened to her every day, calmly looking straight at The King with an ever-so-ladylike smile on her face. When he finished the song, he winked at her and gave a little (very little) nod of his head to me. Jenny and I were both reserved people, unwilling to purposely call attention to ourselves, but I'll admit it was quite a feeling to have even a brief connection with this masterful music man. Part of the enormous price of the ticket included the "foreplay" he provided us all. I wondered if Jenny was thinking what I was: I couldn't wait to get to our room.

After several standing ovations and the final curtain call, the house lights came up and we turned to leave. Nearly a dozen women surrounded Jenny, wanting to know if she knew Elvis. No, she didn't. Was she thrilled? Yes, she was. How dreamy were his eyes? Very dreamy. I stood and watched, realizing that for those who didn't know Jenny, she appeared to be a lady of luxury. Who could know that she was my equal partner in the daily running of two businesses?

In addition to her considerable input regarding the magazine, Jenny was responsible for every detail of our Playgirl Club's dance entertainment. She hired, trained, and managed the schedules and personalities of our dancing women, and often resolved any issues that arose. Our customers loved escaping into the club environment Jenny created; their lives seemed better when they danced and drank and laughed with friends. Jenny was the one to personally comfort our wonderful team of dancers who sometimes heard as many crude remarks from their own boyfriends as they did from a drunken customer. At least Jenny could give a nod to our bouncer and have the rude customer ejected from the club. Not much she could do about the boyfriends except advise the girls to give them the boot.

In both of our businesses, there were highs and lows: gossip, tardiness, sick children, grumpy husbands and wives, or boyfriends and girlfriends. Jenny always knew how to help someone without assuming the burden of another person's problems. She was brilliant but low-key in her work, and she always, *always*, kept us paddling on top of the water, even when the current was trying its best to pull us under.

As Jenny was including the other women in her Elvis moment, I did something rare for me. I lowered my chin just a bit and silently thanked God for this woman. Jenny. My wife. My very life. The woman who'd had an idea that could help possibly change the world's view of women and sexuality. I was so very proud of her, her generous heart, her wisdom, her kindness, and even her ability to kick my ass if needed—and it often was.

Playgirls Speak Up

Jenny: The phone was ringing as we opened the *Playgirl Magazine* office door the Monday after our quick Vegas vacation. We had been closed for business the Friday before due to a national holiday, so it wasn't necessarily surprising to hear the phone going off and see that the mail had piled up behind the door. Though on a second look, we realized the mail had more than piled up—there was a huge mound of correspondence, and we had to gently ease the door open so as not to crush any of the letters. Employees were starting to arrive then too, and they pitched in to help me collect it all. I thought we must have received someone else's mail delivery; this was not normal, even after a holiday.

We collected all the mail and dumped it on the conference room table. I glanced at a few of the envelopes, and sure enough, they were all addressed to *Playgirl Magazine*. Douglas headed for his office to get started with his day, and I picked up one of the still-ringing lines. "Hello?"

"Is this *Playgirl Magazine*?" a breathy female voice asked.

"Yes it is...may I ask who's calling?" I questioned cautiously.

"Your biggest fan! The magazine is incredible! When's the next one coming out?"

My expression shifted from one of concern to one of wide-eyed excitement. I thanked the woman on the phone profusely for taking the time to call in, and before I had so much as hung up the phone, another line lit up. It was more of the same. And when I switched over from answering calls to listening to the voicemails that had been left for us over the weekend, it was still more praise. My cheeks were starting to hurt for how unrelenting the pure joy I felt was, and my hands could barely keep up as I transcribed message after message. After fifteen minutes, I had to wrench myself away from the phone. The news was too spectacular not to share. I grabbed the message pad I'd been scribbling on and found Doug in his office.

I tried my best to conceal my excitement, but he eyed me suspiciously. "What is it, Jenny? What's going on?" he demanded. I could tell he really wasn't in the mood to be playful. But I just couldn't help it.

"Oh, nothing really. I just have a few pages of messages for you," I teased him, slapping the notebook down on his desk. He stared from the book and back up to me several times.

"Since the end of the day Thursday, we've received one hundred and fifty calls from *Playgirl Magazine* readers. Our voicemail only holds one hundred fifty messages though, so there are probably more." I rifled through a few of the notes. "There were one or two negative comments,"

I admitted. "But overall, I'm happy to report that the women of America *love us*! *Playgirl* is a hit, Douglas!" I was beaming from ear to ear now.

He leaped up from his desk and gave me a monstrous hug. As we sat together going through the names, phone numbers, and comments, my wheels started turning. "Let's put three people on phones," I said. "A personal response is so much better than an answering machine." Douglas agreed. Customer service should always be a priority in any business. I also knew it would be productive to have our staff interacting with our readers. They deserved to be part of this heartwarming payoff after all the incredible work they'd done.

"Plus," I added, "we can ask callers questions. If they simply say they like the magazine, let's find out what they don't like too. What are their comments about the missing penis? Did they show the magazine to anyone? To their girlfriends? To a man? What else would they like to see from us?"

Doug nodded. "And at the very least, let's learn the city they're in and where they bought *Playgirl*," he added. "We can perfect our script by the end of the day, but for now let's be sure to cover the basics. Especially where they live and where they bought their copies.

He was already expertly thinking about the demographics of our readers, while my thoughts had now drifted to that heap of mail still in the conference room. I hoped all those letters we'd received contained the same positive enthusiasm as the calls. "Do you know what this means?" I asked him. "We're hearing from real, live Playgirls!" It was an incredible notion to wrap our heads around. And this was only the beginning.

After a long, positively emotional day, it was after midnight when Douglas, our editor-in-chief, and I thanked our great team, said goodnight, and moved into the conference room. Our editor had a shot of scotch, I went with a cup of tea, and Douglas stuck with water.

"We officially have an audience captivated by what we've offered them!" I said excitedly for what must have been the hundredth time that day. "But we can't be complacent. There's always room for improvement."

Our editor agreed and added, "The bottom line is that women want *more*, and they're ready and open to being both informed and turned on by what they see and read in the magazine. And they're making clear through their feedback exactly what they do want to see and read about. And it seems limitless. At long last, women are being given the go ahead signal to explore their sexual desires and ride out their fantasies, wherever they lead."

"As one reader simply put it: 'Hallelujah, it's about time!'" I added. My sentiments exactly.

I locked our notes from our late-night meeting in the office safe, and we said goodnight to our happy editor. It was an incredible moment in our lives, and I was overwhelmed with all sorts of feelings. Douglas hugged me close and said, "We have a success beyond our wildest dreams, Jenny. And the credit is yours."

Returning the hug and sighing deeply, I replied, "And yours. Thanks to us, our Playgirls not only have a voice, but also a place to go to make that voice heard. I love you, my male chauvinist, for many reasons. And right now, that reason is a big one."

"*Ex*-chauvinist," he corrected, laughing. I was so proud to be able to agree with him on that.

Doug: And I was proud to be able to say that and mean it. I was so very grateful to Jenny for bringing me to this point in my character development.

Running through my mind now were images of my sister, mother, and all the other women I knew about who had endured so much and fought so hard for a little bit of freedom, self-respect, equality, and fun. I knew without a doubt Nell would be among those saying, "Damnation, Doug. What took you so long?"

Jenny and Doug enjoying a night out in Las Vegas

Jenny and Tom Jones backstage at Caesar's Palace

Chapter 13

"She's a Lady"

1973

Doug: The women of America had come knocking on our door. Actually, it felt like they wanted to kick the door down and come inside. Through mail and telephone calls, we continued to tally their invaluable comments, observations, and opinions.

It soon felt necessary to lecture our team. "It's one thing to get a person's attention. Holding *on* to their attention is the challenge. We have to be better each month."

Meanwhile, in New York, Fawcett was telling us (selling us on) the realities of measuring sales results. The bottom line in the overly complicated business of magazine publishing is that each month, when a new issue of a "current" magazine arrives at newsstands, airports, drugstores, and grocery stores, the cover of the previous (old) copy is ripped off and kept for accounting purposes. The rest of the magazine, all those pages of advice and wisdom and knowledge and entertainment, are discarded, just thrown into the trash to never be seen again.

The covers that are kept are then stacked with all the other covers of magazines that didn't sell, and they're shipped to warehouses in various places around the world for "safekeeping." These discarded covers become "proof" that the magazines *did not sell*. The *returns* are then counted against the total number of magazines that were shipped. Sales are based on returns. I mention this because it's important information to remember later on.

JENNY: Doug and I had our own measuring stick; we both knew, but couldn't yet prove, that new magazines rarely, if ever, create a response anywhere close to what *Playgirl* was receiving. We began to organize feedback from the letters and calls into an informal but useful marketing study, taking information and unsolicited comments (since the readers were contacting us), and organizing the results into facts, trends, and projections.

It all sounded rather fancy-schmancy, but really, it came to this: We simply tallied the number of women who liked particular topics (sexual education, lifestyle, fashion, fantasy, and advice). As we had suspected, women actually read and absorbed the information in our articles; unlike readers of a men's magazine, where the editorial was there to fill in pages between the pictures. We were touching women's lives, impacting their attitudes, and supporting the personal choices and behaviors that worked for them. Every single reader was an individual and we spoke of her and to her respectfully.

Of course, we couldn't deny that our readers also noticed the pictures, and the topic of the penis did come up in our correspondence with readers. Through all the letters and phone calls, we received a hefty education ourselves about what women like to call "it." We learned that females almost always find an endearing or clever "name" for referring to a man's penis. The list became pretty remarkable:

Weenie	Dong	Wedding Tackle	Summer Sausage
Wee-Wee	Choada	Trouser Snake	Jack-in-the-Box
Pee-Pee	Pecker	Pork Sword	Mr. Happy
Weiner	Prick	Little Soldier	Long John Silver
Ding-Dong	Hog	Baloney Pony	Willy
Mini Twinkie	Cock	Other Head	Godzilla
Winky Thing	Pud	Power Drill	Secret Agent Man
Male Member	Package	Magic Wand	King Kong
Johnson	Baby Maker	Joystick	Dick
John Thomas	Tally-Wacker	Jack Hammer	Man in Charge
Wilson	Beef Bayonet	Frankfurter	Hose
Stick	Wang	Captain Winkie	Love Missile

And we could go on. Really, we could.

We thought about the possible reasons for naming a man's penis. Was it to fool the kids when adults were having sexual conversations? Personalize the thing all men have? Add some humor? We smiled and just accepted that this was probably going on around the world. At least, we hoped it was!

The Whole Enchilada

Some of the calls, of course, were complaints. But not the kind you might expect.

"Your magazine is sold out at the store! I can't find a copy," said many.

"It takes three months to start my subscription?" others complained.

And very often, "Who is the next centerfold?" was demanded.

But the number one complaint was, "Why are you hiding the penis? Show us more! Show us the whole enchilada!"

Only one thing surprised us: Thousands of women were sending us photos of their husbands and their boyfriends and submitting them for a picture layout. They were proud of their guys and were willing to show them off. I figured we had to be the reason Polaroid Instant Exposure cameras were selling out at the stores! Most women wouldn't want to have their husband's "happy thing" seen by the photo guy at the drug store, but our ladies must have been having some good times in private capturing a few rolls of Polaroid pictures of their men. Our resident sex psychiatrist, radio show host Dr. Norton Kristy, said he figured we were doing more to help marriages and relationships than couples counselors.

Doug: In our July issue (number two), Jenny and I slipped in just a sliver of George Maharis' Captain Winkie. But as it was being printed, we were concerned we had shown too much too quickly. We didn't want to offend our readers, but all we were hearing was that the ladies wanted to see more.

And that indeed seemed to be the case.

Playgirl's sales grew dramatically each month. We sold out an unheard of 600,000 copies of issue one, not knowing we would reach an eventual 2,100,000 by issue six. *Playgirl Magazine* was a resounding success. Women around the world were craving our product, and it should have been a time of sunny skies.

But an enormous rain cloud was hovering over us.

Hugh Hefner was not happy about *Playgirl Magazine*. Hef had owned the market of centerfold layouts for enough years that with our new product, his ego must have been badly bruised.

So, he filed another lawsuit against us. And if he won, he would control the Playgirl trademark, lock, stock, and massive inventory of paper. All he needed to do was retool our format, hire a few people, and he'd have "Playboy's Playgirl" dominating an exclusive category in publishing. It's not that Jenny and I hadn't expected this, but I'll admit the reality of it hit us hard.

SHOW DOG

JENNY: News of the lawsuit impacted all areas of our business. At a time when our team needed to be even more clever, creative, and positive about our work, the brewing storm of another lawsuit was dragging us all down. The New York team realized our situation and came up with an idea to lighten us up a bit.

The art director had the team work on a special project that used the upcoming centerfold of George Maharis, but replaced his face with a photo of Douglas. These were the days before the ease of Photoshop as we know it today, so it took quite a bit of time and effort to render the layout and make it appear to be a real photograph.

The team captioned his centerfold as "Show Dog," and when the full color layout arrived at our Hollywood office, the prank not only made us laugh, but it reset the mood. The jokes, comments, and laughter over the picture went on for days. Thankfully, the humor had an uplifting effect on the team, and we moved forward with publishing another great issue of *Playgirl Magazine*.

But we were still facing a very complex situation. We had delivered our top-notch publication and it was making history. Women around the world were responding in a positive way that told us we were filling a void that no one else had identified or attempted to fill.

Yes, we had worked our butts off to see that every detail assured our product was top of the line. Yes, we had an exclusive, original product that was overwhelmingly in demand. Yes, we enjoyed every minute of every long and exhausting day we spent pampering and polishing our baby.

And yet, it was possible that Hugh Hefner's deep pockets, connections, and clout might help him win. What if Goliath took David down this time around? We believed Hefner meant to intimidate us, but we were not backing down.

So, the games began.

Doug: Jenny and I decided on a Chicago law firm to represent us. We were specifically referred to "attorney E.F.," we'll call him. He was from D.C. and had a lot of experience and success in winning antitrust cases. So E.F. took the lead with the Chicago legal team.

We were aware that the case could generate a glut of press exposure, since the lawsuits weren't over the rights to some cleaning product formula. This was about ownership of intellectual property, specifically sexual content, and the press and the public would likely find it more than interesting.

Jenny and I worked hard with the Chicago team to build a successful case. We ultimately made the decision to counter sue Hugh Hefner and Playboy Enterprises on the grounds of an anti-trust violation.

Anti-trust suits go back to early American law. They literally relate to the public "trust" regarding competition in America's business world. Anti-trust law is intended to promote free competition in the marketplace by outlawing monopolies. They prevent business combinations that could restrain competition. This is fundamental to capitalism.

E.F. quickly proved his worth as he was granted by the Order of the Courts to depose Hugh Marston Hefner. That meant Hef would now be required to meet with us in person so that our attorney could question him.

"We'll be face to face with Hef," I said dryly over dinner one night, wrapping my head around that fact. The idea of this meeting was giving me some pleasure and some pain.

But Jenny was more than quick with her cheerful response. "Sounds like fun!"

God, I loved this woman.

Wanna See My Dik Dik?

Jenny: Our attorneys were busy preparing for the deposition of Hugh Hefner, so we flew to New York to meet with Fawcett. We often gathered with the family in their high-rise offices for hours on end for business updates, planning, and strategizing. They were experienced in the never-ending details of launching a national, monthly publication, and we gained valuable knowledge on the process. Many times, we continued on into dinner meetings, always in a private room at some very exclusive five-star restaurant.

The Fawcett brothers were a fascinating group we'd gotten to know over almost a year of prepping *Playgirl*. We worked directly with three of the five siblings, and during this trip we were invited to one of the brother's penthouses for a dinner party. It was Roger Fawcett's penthouse, and Roger was...eccentric.

As we arrived, Roger's staff escorted us into a spacious room where our host personally poured cocktails from a statue with a golden penis as its spout. *Now* it made sense that he called himself Playgirl's number one fan!

I managed to avoid Doug's glance and joined in on the party chatter. It was a very small group: Roger, us, and two women who were certainly not his dates. The women warmed up after a bit and we discussed the differences between living in New York and Los Angeles. I was enjoying their company and observations about how lucky we were to live in Hollywood.

DOUG: Sometimes women were initially intimidated by Jenny's beauty, but it never took her long to share an honest compliment or ask a question that helped them realize Jenny was more than a pretty face and body. She quickly won their hearts and was right at home with the polished women, fine wine, and lovely background music.

Eventually, we moved on to the oversized dining room. Our host, seated in the captain's chair, held court with naughty anecdotes from his grandfather (the *Captain Billy's Whiz Bang* founder). I studied Roger's mannerisms and personality while Jenny's charm captured his attention. As dessert was being served, I swore I heard him ask her, "Do you want to see my dick dick?"

I barely managed to not spit my drink out all over the table. Roger spoke directly to me this time. "Come with me and I'll show you my dick dick," he said again. I attempted to set my anger at his crudeness aside. Hell, I had served in the military in Korea, managed drunk and disorderly soldiers, wrangled go-go dancers when their emotions were out of control, and kept drug dealers at bay. So I maintained my composure, and Jenny and I excused ourselves from the table to follow Roger down a racetrack-long hallway to his private den.

The room was filled with dozens of stuffed species of wild animals. The "trophies," as Roger called them, included big game animals such as tigers, zebras, lions, and other poor, nameless beasts that never had a chance against Roger's team of hunters.

"Here it is." Roger grinned wickedly as he gestured to a tiny deer-like animal posed on top of a marble table. "My dik-dik. A member of the antelope family that I scored in The Bush of East Africa." Roger was thoroughly enjoying seeing us squirm. I noticed that the poor, stuffed *dik-dik* (thank goodness) seemed to be giving Roger a "drop dead" look. That was justified.

Handing us both a brandy he had poured, Roger taunted me. "Have you ever shot anything, Doug?"

I took a pleasurable swig from my snifter. "Sure. I was taught to hunt for my family to survive. I mostly killed birds, as well as deer for the skin and meat. We got through many a winter on deer meat back home in Appalachia." I stared around the room. "You know, I can think of a few human heads I wouldn't mind seeing on your wall."

Roger slapped his leg and laughed. "I hear you on that!" He gestured for us to sit. "And I just happen to have a family member who can take care of that kind of thing. Here, have a bit more brandy." He refilled our glasses and also served himself a hefty pour.

I never was sure how serious he was about that last statement. Nor did I ever intend to find out.

We left soon after seeing the dik-dik, as Jenny and I were scheduled to fly to Las Vegas the next day for a few nights of fun before we got back to the daily grind.

Backstage Access

Jenny: Our editor-in-chief had arranged for us to be guests of Tom Jones at his Caesar's Palace show, a huge hit on the Vegas Strip. Jones was a Welsh singer who gave Elvis and other superstar artists a run for their money. He had many number-one hits and reportedly delivered a show that had every audience on their feet. He performed one of my favorites, "She's a Lady," which had gone gold by selling well over a million copies.

After the show, we were invited to meet Jones in his dressing room. The show's photographer took a photo of us all together, and we made some polite talk about enjoying his performance.

By now, Doug and I had become fairly comfortable with discussing the experience of being a *Playgirl* celebrity centerfold, and Jones seemed genuinely curious when we casually approached him about making an appearance in the magazine.

After graciously explaining that he was flattered but not interested, he told us, "I'm already so busy, and I just don't need the exposure." Then he gently placed a kiss on my hand, and we thanked him again for a terrific show. I decided not to mention his great pun by choosing to use the word "exposure."

On our way back to our room, Doug asked, "Did I imagine it, or was Tom actually blushing as he kissed your hand?"

"He was blushing all right. He's either got nothing or plenty to 'expose.' I guess we'll never know." We shared a laugh and headed to our room.

Trouble Brewing

Doug: Back in Los Angeles, we returned to the issues at hand. In addition to the burden of our anti-trust suit, we began hearing rumors and reading news reports about a newly formed Environmental Protection Agency (EPA). Under the direction of President Richard Nixon, the EPA was initially charged with the administration of the Clean Air Act (1970), enacted to abate air pollution primarily from industries and motor vehicles; the Federal Environmental Pesticide Control Act (1972); and the Clean Water Act (1972), regulating municipal and industrial wastewater discharge.

Of course, long-established paper mills were among the worst offenders on the EPA's list. Naturally, I worried about how all of this would impact our magazine.

But Fred consistently assured me that everything was under control. What he conveniently did *not* tell me was that his company had begun selling off their paper stock in a "liquidation process." Fawcett was selling off assets and contracts and shuffling profits and returns. But I wouldn't learn that until a while later.

So, while I was busy trusting my publishing "partners," I was actually being deceived. Our printer and distributor's willingness to alter a contract for paper would be like cutting off the legs of a man who had trained to run at the Olympics. I just didn't think it would ever happen, nor did I see it coming. Because Fred and his team members were deliberately withholding information from me.

Jenny and I were focused on the last-minute details and decisions that needed to be made to meet our latest print deadline. We were focused on making our early issues professional and polished, as if we had been in business for several years. We were committed to creating the most exciting women's magazine in publishing history.

But Fawcett was working against all that. They knew the EPA could cripple the publishing industry and the production of *Playgirl*.

I was about to become that Olympic runner.

Doug and Jenny receive an award from the Pacific Coast Independent Magazine Wholesalers Association

Chapter 14

"The Hustle"

1975

JENNY: It was finally time for Doug's deposition with Hugh Hefner. Before he left Los Angeles for the Chicago meeting, I reminded him of David and Goliath. I was looking to lighten his mood, as there was so much riding on this outcome. The last thing I said to him when I dropped him off at the airport was, "I packed your slingshot. Use it." I was mildly rewarded with just a small smile as he got out of the car. He was nervous, which was unusual for Douglas. That made me nervous too.

DOUG: Our date to hear Hefner's deposition was marked on our calendar by a big red X. Although we weren't being "heard" in a courtroom, the information collected would be the basis for testimony in front of a judge that might follow. This would be the most definitive meeting since our journey began.

Mr. Hefner was scheduled to arrive at our attorney's office in Chicago at six in the evening. E.F. and I waited until seven. Then eight. Eventually, we made a fresh pot of coffee. The sky turned dark. At nine I threatened to leave, but was advised that Hefner's tardiness was a game he often played to upset his opponent. Over and over, I was told that we should take the high road and wait.

Around ten, Hef finally straggled in with his lawyer and two men who appeared to be bodyguards. They would have appeared much tougher had they not breached the doorway carrying six-packs of Pepsi Cola cans in their big arms.

Hef himself was thin, with long strands of mottled hair. His eyes were deep set and he had what I could only describe as an eerie appearance. We were introduced, and he barely stuck his hand out to accept my shake. He sat with his feet tucked under him, and I felt a moment of sadness for the man I had always admired for his achievements.

Sitting across from Hugh Hefner, the self-proclaimed king of sexuality, I watched and listened as E.F. asked some pointed questions. I quickly caught on that Hefner was skilled at dodging answers.

As the questioning continued, the room took on a fascinating, unexpected mood. I'd had several hours to contemplate the stakes on the table that night. Because in the Lambert-Hefner "match," only one could prevail. No one expected a judge to call this fight a draw.

But no matter who won, they would be facing disturbing times. The situation with the EPA had placed both contenders, at the very least, in the position of dealing with a questionable future. Paper hikes had resulted in my monthly printing costs for just over one million issues nearly doubling, leaving me almost seven million dollars in debt. Hefner, who had established his magazine over many years, was printing approximately seven million copies per month. It wasn't hard to do the math on the paper tab he'd run up.

Of course, the most ominous issue in front of me was that we could possibly lose the anti-trust case, and that would trigger unspeakable actions, including the loss of the Playgirl trademark.

But I had learned to just sit tight and let E.F. do what he did best, so I managed to keep myself quiet during all the legal back and forth. More than an hour later, Hefner and his bodyguards were dismissed, and they scooted out the door, leaving behind their remaining cans of Pepsi.

"What do we do now?" I asked E.F.

"We wait, Doug. We wait."

Disco Daze

JENNY: Doug and I returned to our demanding schedules. While *Playgirl Magazine* was climbing in distribution and sales, the Playgirl Club was continuing to feel the squeeze of disco.

The trend of disco music included special dance floor lighting techniques, and the dance moves were specific steps that echoed lyrics, such as a line dance choreographed to the song "The Hustle," recorded by Van McCoy. This song and dance routine was sweeping America. McCoy's manager had coordinated several clever marketing moves that made the song and the artist a smash hit in New York City, a hit-making market. The song climbed to number one on the Billboard Music Chart and became hugely popular around the world.

"The Hustle" was just one of the countless disco hits changing America's music and lifestyle scene. Much of our Playgirl Club crowd was moving on to disco dance clubs, and Doug and I faced the reality that we might need to sell our club while it still had value. While we considered the possibility of converting to a disco style club, our hearts just weren't in it. Besides, nearly all our time, creativity, and energy were devoted to the magazine. It was personally very difficult for us to accept that the Playgirl Club, our beautiful hen that kept laying golden eggs, was taking a backseat to her namesake. But facts were facts. So, we continued to concentrate on the magazine.

As if we needed another challenge, in response to the many requests for more explicit sexual material, Douglas and I created a series of what are known in the publishing world as "one-offs." *The Playgirl Advisor* was a smaller magazine, matching the size of *Reader's Digest* at that time. Its purpose was to give women what their letters and phone calls indicated they wanted, in addition to the monthly celebrity centerfolds, articles, and features found in the larger magazine. The primary call seemed to be for escape through sexual fantasy.

I remember discussing with our editor two letters in particular. In one, the writer described a two-mile high adventure where she and her partner managed full orgasms under a blanket while in their airplane seats. The writer was particularly skilled with describing this "adventure," including the intensity of her own orgasm, heightened by the fact they were doing something untoward, if not illegal. It was similar to the turn on some experience from having affairs with someone married, of a different race, of the same sex, much younger or older, or even someone like your priest or doctor.

The second letter described the reader's memorable night out. She was provocatively perched on a barstool when a handsome man took the seat next to her. They shared cocktails, each taking a bite of the cherry in hers. The nibble led to a passionate kiss, then to hands all over bodies, and finally culminated in stepping into a stall in the ladies' room. There, the bathroom attendant got an earful of moans, heavy breathing, panties dropping, and the obvious sounds of relief from both man and woman.

Clothes back in place, they smugly left the bar under the incredulous eyes of many of the customers, who had already heard reports of the action. Walking her to her car, the gentleman chuckled as she removed her wig and gave him a last kiss. "See you at home, honey. Make sure you watch the sitter until she gets safely across the street and all the way into her house, okay?"

The three of us, Douglas included, were bowled over at the clever, bold, and boundary-pushing sex plays many of these readers shared with us. And the most interesting part was that they wanted even *more*. They not only wanted to share their stories, but they also wanted to hear about stories from other women. Erotica was easily the most popular genre our customers wanted to read.

From this feedback, the *Playgirl Advisor* was born. Our "fantasies" described in detail sexual encounters between heterosexuals and homosexuals alike, plus tales of multiple partners, self-stimulation, and sex toy use. We carefully avoided fantasies that involved harming or being harmed.

It seemed the sexual creativeness became, well…more creative with each batch of new mail. We found ourselves quite impressed with the range of stories and scenarios submitted to us—not to mention, the pure artistry of the writing.

In addition to mildly graphic fantasy, we were often ahead of our time in our feature articles. One such article was by Canary Conn, who profiled with remarkable sensitivity and specific details the life of a transvestite—a subject rarely talked or written about at the time. Documented in the article were the memories of Julie as a young girl on her journey to becoming Jude. This poignant life experience appeared at a time when no other widely published magazine would approach the topic.

To our knowledge, *Playgirl* was also the first to take graphic cartooning into the world of female sexuality. "Sex Trek," which appeared in an issue of *Playgirl Advisor*, presented a tale of space travelers confronted by aliens demanding sex from the Earthlings. Placing love and loyalty before the payoff of quick pleasure, our hero is eventually rewarded by his Earth mate.

During our years of ownership, *Playgirl Magazine* broke many of the publishing rules and records that were in play at that time. Simultaneously, in what seemed like a cruel twist, we constantly battled in the courtrooms for its right to exist.

Waving the White Flag

Doug: My assistant stepped into the door of my office. "Your attorney is on line three." I didn't hesitate, even though I never knew what new and terrible information E.F. might have to report.

"Doug...Hefner wants to drop his lawsuit if you'll drop your anti-trust suit against Playboy. He's calling a truce. What do you think?"

I didn't need a beat to think. "I agree if you agree."

"Smart move, Doug. *Playgirl Magazine* is all yours now." He chuckled. "I'll wait until tomorrow to give them the news. Let them sweat a little bit."

"Great. Let's wrap it up...on their dime, yes?"

"You bet. I'll send you the paperwork. Congratulations, pal. You've done it again."

It was hard to fathom how we'd managed to beat out ol' Hef no less than three times. Regardless, Jenny and I were grateful as hell for yet another victory, and we were sure to send a note of thanks to E.F. for his outstanding performance as our savior.

It was finally over, once and for all...or so I thought.

A few days later, I was just finishing a meeting when my assistant popped her head into the room. "Mr. Hefner is on the phone. Line one."

Hugh Marsten Hefner, Mr. Playboy, was calling me personally. I hadn't necessarily been expecting his call, but I wasn't surprised either. The conversation between us was simple, blunt, and without much emotion.

"This is Hef," he said. I waited, silently pushing him to his point. "I wanted to ask you how much you want for your magazine."

Well, at least he was admitting he knew it was *my* magazine. I quoted a number that will forever remain our secret. Hefner's exact response was, "Fuck off!"

We both hung up.

This time, it was over for good.

JENNY: That night, Douglas and I enjoyed an impromptu champagne celebration. I knew without ever saying it that he felt more than a little smug that Hugh Hefner had wanted to buy the magazine. This was more than just a David and Goliath moment. This was my husband, partner, and best friend experiencing a true and lasting victory. I embraced the man who had the courage to take my ideas and make them our reality. And in doing so, he had played a huge part in changing sexuality for women around the world.

I was feeling sentimental. "We've come through a long, hard journey," I reflected to him. "But more important than our business success is how proud I am of the man you are, Douglas." We snuggled in front of our living room fireplace, and I could feel the tension leaving both our bodies as he wrapped me in his arms.

"You've always been smart, kind, and handsome," I continued. "But now, you're open to new ideas, including the real potential of women. You really do view us as equals, which I can't say about a lot of men." I gazed into the popping fire in front of us. "Of course, there are basic scientific differences between men and women. That's a given. And I see how women show their independence in different ways than men. But you really get that we are of equal status, importance, and value. I couldn't be more in love with you, Douglas."

Doug: Jenny's words really took me by surprise. I thought for a few minutes before I answered. "That means everything to me, Jenny. But I would never have had the chance to improve if you hadn't had the idea for *Playgirl Magazine*." I paused, choosing my words carefully. "And if you hadn't believed that I could change enough to really get behind your idea." She finally turned to face me. "And I have never loved you more than I do right now. I will always love you."

Any other night, Jenny might have shed a tear or two. I didn't talk about my emotions very often. So I was a little surprised that my openness didn't appear to move her. Then I had the thought that Jenny was feeling her own strength, her power as the person who had taken an idea from concept through creation and into unmatched success. Because of her, *we* were celebrating our mutual success.

We both went silent, basking in the reality that we were two people sharing in the pain and pleasures of building an unusual but amazing business and life together as one.

Feeling Honored

Jenny: As publishers of the most provocative and fastest growing magazine on Earth, we landed on the party list of many of the movers and shakers in Hollywood.

Allan Carr was one of the most respected and successful producers in the world. He enjoyed hits on Broadway before he turned his talents to filmmaking to create hits like *Saturday Night Fever* and *Grease*. He also produced the Broadway smash *La Cage aux Folles*, which was later made into the classic movie *The Bird Cage*. Alan was a short, rotund, dynamo of a man. He was both brilliant and kind, and his network of friends and contacts was staggering. His home was designed for a party crowd. The stairs to his private quarters were always guarded by serious men in suits, and the party area was meticulously cared for during the festivities.

Douglas and I were regulars on Allan Carr's invite list and over time we had memorable conversations with the likes of Peter Sellers, Zsa Zsa Gábor, George Hamilton, and the always attention-grabbing Charo. Ann-Margret, Herb Alpert, and a rising comedienne named Joan Rivers were also among Carr's clients and party guests. Casual conversations could turn toward career interests at these parties, and business cards were often exchanged. I sometimes felt these events were as much work as they were play, but it was always interesting to be face to face with TV, music, and film stars.

Doug: Every business has highlights like the great events we attended, but the lows were unfortunately more common, and one of ours was looming. The first time I became aware of the seriousness of the EPA storm that was brewing was in the fall of 1974, when Jenny and I accepted a prestigious award from the Pacific Coast Independent Magazine Wholesalers Association (PCIMWA). The event was held in San Francisco, and because we valued our wholesalers, we were willing to take that rare step into the spotlight to honor their recognition of us. The award we received was inscribed: *To Douglas and Jenny Lambert; In Recognition and in Honor of the Many Everlasting and Enriching Contributions Their Magazines Have Made to Inform and Disseminate the Lifestyle and Culture of the West, Throughout America and the World.*

Jenny and I did not miss the thoughtfulness of the group's message. They acknowledged their place in our success and graciously included our impact and influence. It got us thinking about just how far-reaching our little project might really be.

On our flight home, Jenny and I talked about how in the previous eighteen months we had moved in circles of celebrity power and business clout. We had met some of the best-known faces among the ranks of people who were making news. We had been included at exclusive, small cocktail parties and at galas in grand ballrooms. But there were a lot more people involved and intertwined with the magazine than the bigwigs we wined and dined with. The reality was that we were running a business that created jobs for people we'd never even meet.

"On this trip, we met people we relate to. People who work hard, put in overtime, and are grateful for good jobs so they can provide for their families," Jenny said.

Without thinking, my next words fell from my mouth. "I learned that on a train." I was remembering my cross-country railway trip. "When an entrepreneur founds and funds an enterprise, they're creating opportunity and employment for other men, women, and their families. It means more than they realize." I put my head back and reflected on just how much my life had changed since that first train ride.

THE EPA MONSTER

Setting my mind in the present, I threw myself into understanding the ramifications the EPA could have on our magazine business. At the PCIMWA awards, I overheard comments from wholesalers about the "paper squeeze" and "do-gooders attacking the tree farmers" and "paper becoming as valuable as gold." My mind was constantly ticking. Why hadn't Fred warned me about these problems? What was our plan to deal with the financial challenges headed our way? Why wasn't my New York ally keeping me in the loop? I knew there weren't any good answers to those questions.

My phone rang at the early hour of 7:00 AM. I picked up, realizing that New Yorkers had already been up and working for hours.

"You answering your own phone, Doug?" I recognized that voice.

"You bet, Fred, and I can still wield a mean broom if there's any trash lying around."

Fred sensed I wasn't up for his usual BS chitchat. "Listen, I want to update you on the paper situation." He went on, stammering his way through his version of the facts. Obviously, he was forced to finally call me because time had run out. I stayed quiet because I didn't want to interrupt him and miss one detail of the fiasco we were now facing.

The bottom line of my conversation with Fred didn't reveal anything Jenny and I didn't already suspect or know for certain. Our current dilemma was that in recent months our paper and production prices had soared and, of course, we had to maintain our overhead to deliver a top-quality magazine each month. As a result, *Playgirl* had shifted from functioning "in the black," where profits were strong, to being "in the red," a gully where our financials were bleeding ink daily.

The shocking news from Fred was that in addition to the sea of debt, Fawcett had sold my contracts for printing and distribution to some company called Hall Printers. They had literally moved my dealings into the hands of strangers. In doing so, Fawcett was in breach of our contract, and Hall was a company where I knew no one, had no relationship, no history, no bargaining chips, and really, no interest from them in *Playgirl's* continued success. It was a nightmare.

My conversation with Fred ended with more concerns and questions than answers. When we hung up, I shared the devastating news with Jenny.

"It feels like my child has been ripped from my arms." She was furious about the situation, and I was even angrier than she was. We had delivered a record-setting winner in the publishing world. We had plans for expanding our brand into products for merchandising worldwide. Jenny felt strongly that our books of erotica for women would continue to be successfully translated for an international market.

With those goals still in mind, we fervently agreed to stay the course. It was all we knew to do. We *had* to keep moving forward.

Our next plan was to expand our centerfold reach beyond famous people. Jenny continued to remind our team and me that we had clearly heard from our readers that "real" men, not just celebrities, would be welcomed. "We should find a middle ground between famous and family." Jenny was making the point that we didn't need to spotlight husbands and boyfriends as centerfolds, but that we could find everyday men who would be more like the guy next door.

Our centerfold team began exploring interesting men at local gyms, on sports teams, and dancers at male strip clubs. We were determined to keep our momentum going strong as best as we knew how.

$1,000 Per Inch

My phone calls were screened, so when my secretary stepped into my office with a smile and the suggestion that I pick up the phone, I played along. Jenny was sitting in my office, so I put the caller on speakerphone. He politely identified himself as Jim Brown, and Jenny and I exchanged a knowing look. He was a wildly famous football star.

Jim cut right to the chase. "I'm interested in being one of your centerfolds and I guarantee you the ladies will be very happy with my photos. How much do you pay?"

We'd never conversed with a potential centerfold so confident and direct. It was comically shocking, and Jenny cupped her palm over her face to keep her laughter from being heard.

"Well, we don't usually pay our celebrities," I said as straightly as I could manage. "But if you have what you say, I'd offer $1,000 per inch." I held up my hand to signal Jenny to stop laughing—I was about to lose it myself.

Jim was obviously doing the math in his head. Finally, he came back. "So that means you'd pay me $10,000. And we do this in one photo session. Agreed?"

"Agreed. How about I have our centerfold team call your agent to send you a contract and arrange the photo shoot?"

"No, have them call me directly." He provided his number. "You don't want to meet with me first?"

"Nope." I replied. "I'll take your word for everything you've so willingly shared."

At this point Jenny almost fell out of her chair and was gasping for breath.

When we said a friendly goodbye, Jenny and I finally exploded with laughter. She had tears rolling down her cheeks and I was having a rare laughing fit.

A few weeks later, the centerfold photos were completed, and I phoned our NFL star to invite him to lunch so I could pay him directly, as requested.

He sounded happy. "Can you pay me in small denominations?"

And odd request, but not entirely unreasonable. "Sure." I glanced at my calendar. "How about Tuesday at noon at the Cock 'N Bull?" That was a deliberate restaurant choice.

I was fashionably late for our lunch. After all, I was the one with the paper bag containing an assortment of small cash bills. Our very famous running back was nothing if not easily recognizable, so I stepped around the hostess and joined him at our table for two. His handshake could have put anyone under that table. Even with his unmatched winning record and large stature, he was blessed with a gentle confidence in person.

I plopped the brown paper bag down on the table between the two of us. He gave me a questioning look. "You expect me to count it here?"

"You said you wanted cash. Better make sure it's all there."

The gentle giant was looking a little hot under the collar as he leaned across the table, obviously not comfortable with a sack of money sitting between us. "Well, is there $10,000 in there?"

I could feel his excitement growing. "No. $9,000." I replied with all the intended innocence I could muster.

My guest's indignation flared. "You're a thousand dollars short of our agreement."

"Actually," I replied, "You were an inch short of our agreement."

We both let out a laugh and I sat back to enjoy lunch with my new favorite celebrity athlete. I guess not everything about this business always had to be so tough.

Magazine returns were stored in this old sugar mill in Barbados

Jenny, Doug, Eric Chung, Playgirl Magazine's attorney, and Jim Summers in Barbados

Chapter 15

"Fight the Power"

1975

Doug: Our international distributors were shipping hundreds of thousands of issues of *Playgirl Magazine* to Europe each month. Jenny and I were very encouraged by the worldwide response to our ideas and our spectacular photographs of men. Letters from women and men in France, Germany, Italy, Russia, and beyond shared their excitement about receiving their next issue of *Playgirl*. We had an international mix of ethnic groups who were loyal fans. The world was still decades from the internet and social media, yet we had created a product that people were excited about and were telling their friends about…who then told their friends. Jenny's crazy idea was influencing the sexuality of societies around the planet.

But troubling us both was that Fred had put me in a position where he expected me to take his word on the totals of our sales versus returns, and how they were tallied up for payment. He wanted to use the honor system instead of cold, hard numbers, and that felt hinky.

I continued to hound Fred and his associates, but he wouldn't budge at all. "You just don't understand the international publication model, Doug." Fred was more than condescending in his conversations with me. "In this business, a sale is only counted after we subtract the returns from your total."

I understood all right. Returns were based on counting our covers; covers that were ripped from the magazine, bundled at an unknown location, and shipped to Barbados, a remote island in the Caribbean, for storage. When I confronted Fred about tracking the returns myself, he barely stopped short of laughing. "Are you crazy?" he asked.

Aha. The magical words that told me I was getting close to my answer.

"Fred, I'm telling you one last time: Either you get me some explanation and accounting, or I'm prepared to get a court order to stop all distribution to Europe until we settle this."

The French Connection

Fred's assistant told us to expect a call from Hachette, our European distributor based in France. The man who would be calling us headed the largest magazine publishing company in the world.

The call came at midday. "Monsieur Lambert." His English was surprisingly good and his tone projected warmth. "What is the situation? I have learned you have concerns."

"Thank you for calling," I replied. "I'll cut to the chase: There's no money coming in, and lots of magazines going out each month."

The Frenchman didn't hesitate. "There is quite a large number of magazines that are unsold and returned but, as you are aware, the return process is complex and also…irregular…in its time schedule."

I had heard all of this before, so I stayed quiet.

"Monsieur Lambert, we should meet and discuss this in person. I will be in California in two weeks. I would like to meet the man who brought America into the 20th Century." His flattery was wasted, but I agreed because I wanted to look this man in the eyes as I made my case.

With two weeks until our face-to-face, I went to work learning more about my international distributor. As a teenage boy, he was a printing press apprentice, and that apparently whet his appetite for publishing. Little was known about his loyalties or his activities during World War II, but after the war he set an upward path in both business and French society. As an expert in jazz, he hosted a radio show on the topic, then purchased *Jazz Magazine*, which would become a hit and the flagship of his publishing empire. Ultimately, he would buy or start magazines for teens, sports enthusiasts, and with themes including photography, boating, and cooking. With *Playboy* and *Penthouse* on his international distribution roster, it seemed sensible that he also represent *Playgirl Magazine.*

"Sensible can sometimes be a code word for safe," Jenny told me over dinner at our favorite sushi restaurant. "And safe rarely leads to success." We were both aware that Mr. Frenchman could have easily diluted our payments and profits by reporting increased returns. It was one of the oldest tricks in dishonorable bookkeeping and difficult to expose because we were thousands of miles away from the books...not to mention, the supposedly returned magazine covers.

Discrepancies

Our lunch meeting was scheduled at the Beverly Wilshire Hotel, famous even before the movie *Pretty Woman* was filmed there. Moving south on Rodeo Drive, I drove past the most famous designer stores in the world just before dead-ending at Wilshire Boulevard, where the hotel majestically spanned an entire block of prime Beverly Hills real estate.

The Frenchman greeted me with a friendly smile and handshake. Despite our vast cultural differences, we moved into easy conversation discussing our backgrounds as we enjoyed our lunch. Several times he reflected on his days as a disc jockey, and I told him about the jukeboxes that had made an impression on me.

He asked me how the idea for *Playgirl Magazine* occurred, and I spent some time remembering out loud how our club led Jenny to the idea of a magazine for women. I even filled him in on my battles with Hef and he sat back in his chair to listen.

"So you win the battle, start a magazine, and change the world, no?"

I sensed my opportunity. "It would be a much sweeter success if I got paid for every magazine sold, but there's quite some discrepancy in magazines shipped, sold, and returned under your watch in Europe."

He paused. "How much do you want?"

"For what?"

He retrieved an elegant Montblanc pen from his pocket and picked up the paper napkin sitting under my empty glass of iced tea. He wrote a number on the napkin and passed it to me. The first number was low, but it was followed by six zeros before hitting a decimal point.

"No, thanks." I pulled a twenty-dollar bill from my wallet for the tip and tossed it on the table. I had done the numbers and estimated that *Playgirl* would be worth millions if she went up for sale on the market. I was insulted that this man would think I would sell our baby short.

Before I turned to walk away, I saw a perplexed look on the Frenchman's face. He appeared to be most confused by my decision. But I was too angry to interpret his look further and stormed off to the valet for my car.

I returned to the office where Jenny was waiting. "It didn't go well," I told her.

Jenny didn't ask for details, and I was grateful, since I had an unusual sense of discomfort about how the lunch meeting had ended. I experienced a nagging thought of regret that I hadn't stayed to hear more from him…

That's when I decided it was time for us to take matters into our own hands. "We need to go to Barbados," I told Jenny.

She was remarkably calm about this decision. "I'll have Helen check on flights for a few weeks from now," she replied as she stood to leave, giving me space to ponder my thoughts. But I forced myself to put my negative feelings about the lunch meeting aside, and spent the rest of the day further investigating the process of returns in the publishing industry.

I came across a fact that was devastating. I learned that the magazine covers shipped to Barbados and other remote locations were destroyed after they had supposedly been counted. I struggled to calm my mind so I could get through the details.

Why were magazine covers sent to such remote locations? Why wasn't the counting done at the distribution centers where they were originally shipped? Who in the hell was doing this so-called counting? Why were magazine covers bagged as trash and thrown away or burned? Couldn't the most successful publishing company in the world afford to store these covers for tracking and payment? Didn't they have the means to create a reputable and trustworthy system for keeping track of their own products?

Of course they did. And that being the case, I instinctively knew the answers to these questions.

As the saying goes: I was being royally screwed.

The Sinking Ship

Jenny: I had rarely seen Douglas so distressed. We began to discuss the strategies of developing a strong legal offense rather than waiting for possible enemies to put us on the defensive. We extended our legal team to include a man named Eric Chung, an attorney who had successfully challenged publishing industry payments in complex court cases. His legal expertise was as much of a specialty as becoming a surgeon qualified to reattach a limb to a body.

Together we were presenting a case that was very time sensitive. Our intent was to stop the destruction of *Playgirl Magazine* covers that had been in international distribution.

We actually saw a few immediate, positive results. Reacting to our offensive move, our "new" printing company, Hall Printers, got cold feet and returned legal responsibility—our contract—to Fawcett. At least we had our printing back on track and the original company was forced to again be accountable for advances, bookkeeping, payments, and profits. And they knew we were paying attention now.

Our ultimate goal was to win the separation of *Playgirl* from both our printing and distribution contracts. By clearing the slate, Doug and I could continue publishing *Playgirl* while old contracts and dealings were carefully examined and evaluated by the courts. For starters, we filed the suit needed to freeze the distribution of international copies of *Playgirl*, as they were being reported as having been returned rather than sold. Our bold actions resulted in Fawcett giving us the go-ahead to visit the Barbados location and see for ourselves what was really going on there. They weren't happy about it, but we weren't backing down, and got them to realize their hands were tied.

Also, while not surprising, we finally confirmed the other disturbing news about the activities of Fawcett that we should have been privy to from the beginning. Douglas brought me up to date late one afternoon.

"Our buddy Fred Klein began a 'liquidation process' some time ago. Fawcett is selling off their contracts and moving profits and returns around with abandon, and it's been going on for months. We really need to step up our Barbados schedule."

I was frustrated, but no more surprised about this than Douglas had been.

The center point of our legal case was specific to the issue of advances. Advances were defined as payments owed to us to produce current and future magazines. But with the huge lag times caused by shipping "returned covers" to Barbados, then attaining any sort of numbers and relaying that information back to us, there were huge holes of time and information that were being used to dilute payments. This method was surely tricky—but not illegal unless we proved it was intentional.

We had our enemies on the run over profits, distribution, and accounting in Europe, while we were carefully developing a breach of contract (and worse) case in the U.S. The entire scenario was daunting.

Douglas and I took a rare Sunday drive to Marina Del Rey to gaze at rowboats, sailing vessels, and mega yachts. I recalled telling Douglas years ago how I longed to one day own a boat as beautiful as one of these. We then chose a favorite restaurant to dine in and enjoy the magnificent California sunset. It was a relaxing evening, which were few and far between these days.

On the ride home, I played disc jockey to our radio, taking us in and out of hit songs. "Listen to this one, Douglas. It's about us," I said as I turned up the audio and turned my ear to the lyrics of The Isley Brothers hit "Fight the Power." It made me sad to feel like we were always fighting someone, but we couldn't deny the truth of that fact.

We certainly had success: money, influence, and the joys of achievement. But it all seemed overshadowed by the heavy hitters surrounding us. These people had been playing tough for years, if not generations. I didn't like the idea of getting ready for another fight every day of our lives. My nature was to be kind, and I genuinely liked most people. But the man in my life had been unwillingly pulled into a business war, and I was not going to crumble.

DOUG: As we hoped for an ultimate outcome that would save our precious publication, Jenny and I watched as the dollars flew out of

our bank account each month. Counter to every principle we had always practiced, we were building debt. This was foreign to both of us, whether we were managing a monthly grocery budget, a thriving nightclub, or an international magazine. As the negatives piled up and our spirits sank, we were becoming increasingly more alarmed.

But as it has been said, often the only way out of a problem is to go through it. So Jenny and I suited up every day to turn out another great issue of *Playgirl Magazine*. Sometimes we put on false but happy smiles for an occasional check in at the Playgirl Club, and some days we donned war armor to take on legal monsters. I noticed how all of this was affecting us. Jenny and I were missing dinners together. Sunday mornings in bed and other relaxing times were only memories.

But suddenly, it seemed a small slice of sunshine appeared in all the darkness.

Let's Make a Deal

"Jenny, we may have an exit plan. Meet me at home."

I was at the magazine office and Jenny was meeting with the dancers at the club. There were times when we both wondered which atmosphere was more frustrating than the other.

We ordered in pizza and Jenny sipped on a nice red wine while I explained the reason for my excitement: E.F. was in contact with Warner Distribution, a major company interested in distributing up-and-running magazines. We fit their bill, and signing with them could resolve several of the issues we currently faced—a big one being the issue of actually trusting our printer and distributor.

We discussed our plan for me to go to New York to present *Playgirl* in another pitch meeting to Warner, and Jenny was as intrigued as I was about this prospect. "I think there are two major differences this time around," Jenny noted, taking a healthy drink from her glass. "One." She held up her pointer finger. "You're presenting the most innovative and successful women's magazine launch in history."

I honestly wondered what was more important than that one fact.

But she held up a second finger. "And two, my love, you have the future of women and their sexuality in the palm of your hand. Erotica, calendars, books, and 'best of' issues. There's so much more than meets the eye. Any distributor worth their salt will be able to see that."

I nodded vigorously. Jenny was one hundred percent correct. *Playgirl Magazine* would be a great investment for a distribution deal. Our publication was known as the leader in reaching women who were forward thinking. We provided an option for a way of life enjoyed previously only by men, unburdened by personal judgments or boundaries.

I grabbed Jenny's still-outstretched hand from the air and spun her around. We enjoyed a belly laugh for the first time in longer than I wanted to remember.

E.F. and I arrived early for the meeting at the Warner Distribution New York offices. Exiting the taxi, I spent a few minutes under the towering building emblazoned with the name of the company who I might next trust with my magazine's distribution.

For whatever reason, I flashed back to that night I drove the honky tonk truck to the moonshine dealer's shack. I chuckled to myself at the memory of that gawky kid, terrified but willing to take a risk. "Hell," I mumbled to myself. "Too late to think about being scared now." And I wasn't.

In fact, I felt confident during my brief presentation. I had worked my pitch to the bare bones. My goals were distribution and advance payments. After stating a few facts about our glowing and growing sales and advertisers, I pivoted to the real opportunity.

"Here's the bottom line," I stated to the room full of decision-makers. "Playgirl has cornered the international market on women's...lifestyle." I lingered on that last word, then stood up and took deliberate time putting my hands in my pockets. Then, I added a hint of a smile. No one moved a muscle. In the time it took me to stand, I had created the needed space for everyone in the room to mentally substitute the word "lifestyle" with the real word: sex. And as I recapped our success, I included words that were always banned in business: male nudity, erotica, sexual partners, nude centerfolds, birth control, sexual fantasies, and the like.

"I think I've covered it all," I finally stopped myself. "Or rather, uncovered it all." The head guy let out a warm laugh and the rest joined in. The women in the room had already relaxed and the laughter helped the guys loosen up a bit. I took my seat and waited for the laughter and side jokes to finish. I chose my next words carefully. "So, we're exploring the idea of an arrangement with a company not unlike yours." I wanted them to think they weren't the only team on the court.

It was their turn, so I accepted a fresh cup of coffee and sat back to listen to a group of strangers lay out their plan for *Playgirl's* future. The team did not hedge on the realities of our legal issues, and all terms proposed were contingent on winning our lawsuits against Fawcett. Yet, their offer was generous. I thanked them for their time and assured them we would give their plan serious consideration and get back to them soon...even though I already knew our answer would be a resounding, "Yes." It was the smartest move available to us at that time.

After the meeting, I found my way to a diner that had small jukeboxes on each table. I ordered a burger and a cola and scanned through the songs to find three that were deserving of what would now cost me a dollar. As I ate my meal, I reflected on the meeting and considered the variety of possible outcomes. Even the music couldn't distract me from what the future might hold.

Warner Distribution seemed just as eager to settle the deal as Jenny and I were. Before I even left New York, I found myself back in their office signing the papers that made things official.

From what I understood, our deal for *Playgirl's* continued distribution would be under Warner as the parent company, but the actual printing and distribution would be carried out by Wisconsin Cuneo Press, located in Milwaukee. This was a fairly normal practice for the publishing and printing industry at this time, and as such, the arrangement was deemed just fine by me and E.F. both.

After providing my John Hancock and a lengthy round of good-willed handshakes, I left the New York office feeling more chipper than I had in months. Amid the ongoing lawsuit against Fawcett, the switch-over to Cuneo would begin almost immediately, and hopefully that meant *Playgirl* would be getting back on track, as she so rightly deserved. We were finally kicking our way back to the surface of the water, where we could take a nice, big gulp of air.

With the deal done, Jenny and I now had other fish to finish frying, so I was happy to let Cuneo get started and do their thing.

But I would come to find out that you can never know you've made a grave mistake until you're on the other side of it.

Counting in the Caribbean

Jenny: While Douglas was in New York, I prepared for our inquisition journey to Barbados. The time had finally come. We had no idea what to expect, but our goal was to inspect and evaluate the shenanigans going on regarding the returns and the accounting of our magazines' sales. The very future of *Playgirl Magazine* was in question.

Doug arrived home from New York, and the next day the limo arrived to shuttle us to Los Angeles International Airport, where we would depart for the Caribbean. Our inspection team consisted of myself, Douglas, our attorney Eric Chung, our accountant Jim Sommers, and Doug's nephew Larry Greer, who would assist with counting magazine covers.

Barbados was a lovely island where the ocean and balmy weather set an immediate tone of relaxation and fun. When we arrived, the sun was setting and tourists were laughing and enjoying vacation time while the locals welcomed their business. We checked into a hotel near where the magazines were stored.

Our group convened in the lobby at eight the next morning and we introduced ourselves to Jason, Fawcett's representative who was foolishly dressed in a business suit. The rest of us were wearing khaki pants and shorts to combat the heat and humidity. I completed the look with knee-high boots and a camera around my neck.

The drive to the location took us past tourist attractions, historical buildings, jewelry and clothing shops, scuba rentals, and helicopter rides. Golf, cave exploration, bars with exotic drinks, and restaurants with freshly caught fish were all poised for visitors' pleasures. But no one in our group was in the mood for island festivities.

We arrived at the building, a rotted-out sugar processing facility in the middle of large fields of sugar cane and other indigenous plants. The caretaker was waiting for us and had already unlocked the doors. Everyone was nervous over what were about to find.

Inside, we were immediately greeted by the putrid odor of decay. Stacks and stacks of cardboard boxes were piled on top of and against each other, soggy from rain penetrating the leaky roof. The place was also infested with rats. Not off to a great start.

Larry passed us each a clipboard of paper and some pens, in case we found something worthwhile to record. I glanced at Doug in his expensive loafers, which were now ruined by the mush and slush on the concrete floor. I said a silent thanks to myself for thinking to wear tall, protective boots.

It didn't take long for us to discover that, yes, there were stacks and stacks of *Playgirl* covers bundled together into mushy mounds of pulp. They were there...but they were not as had been reported. To me, it became almost immediately evident that the number of returned covers housed here was far below the number of returns that had been reported to us. I felt some sense of hope, but made sure to contain my emotions. We still needed to count to be completely sure.

Jason had been assigned to this mission on behalf of the New York team to prove that hundreds of thousands of copies of *Playgirl* had not been sold, and that those returned magazine covers were stored here in this old building. The rest of us were there because our attorneys had demanded the right to physically count those covers to be sure the returns deducted from our revenues were accurate. That meant Jason was certainly on the "other team." We could consider him the enemy, and yet, I felt grateful he was here to witness the true outcome.

Sweat rolled out of every pore on our bodies as we diligently counted the inventory. Then Jason, Douglas, and I compared our totals. "Well, what we have here, witnessed by each of us is that, yes, every issue of *Playgirl Magazine* did not sell out. We have covers of the magazines to show that," Doug stated. Then he exhaled, and I was sure I caught a small smile crossing his face. "But we have also proven that while perhaps thousands of magazines didn't sell and their covers were shipped here, it's nowhere near the *hundreds* of thousands of magazines being deducted from our profits." Now I *know* he smiled. "We are, in fact, owed back payments for sales. That fact is confirmed by the returns counted in this very building."

I was beaming. Larry pumped his fist. Eric was nodding his head, and even Jason looked resolved to the outcome. Meanwhile, the building caretaker was fiddling with his keys in hopes we were adjourning for the day. Satisfied with the outcome, yes, we could adjourn.

Back at the hotel, we had showered and were seated for dinner. Everyone settled in to relax with a tropical drink, and I proposed a toast to the success of our trip. I watched Jason's reaction, and he was actually nodding in agreement. Under the table, Douglas squeezed my hand.

Doug: On the flight home, Jenny and I discussed our past and our future. We wondered if other magazine publishers were being cheated because they didn't have the resourcefulness (or maybe the stubbornness) to actually fly to a reclamation site and calculate their returns. This part of the business world seemed far filthier than that of my old moonshine buddies', who could at least trust each other's word and handshake. Hell, I was even raised around farm animals, which meant slipping and sliding in muck and manure often. Dirty business wasn't a new experience for me, and, yet, this felt much dirtier than anything I'd been through before.

But no matter what, when I would fall right in the middle of a pile, I always got back on my feet. So, I figured I'd do the same if I landed on my butt in this particular dung heap.

Doug's favorite honky tonk angel

Chapter 16

"A Teardrop on a Rose"

Doug: A few months had gone by since our telling trip out to Barbados, and Jenny and I were trying to be patient as our lawyers continued to work hard on the lawsuit against Fawcett. In the meantime, distribution with Warner/Cuneo was under way, and all seemed to be going just fine.

Until it wasn't.

I received a call from Warner Distributors saying that it was urgent I be in New York in the next two days. An instant feeling of dread swept over me.

My accountant Jim Sommers and I flew in and made our way to the Warner Distribution office. We entered the fancy conference room, but this time, instead of a welcoming group, there were two disgruntled men waiting for us. The first was a corporate executive type, but the second was more rough looking. The formalities of handshakes and introductions were honored, and I learned that these two gentlemen were actually in from the Cuneo office to "hash out business themselves." That had all sorts of inklings that didn't sit well with me.

Sure enough, as we sat down, I caught a glimpse of a pistol under the belt of the second attendee. A gun at a business meeting in a New York high-rise? My inklings seemed to be spot-on already.

The executive got right to the point. "Doug, you owe us millions in paper and printing costs. It's time for you to pay up."

I digested this demand carefully, actually understanding where it was coming from. With the back payments still owed to me by Fawcett, I had been unable to pay Warner/Cuneo the dues they were owed for their role in the magazine. But at the same time, I was perplexed by this sudden demand—it had been made clear to Warner from the beginning that I was in the middle of a lawsuit, and the money could be tied up for a while. Even knowing this, they had still agreed to take *Playgirl* under their wing.

So I chose my words carefully, but spoke with intent. "You will get your money. I'm just waiting for final count results from Fawcett, our previous distribution company. They owe me more than I owe you."

But by this point, we all knew we weren't talking about making a fair and balanced list of who owed who what. The situation was too far gone to even think of a friendly solution.

"Well, Doug, we're calling in the cash or collateral for the current debt *now*."

I remembered back to the time when we had been shaking hands and patting each other's backs in this very room. Now across the table, I was facing two veritable thugs packing heat. While one of them was threatening me, I reminded myself I had faced a multitude of men waiting for a fight in the past, from the rough and ready Appalachian Mountain moonshiners to Hells Angels members to Hefner's lawyers. No time to quit now.

I didn't blink. Finally, the loudmouth executive started again. "Put it like this. We want *Playgirl's* trademarks and copyrights signed over as payment for the debt."

Alarm bells went off in my head and my stomach flip-flopped, but with great effort, I kept my tone even to accentuate his ridiculous demand. "How about instead, I have my accountant explain our repayment plan to you, because I am not giving up my trademarks or copyrights. And if you shoot me, you get nothing. So I'd listen to our plan very carefully."

He took a pause to consider what I'd just said, but still didn't budge. "We want trademarks and copyrights. Or we'll force you into bankruptcy. It's that simple."

Now I did raise my voice. "Here's how simple it is. You geniuses didn't do your homework. Way back when I opened the Playgirl Club, I created two corporations: Playgirl Corporation, and Playgirl Key Club, Inc. Your contract is with my operating company, Playgirl Corporation. But Playgirl Key Club, Inc. owns and licenses any trademarks and copyrights to the operating company. Should there be insolvency or financial concerns of any kind, including moral turpitude or criminal activity, *all* rights revert back to the holding company. All rights."

I stood to leave. More yelling wouldn't accomplish anything, and both sides had said their piece. I took Jim by the arm. "Keep walking unless they shoot," I whispered, joking. At least, somewhat joking.

The last thing we saw was a furious face as the elevator doors closed. Jim and I walked quickly to our hotel, collected our bags, and headed straight for the airport. With a few minutes to spare, we stopped at the terminal bar for a quick cocktail. Just as the booze started to take the edge off, I noticed none other than the two men from our meeting sitting on the far end of the bar, watching us.

Needless to say, we downed our drinks and headed for the gate to board our flight. It was time to get the hell out of Dodge.

Beverly Hills Showdown

Jenny: Douglas and I were finishing up with a meeting when our secretary notified us that Fred Klein was on the line.

Doug's communications with Fred had been limited to Fred's attempts to persuade Doug to drop his lawsuit against Fawcett, so we were very curious about what he might have to say now.

Fred was friendly on this call and took a more personal approach. "Doug, I'd like to meet with you and Jenny. I'll be in Los Angeles next week. I'm staying at the Beverly Hills Hotel. How about Thursday night for dinner?"

Without pause, Doug told him, "Sounds good. We'll pick you up at seven, and I'll pick a nice place." His almost upbeat willingness surprised me, so I was more than curious to see how this dinner would play out.

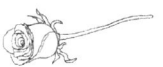

Doug: I could have chosen the Polo Lounge for our meeting. It was right there inside Fred's hotel, and the food was great. But two things influenced my decision to select another restaurant: Memories of our very first meeting with Phil and Marveen at the Polo Lounge might cause nostalgia, and I wanted all my focus on the issues at hand. Also, the Polo Lounge was bright and busy with the Los Angeles social scene. It was not a place to remain low-key and private.

We decided to make reservations at Perino's, a fine dining Italian restaurant where the food was amazing, with an incredible wine list and sommelier to match. The service was always impeccable and nonintrusive.

Jenny and I arrived to pick up Fred in a stretch limo that was only important because it gave us enough legroom and space to look each other in the eye. I stepped out of the car to shake Fred's hand, and he moved inside to place a gentlemanly kiss on Jenny's cheek. After admiring Jenny's appearance, Fred sat forward and presented her with a box wrapped in elegant linen paper.

JENNY: Fred gestured for me to open the gift. The box was lacquered black with two words on the top: Waterford Platinum. They made the finest crystal and China in the world.

Inside I found a crystal decanter. It was thin and stylish, bevel cut, and had a rouge colored based. The piece pulled a sparkle from every light source available, from the interior car lights to the reds, blues, and greens of the neon lights decorating Sunset Boulevard. It was brilliant, magnificent, and captivating. And just like *Playgirl*, it was fragile. It was both a beautiful and a suggestive gift.

We arrived at Perino's and were graciously welcomed by the maître d'. As we had requested, we were seated in the most private area of the dining room, allowing us to catch up on old times without interruption. We enjoyed our food, shared memories, and even had a few laughs.

As the after-dinner liqueurs were placed before us, I made a move to go to the powder room. But Douglas gently placed his hand on my wrist so I would stay. I knew what that meant.

DOUG: When he finally decided it was time to talk business, Fred got right to the point. "Doug, we have a big mess on our hands. This lawsuit can ruin everything for us all. You have to end it."

I shook my head. "Fawcett owes us money, Fred. Lots of it. And by the way, so does Hachette. Millions of dollars are missing from the Barbados reclamation center. Plus, you broke our contract when you sold my printing contracts to Hall Printers. And your creative accountants can't continue their shell game with *Playgirl's* sales and returns numbers forever." Fred stayed quiet. "I learned that term from the folks out here in Hollywood. They know all about the shell game distributors use on their clients." Fred took the lashing, remaining submissive just in case I had one more bullet in my verbal gun. Which I did. "And they say that you stuffed shirts in New York invented the game." There. I was finished.

Fred spoke quietly now. "Doug, as your friend, I'm asking you to listen to me. Carefully." He glanced over his shoulder. "I know you're a straight shooter, but this situation is way over our heads. We're *both* in the line of fire. There's a certain degree of...'family involvement' that puts us there. Do you understand what I mean?"

After my last meeting in New York and practically being chased to the airport, I did understand what he meant. Though I didn't want to. What he meant was that there were people who had no right to our business now acting as big players in our game. People who often operated outside the law, who created their own sets of rules, and who weren't afraid to hurt those who stood in their way. And it appeared that those were exactly the type of people we were dealing with now. Those "family" people Fred was clearly so terrified of. And with good reason. I had refused to be terrified up until this point. But now, seeing Fred's reaction in the flesh was finally making me truly nervous. And my nerves threatened to display themselves as anger.

"You have to settle this lawsuit before it goes to court. The...implications...are too severe," Fred nearly whispered.

Jenny must have noticed my fumes rising, because under the table, she put her hand on my leg and squeezed me into continued silence.

Fred's tone became even more serious. "Look. Everything has a time, and *Playgirl* has had hers. You just can't continue to run an international magazine like a nightclub."

Fred's point was like a dagger in my heart. Sure, the nightclub business often involved decisions based on family, connections, bones buried in concrete, deathly secrets, and uncovered skeletons. But we *always* tried to be better than that.

Even so, we had dealt with our share of scoundrels, creeps, and scum. In our nightclub, we had faced down bad guys who wanted to be on the take for a cash kick back for every liquor delivery, and dancers who would have prostituted themselves had we not banned it. Over the years, we found our way through incidents of defending our sales receipts, our negotiations with vendors, and through literally having our lives threatened. While we ran a reputable club business, it was fair enough for Fred to assume that ours was the same as any other nightclub. And he was right—no international magazine should be run *that* way.

"And," Fred continued speaking his mind, "there cannot be depositions. We cannot put all the parties who are involved in this deal under a microscope." He took a deep breath. "It's just too widespread, Doug. We could be hurt beyond our pocketbooks."

There. The *real* threat had finally been laid out in full.

Jenny and I sat quietly as we absorbed the seriousness of his words: If we continued to fight, bad people would make bad things happen. Things that should never belong in the world of legitimate business.

Fred closed the meeting out and sought to conclude on as high a note as possible. "Doug, Jenny, we all had a great run. Let's go on and do other things."

I wanted to continue being fuming mad at Fred. But as we shook hands, I reminded myself that in this scenario, Fred was now just the messenger. And we all know what can happen to messengers.

The Curtain Falls

The next morning, I phoned my attorney Eric to recap our meeting with Fred. We acknowledged the threat of what was really at stake. Eric was pragmatic, but we both had serious concerns. "We don't even know all of the true players here," I told him.

Eric began ticking off our problems. "Paper is trucked to the printer, then the magazines are trucked to distribution hubs, then to sales locations. There's lots and lots of room for 'family involvement' along those routes. Palms get greased, payoffs are made, and percentages are siphoned off. And that's just here in the States. I don't see them ever giving you accurate accountings, Doug." He gave me his bottom line. "Regardless, I can't see us filing lawsuits that won't be endlessly countered with appeals on both sides. Your life will be living in courtrooms with millions of dollars of debt and payments in dispute. Whatever you win will be eaten up by attorney fees, unless you win every battle." He sighed heavily. "Then, when I factor in the, uh, 'family involvement,' I just can't recommend fighting this any further, Doug. Not anymore. I'm sorry."

I knew this was coming. I hadn't wanted to know, but I'd felt it in my country bones for some time. And I couldn't begin to imagine how I was going to break it to Jenny.

So instead, while driving home that evening, I thought of how proud I was of her. Jenny had developed a concept that inspired women and changed their lives forever. And I was admittedly proud of myself, too, for putting every ounce I had into building *Playgirl* into a sensational success. I recalled the time I had jokingly suggested we use the image of Rodin's "The Thinker" as our first *Playgirl* cover. Ultimately, "The Thinker" had represented my willingness to strip down my male ego in order to support Jenny's forward-thinking ideas. We had both come so far together—now where would the path we walked lead us? It was hard to fathom a life without the thing we had ingrained nearly every part of ourselves into.

At home, Jenny listened quietly while I gave her the details of my conversation with Eric. Only a few tears fell as she did, but I suspected she was saving the rest for a more private reflection, and understood that fully. As I left the room to let her be, I glanced around to see if she had placed her lovely Waterford gift from Fred on display. It was nowhere to be seen.

The next day, Eric and I worked on settling the lawsuit with Fawcett. As we worked, I thought of an old business saying: "It's a good deal when both parties leave dissatisfied." I was plenty dissatisfied, but I can't say the deal felt good.

The showdown was resolved, and within weeks, an interested buyer for *Playgirl* contacted Eric. The mystery corporation was fronted by *Playgirl's* Vice President Ira Ritter. Negotiations were on the table, and it was just a matter of price.

It really was time to close the door on the past.

Less than a year later, we heard the Fawcett family wanted to get out of the magazine distribution business, and that they had been purchased by CBS in a $50 million cash deal. No wonder Fred felt we were both in the line of fire if we didn't resolve Fawcett's legal issues with *Playgirl*. Not to mention, all the additional parties who'd latched themselves onto it.

Still, getting out of that line of fire was one of the most difficult decisions Jenny and I had ever had to make up to that point. In fact, I would call it the single most heart wrenching reality we ever faced. Though we weren't public with our emotions about the whole endeavor, in the privacy of our own home, sometimes it was hard to even summon a smile.

Together, we had built something beautiful, meaningful, creative, and financially successful. We had poured every ounce of ourselves onto every high-gloss page, and in doing so, had played a part in moving the needle further along in helping women achieve some semblance of the equal footing men enjoyed.

To have all that so suddenly wrenched away wasn't just deeply disappointing and disillusioning to us—the suddenness and finality of it left me a bit dazed and feeling a deep hurt that I knew would stick around for a good while. Losing the Playgirl trademarks we had fought so hard to win was like losing my identity. Playgirl had become who I was. So...who would I now become without it?

On top of that, thinking about what might happen to *Playgirl Magazine* once it was out of our hands scared the daylights out of me. We had so carefully shaped its image and message and had planned for its future. What would it become now? We all too soon found that out.

All this was a strange space I had not yet entered in my life—having something forcibly taken away from me before I decided I was ready to let it go. Yes, we admittedly walked away with a pile of money, but money had become secondary to the importance of *Playgirl* in our lives. The whole thing didn't sit well with me, and I knew Jenny was hurting even more deeply than me. I felt so helpless as to how to make it right. If there was even a way to do so. And feeling helpless was another element in my life I had not experienced, at least not since the days when I was a young boy and my father would take his unholy wrath out on our family.

JENNY: During the weeks following the final signatures that officially severed our ties with our beloved *Playgirl Magazine*, Douglas and I sorted through the amazing evidence of our five-year adventure. As a phenomenally successful publication from the beginning, *Playgirl* was the world's first male nude celebrity centerfold magazine and, of equal importance, it was filled with page after page of articles and advice for women. As such, it was a go-to for women in search of new options to enhance their lives. And along with these important firsts, we had published and successfully sold seven male nude photography books, centerfold calendars, and books of erotica where women could fantasize about the sexual aspect of their natures and come to feel that being a sexual being, along with all else they were, was not just okay—it was empowering! For the time, it had all been quite a feat, by anyone's definition.

But that kind of success didn't come cheap. We had poured our hearts and souls, our time and energy, our passion, our whole lives into everything this magazine had become. Yet, we were forced to relinquish the whole kit and caboodle to those who neither contributed to the success of, nor shared in the vision for this groundbreaking publication.

But my disappointment and disillusionment reached down deeper than just mourning the loss of a successful business venture. It was this empty feeling of having the very *intention* of our magazine invalidated by it being ripped so callously from us. Was our whole vision of making women's lives better pointless?

We had created an exciting, safe, and reliable place for women to come and be informed, to have fun, to feel empowered, and to realize the beautiful, intelligent, sensual beings they are as they immersed themselves in the pages of *Playgirl*. We had shown what women of this world desire in all arenas of their lives: equal standing, an even playing field, fair play; freedom to sexually express and enjoy themselves without condemnation; power to make a difference; respect, recognition, and appreciation for who they are and what they do; and, in general, the aching craving women had for richer and fuller lives.

The pages of *Playgirl Magazine* had not only helped show women the way to get what they wanted, but, importantly, helped them realize that all these desires are acceptable and can be a reality in their lives. We waved the pages of our magazine like a flag, with every word on those pages chanting, "Yes you can!" And now here we were, empty handed and whispering to ourselves, "But maybe *we* can't..." It felt awful. It was an agonizing and gut-gripping time the likes of which I hadn't experienced before. There were days I didn't want to get out of bed and face the reality of what we had lost, or the gloom that had settled over us. I worried about what the magazine would now become—something I intuitively knew would be very different than what we had created.

However, one critical thing Douglas and I had in common was a stubborn fire in our bellies that never went all the way out, regardless of how beaten down we became. And although it was gradual, that fire within each of us began igniting again. So, we poked our heads up, looked around, and realized we were now in a position to do just about anything we wanted to do.

To completely dispel the gloom and doom, Douglas sat me down one day and put *Playgirl Magazine* into perspective: "We provided a beacon to women who wanted a brighter life. We made a difference. We did no harm. We broke some publication records. We made some money. We had fun, and most of all, we now love each other more than ever. Don't tell me it was all for nothing, Jenny. It's just time to move on to whatever's next." Then he pulled me in close, sighed, and said, "But it's going to be goddamn hard doing anything that good again."

I couldn't help but find myself agreeing with him. On every front.

Eventually, though, our lives did become lighter. There began to be more play, laughter, and passion. We realized how much we appreciated and depended on each other; how much we loved being together; how totally we complemented each other. It wasn't that we didn't know or feel these things before, it was that we had been too too caught up in the constant drama to truly bask in them.

We soon realized that drama had been pushing in on the magazine from every angle, compressing our relationship into a mold that worked at the time, but desperately needed to be reshaped.

And now we had all the time and leisure we wanted to do just that.

Jukebox Music

Doug: Not too long after that, Jenny and I stood at the panorama window of our Bel Air home taking in the view of the Hollywood Hills. Beyond them, the land stretched all the way to the Pacific Ocean, shimmering under the hot sun of the too-quiet afternoon.

And standing in its own majestic glow in the corner of that very room was our jukebox—our old friend we had toted from place to place along our journey. That beautiful, magical music machine represented all things good in my life so far: my boyhood spent in the honky tonk, my time in the ol' Quonset hut in Korea, meeting and falling in love with Jenny at the wildly popular Playgirl Club, and the thrill of creating something as phenomenal as *Playgirl Magazine.* All its songs were woven over decades as the threads of our lives.

Jenny: I sat on the arm of the leather sofa gazing out at the view from our window. Glancing around at Douglas walking to the jukebox and taking a coin from his pocket, I wondered what he would play. The thought ran through my head that every song available related to a time, place, or event in our lives. *Music is much better than a photograph, or even a video,* I thought. Music brings back not only a visual memory, but it can stir up and intensify the memory of all the senses and rekindle the emotions we experienced at certain times in our lives. When Nell told Douglas so many years ago, "Ain't nothin' else but music that helps us get all that pain out of our soul and puts all the joy in it," she was so right.

DOUG: I pushed the A-1 button of the jukebox, calling up the song that started everything for me. Damn, had life changed since Hank Thompson recorded the one-sided, male-minded hit "The Wild Side of Life"! The old, worn 45 record dropped into position, the needle arm moved into place, and the scratch that sounds just before the song sent a chill up my spine, as it always did. I nodded to Jenny and she was in my arms in a flash. We danced so close, not a puff of air could get between us.

JENNY: Doug was quiet. But I had an inkling of what was on his mind. "Thinking about Nell?" I asked as I pulled back to look at his face.

He nodded. "I'm thinking about Nell, my mother, your mother, and all the women who've had such hard times at the hands of men. How unbalanced life was and, thankfully to a lesser extent, still is for women. It pisses me off that I didn't get it sooner."

"Yes, but you get it now, and that's all that matters." I rested my head back on his chest. "And let's be grateful to Kitty Wells for shaking things up with 'It Wasn't God Who Made Honky Tonk Angels' and starting to help some people along back then." As the song ended, I held my palm out for a quarter and laughed. "Besides, you had to meet me, grow up, and fall madly in love before you could see the light. In that order!" He laughed and handed me a quarter.

I knew exactly which of our favorite songs to play now. The lyrics and tune had been roaming around my head for the past several days. Searching for the button, my mind flashed through the events of our lives. As I was making my way from Indonesia to Holland to America, and ultimately to Los Angeles, Douglas was making his way from the mountains of Appalachia to South Korea and on to California too. The odds of us finding each other, considering the different worlds we came from and the paths we traveled, were astronomical. But we did find each other. Was it a miracle, blessing, or destiny? Who's to say. But once our lives finally did come together, we began an incredible journey. One that I knew was far from over.

But for the moment, as Douglas and I worked to put the pain of our broken hearts behind us, we had one last tear that needed to fall.

Doug: At one point in her life, Nell had particularly liked and related to songs about heartbreak and picking up the pieces. One time in her small apartment in Baltimore, when things were looking particularly bleak for her and the kids, I remember Nell strumming and singing a poignant Hank Williams hit. It stayed in my memory, and later in life I was particularly impressed by the poetic symbolism in the lyrics.

A walk in a garden becomes a metaphor for life, and a teardrop that falls on a rose represents sorrow stemming from a broken heart. Jenny often said our life together was like a "beautiful red rose," which, in her opinion, was "Mother Nature's perfect creation." The rose blooms to reveal exceptionally delicate and sweetly fragranced beauty because of its own strength, but that beauty is protected by intimidatingly sharp thorns that keep what threatens it at bay. From my perspective, Jenny was my life, my perfect rose, and I'd done my best to be the big, bad, prickly thorn that protected my beautiful flower and our incredible life together. I didn't always do it right. I too often overplayed my big, bad role, and pricked at the world even when there was really no threat. But I never, ever let my guard down when it came to the most precious treasure to me.

Now, I smiled as this perfect woman played the most perfect song she could have chosen for this moment.

Jenny: It's always especially meaningful when we find a song that's perfect for the moment. A song that expresses shared feelings, hard truths, sorrow, joy, lust, and all else that life holds. I silently thanked Mr. Hank Williams for his beautiful song "A Teardrop on a Rose."

As we we held each other close and moved in time to the slow rhythm of the music, we were not ashamed of the tears that rolled down our cheeks. By the time the song ended, I knew we were ready to let go of where we had been, and begin focusing fully on where we were going.

I asked Doug for one more quarter, walked over to the jukebox, hit a different button, and danced my way back to my man. "This is our theme song now!" I declared.

Doug: With Hank's lonesome voice still in my head, that magnificent music machine burst out the fast beat and treble voices of the Bee Gees singing "Stayin' Alive"! Jenny had jacked up the volume and the beat now shook the room. Then and there, my incredible wife started an unbelievably seductive dance just for me. I realized then that we were more than alive—we were on fire! We had each other a whole lot of life to yet live.

And come what may, we would live it together.

In Memoriam

Douglas Lambert, 1934-2021

Douglas and Jenny spent over a decade working together on all the details of their story for this book. When Jenny's illness kept her from doing the challenging work it takes to plan and write a manuscript, Douglas remained steadfast in his effort to complete the book. Even following Jenny's death in July, 2020, under devastating circumstances and in the face of his own progressive illness, Douglas continued on.

Seeing *A Teardrop on a Rose* published was his final dream and most fervent wish, for Douglas wanted the world to know what an extraordinary woman Jenny was and for others to adore her as much as he did. He felt their incredible love story and where it led them might inspire others to reach for the stars. So Douglas continued working endless hours, giving attention to every detail and nuance, until his death in October, 2021.

Fortunately, Douglas did have a chance to hold a preliminary copy of the book in his hands before he died, and knew their story would live on in those pages. His last words before giving in to unconsciousness were, "Do you think Jenny is waiting for me?"

The answer was a resounding, "Yes! Indeed, she's waiting—with her big, beautiful smile and outstretched arms."

It is our privilege to finally share Douglas and Jenny's story and some of their groundbreaking achievements—just as that shy little girl from the exotic island of Java and that good ol' boy from the Appalachian Mountains intended.

Your Voice Matters

It's important for independently published books like this one to have a chance at being discovered by eager readers. This is especially true when it comes to sharing messages of hope, love, and equality for all.

One of the best ways to achieve that is through readers like you leaving an honest rating or review of the book on Amazon. More reviews of the book—no matter what they have to say about it—means more visibility. Your honest opinion of this true story and how it's portrayed in these pages not only means the world to the people whose legacy it explores, but to the people who've worked hard to make sure it's shared with others. Thank you for your support.

www.ingramcontent.com/pod-product-compliance
Lightning Source LLC
Chambersburg PA
CBHW060647150426
42811CB00086B/2447/J